SEVEN DAY LOAN

This book is to be returned on
or before the date stamped below

UNIVERSITY OF PLYMOUTH

PLYMOUTH LIBRARY

Tel: (01752) 232323
This book is subject to recall if required by another reader
Books may be renewed by phone
CHARGES WILL BE MADE FOR OVERDUE BOOKS

AGRI-ENVIRONMENTAL POLICY IN THE EUROPEAN UNION

This book is dedicated to the children born during the course of this project:

Erik

Maria Sofia

Marie

Rose

Stella

Agri-environmental Policy in the European Union

Edited by
HENRY BULLER, *Université de Paris 7*
GEOFF A. WILSON, *King's College London*
ANDREAS HÖLL, *Danish Forest and Landscape Research Institute*

Ashgate

Aldershot • Brookfield USA • Singapore • Sydney

Published by
Ashgate Publishing Limited
Gower House
Croft Road
Aldershot
Hampshire GU11 3HR
England

Ashgate Publishing Company
Old Post Road
Brookfield
Vermont 05036
USA

Ashgate website: http://www.ashgate.com

British Library Cataloguing in Publication Data
Agri-environmental policy in the European Union. -
    (Perspectives on Europe)
    1. Agriculture and state - Environmental aspects - European
    Union countries
    I. Buller, Henry, 1956- II. Wilson, Geoff III. Höll, Andreas
    338.1'84

Library of Congress Catalog Card Number: 99-76158

ISBN 1 84014 504 8

Printed and bound by Athenaeum Press, Ltd., Gateshead, Tyne & Wear.

Contents

List of Figures

List of Tables

Portugal

Regulation 2078: patterns of implementation

List of Contributors

Javier AGUIRRE   Dep. de Ecologia, Universidad Autonoma de
                         Madrid, 28049 Madrid, Spain

Erling ANDERSEN   Department of Economics and Natural Resources,
                         Den Koniglige Veterinaer- og Landbohoejskole,
                         Rolighedsvej 26, 1958 Frederiksberg C, Denmark
                         erling@morgana.kvl.dk

Nicos BEOPOULOS   Department of Agricultural Economics,
                         Agricultural University of Athens, Iera Odos 75,
                         118 55 Athens, Greece
                         nbeop@auadec.aua.gr

Hélène BRIVES   LADYSS-CNRS, Université Paris X, Nanterre,
                         France
                         helene.brives@wanadoo.fr

Henry BULLER   Département de Géographie, UFR GHSS,
                         Université de Paris VII, 2 Place Jussieu, Paris,
                         France; Laboratoire de recherche LADYSS, CNRS,
                         UMR-7533, Université de Paris X, France
                         buller@paris7.jussieu.fr

Helene CARLSEN   Department of Economics, The Swedish University
                         of Agricultural Sciences, PO Box 7013, 75007
                         Uppsala, Sweden
                         helene.carlsen@ekon.slu.se

Peter EDEN   Instituto para o Desenvolvimento Rural e Gestao
                         Ambiental, Avenida Dr Jose Pontes 43, 2720
                         Amadora

Annegret GRAFEN   Institut für ländliche Strukturforschung,
                         Zeppelinallee 31, 60325 Frankfurt, Germany

Michael GROIER — Bundesanstalt für Bergbauernfragen, Möllwaldplatz 5, 1040 Wien, Austria
michael.groier@babf.bmlf.gv.at

Kaley HART — Council for the Protection of Rural England CPRE, Warwick House, 25 Buckingham Palace Road, London SW1W 0PP, UK
cpre@gn.apc.org

Knut Per HASUND — Department of Economics, The Swedish University of Agricultural Sciences, PO Box 7013, 75007 Uppsala, Sweden
knut.per.hasund@ekon.slu.se

Anita HENNINGSEN — Den Koniglige Veterinaer- og Landbohoejskole, Rolighedsvej 26, 1958 Frederiksberg C, Denmark

Andreas HÖLL — Danish Forest and Landscape Research Institute, Horsholm Kongevej 11, DK-2970 Horsholm, Denmark
anh@fsl.dk

Bernard LEHMANN — Institut für Agrarwirtschaft, Eidgenössische Technische Hochschule Zürich, Sonneggstr. 33, 8092 Zürich, Switzerland
bernard.lehmann@iaw.agrl.ethz.ch

Elisabeth LOIBL — Bundesanstalt für Bergbauernfragen, Möllwaldplatz 5, 1040 Wien, Austria
elisabeth.loibl@babf.bmlf.gv.at

Leonidas LOULOUDIS — Department of Agricultural Economics, Agricultural University of Athens, Iera Odos 75, 118 55 Athens, Greece
louloudis@auadec.aua.gr

Juan E. MALO — Dep. De Ecologia, Universidad Autonoma de Madrid, 28049 Madrid, Spain

Juan J. OÑATE   Dep. de Medio Ambiente, Universidad Europea de
Madrid (CEES), Villaviciosa de Odon, 6207
Madrid, Spain
jjose.onate@amb.cie.uem.es

Begoña PECO   Dep. De Ecologia, Universidad Autonoma de
Madrid, 28049 Madrid, Spain
begonna.peco@uam.es

Jørgen PRIMDAHL   Department of Economics and Natural Resources,
Den Koniglige Veterinaer- og Landbohoejskole,
Rolighedsvej 26, 1958 Frederiksberg C, Denmark

Hansjörg SCHMID   Institut für Agrarwirtschaft, Eidgenössische
Technische Hochschule Zürich, Sonneggstr. 33,
8092 Zürich, Switzerland
hansjoerg.schmid@iaw.agrl.ethz.ch

Jörg SCHRAMEK   Institut für ländliche Strukturforschung,
Zeppelinallee 31, 60325 Frankfurt, Germany
schramek@em.uni-frankfurt.de

Francisco SUÁREZ   Dep. De Ecologia, Universidad Autonoma de
Madrid, 28049 Madrid, Spain

Miguel VIEIRA   Instituto para o Desenvolvimento Rural e Gestao
Ambiental, Avenida Dr Jose Pontes 43, 2720
Amadora
idrga.mv@mail.telepac.pt

George VLAHOS   Department of Agricultural Economics,
Agricultural University of Athens, Iera Odos 75,
118 55 Athens, Greece
gvlahos@auadec.aua.gr

Geoff A. WILSON   Department of Geography, King's College London,
Strand, London WC2R 2LS, UK
geoff.wilson@kcl.ac.uk

Acknowledgements

The authors of the nine EU countries represented in this book would like to thank the European Commission (DG VI) for the funding of the project on 'Implementation and Effectiveness of EU Agri-environmental Schemes established under Regulation 2078' (FAIR 1CT95-0274) upon which this book is based. The Swiss team is particularly grateful to the Swiss *Bundesamt für Bildung und Wissenschaft* for funding their part of the research.

Many thanks also to Roma Beaumont and Carolyn Megan for help with drawing the figures, to Joanne Hay for assistance with the final formatting, and to Anne Keirby (Ashgate Publishers) for help with preparing the camera-ready copy of this book.

Especial thanks must go to Professor Dieter Biehl and Jörg Schramek (Institut für ländliche Strukturforschung, Frankfurt, Germany) for co-ordinating the above-mentioned EU project.

Last, but certainly not least, the three editors of this book wish to thank the individual country teams for their chapter contributions, and particularly for their co-operation in the production of the final versions of individual chapters.

List of Abbreviations and Explanation of Terms

AEP	Agri-environmental policy
BMELF	Bundesministerium für Ernährung, Landwirtschaft und Forsten (Germany)
BMLF	Bundesministerium für Landwirtschaft und Forsten (Austria)
BSE	Bovine spongiform encephalitis
CAP	Common Agricultural Policy
CPRE	Council for the Protection of Rural England (UK)
CSS	Countryside Stewardship Scheme (UK)
DBV	Deutscher Bauernverband (Germany)
DSPEP	Directorate of Spatial Planning and Environmental Protection (Greece)
EAGGF	European Agricultural Guidance and Guarantee Fund
EC	European Community (period between the Single European Act 1987 and the Maastricht Treaty 1992)
ECU	European Currency Unit
EEC	European Economic Community (period between the Treaty of Rome in 1957 and the Single European Act 1987)
EMP	Environmental management plan (Greece)
ESAs	Environmentally Sensitive Areas
EU	European Union (since the Maastricht Treaty 1992)
FCGS	Farm and Conservation Grant Scheme (UK)
GAK	Gemeinschaftsaufgabe zur Verbesserung der Agrarstruktur und des Küstenschutzes (national agri-environmental policy framework in Germany)
GATT	General Agreement on Tariffs and Trade
GDP	Gross Domestic Product
ha	Hectare
HEKUL	Hessisches Kulturlandschaftsprogramm (Germany)
KULAP	Bayerisches Kulturlandschaftsprogramm (Germany)
LFAs	Less favoured areas
LU	Livestock units
MAFF	Ministry of Agriculture, Fisheries and Food (UK)
MAPA	Ministry of Agriculture (Spain)

MEKA	Marktentlastungs- und Kulturlanschaftsausgleich (agri-environmental scheme in Baden-Württemberg, Germany)
MECU	Million ECU (European Currency Units)
MLC	Scheme for landscape conservation (Sweden)
N	Nitrate
NGOs	Non-governmental organisations
NOLA	Scheme for nature conservation measures in the agricultural landscape (Sweden)
NUTS	Nomenclature pour Unités Territoriales Statistiques (Nomenclature of Territorial Units for Statistics in the European Union)
ÖPUL	Österreichisches Programm für Umwelt und Landwirtschaft (Austria)
P	Phosphate
PDD	Sustainable farm development plan (France)
PPG	Payments-for-public-goods-principle
PPP	Polluter-pays-principle
RSPB	Royal Society for the Protection of Birds (UK)
SSSIs	Sites of Special Scientific Interest (UK)
UAA	Utilised agricultural area
UK	United Kingdom
WWF	Worldwide Fund for Nature

1 Introduction: the emergence of Regulation 2078

Henry Buller, Geoff A. Wilson and Andreas Höll

Aims of the book

This book is about the adoption, implementation and achievements of the European Union (EU) agri-environmental Regulation 2078/92 (hereafter Regulation 2078), introduced as part of the 1992 reforms to the Common Agricultural Policy (CAP). Regulation 2078 is, at the time of writing, some seven years old. Most of the countries featuring in this book, have arrived or are arriving at the end of the first of the five-year agri-environmental programmes[1] that the Regulation imposes. All of the countries featured in this book are facing the prospect, over the next few years, of substantial changes in the way in which European agriculture is funded and regulated. What is clear from the European Commission's *Agenda 2000* propositions and indeed from national responses to these propositions, is that the political and financial priority given to the role of farming in maintaining and protecting the rural environment is likely to increase rather than decrease in coming years. Regulation 2078, and its preceding legislation, Regulations 797/85 and 1760/87, are therefore, we would argue, highly significant to the

---

[1] It is important to briefly clarify our use of the three terms 'agri-environmental programme', 'agri-environmental scheme' and 'agri-environmental measure' in this book:

Agri-environmental programme: this term refers to the national agri-environmental policies implemented by nation states (e.g. the UK agri-environmental programme; see Ch. 6). An agri-environmental programme is usually comprised of several **agri-environmental schemes** although there may be exceptions (e.g. the Austrian ÖPUL programme only has individual **measures**; see Ch. 9).

Agri-environmental schemes: individual schemes that usually apply within specific geographic contexts in nation states (e.g. ESA scheme in the UK, Denmark or Portugal). In some cases, a scheme may target the entire country (e.g. many organic aid schemes). Usually, several agri-environmental schemes have been implemented within one country. Agri-environmental schemes usually comprise several **agri-environmental measures**.

Agri-environmental measures: these form the 'smallest' policy unit of agri-environmental policies. Agri-environmental schemes may specify individual measures (e.g. delaying of hay cutting on flower-rich hay meadows, restrictions on N-fertilisers, etc.) or may be comprised of different 'tiers' each of which in turn may contain several measures (e.g. a basic tier may include a measure for livestock reduction for a given forage area).

1

current evolution of European agricultural and rural policy despite the fact that until now they have not constituted a major component to the total CAP budget.

In 1996, Whitby examined the emergence of European agri-environmental policy (AEP) in eight Member States (Whitby, 1996a). At the time, in many of the countries studied, the implementation of Regulation 2078 was planned rather than operational. At the end of his book, Whitby suggested that further examination of the design and implementation of the policy were required before any assessment of its effectiveness could be made. The current volume is a contribution to that examination.

This book reviews the implementation of Regulation 2078 in nine EU Member States and the implementation of parallel agri-environmental mechanisms in Switzerland. The book derives from a research programme entitled 'Implementation and effectiveness of agri-environmental schemes established under Regulation 2078/92' which ran from 1996 to 1999 financed under the FAIR programme of the DG VI of the European Commission (DGVI, 1999). All the authors are drawn from members of that research programme. The chapters reflect the views of the individual authors which are not necessarily those of the European Commission.

The origins of Regulation 2078

The full title of Regulation 2078 is as follows: 'Council Regulation 2078/92 on the Introduction and Maintenance of Agricultural Production Methods Compatible with the Requirements of the Protection of the Environment and the Management of the Countryside'. Introduced on the 30th June 1992, the Regulation seeks to:
- accompany the changes to be introduced under the market organisation rules
- contribute to the achievement of the Community's policy objectives regarding agriculture and the environment
- contribute to providing an appropriate income for farmers (EC, 1992a, Article 1).

As we have argued elsewhere (Buller, 1999a), behind these three goals lie three very different policy concerns each with its own, largely independent, political trajectory. To understand the Regulation and its impact, we need to place it in terms of these different contexts.

CAP reform

Regulation 2078 is one of three 'Accompanying Measures' to the 1992 reform of the CAP. As such, it forms an integral part of a wide-ranging reform whose principal driving concern at the time was to reduce the overproduction of certain farm products within the EU and thereby reduce the overall costs of the CAP (EC, 1985a). Reductions in costs meant changes in the ways in which farm aid is shared out, and the European Commission – in response to growing criticism of the regional and structural imbalances built into the manner in which agricultural support was distributed amongst European farmers at the time – were also mindful of the need to increase, relatively, the support of the less economically strong sectors and regions of European agriculture (EC, 1991b). A further concern underlying the 1992 reforms was world trade and the growing demands (particularly from the United States) that EU subsidies for agricultural production and export costs be reduced (Potter, 1998). All in all, these various concerns amounted to a relatively fundamental challenge to the original principles of the original CAP.

The 1992 agri-environmental Regulation 2078 fits into this reform agenda in a number of ways. First, it was an element in the general reform goal of reducing or stabilising certain agricultural production levels. As such, it sought to promote extensive farming practices and the reduction of entrants, leading to agricultural de-intensification. Second, agri-environmental aid, offered under Regulation 2078 (like its predecessor Regulation 797/85), was conceived as a 'direct payment' to farmers, compensating them for income foregone and the costs of compliance. This too fitted in with the newly designed system of direct compensatory and other payments for farmers as a replacement for former volume-related market support mechanisms. Finally, in focusing specifically upon environmental objectives, Regulation 2078 provided a possible mechanism compatible with the General Agreements on Tariffs and Trade (GATT) for supporting European farming and, specifically, those areas and farming types that would be most threatened by further alignment with world prices and by a more market-led agricultural policy.

Environmental policy integration

An additional concern to which Regulation 2078 offered a partial response was the need to address the issue of environmental damage caused by modern agricultural techniques (EC, 1997b). Here, a number of different elements can also be identified.

First, increasing public and political recognition of the role of the CAP in encouraging environmentally damaging agricultural intensification, together with the manifest failure of the CAP to support and sustain those more 'traditional' modes of agricultural production considered to be more environmentally friendly, were clearly emerging as dominant concerns during the 1980s; concerns that the European Commission itself acknowledged (EC, 1991b, 1992b). The expanding financial cost of European agricultural policy was becoming more and more difficult to justify in the face of such environmental disbenefits.

Second, up until the late 1980s, European Community (EC) environmental policy had developed essentially independently of EC agricultural policy (Buller, 1998c). Although certain changes in the CAP might have had positive environmental consequences (notably extensification), this was not the primary aim of these CAP changes. Agriculture under the CAP had often 'escaped', as it had under national policy, the mandatory imposition of regulatory controls relating to environmental quality maintenance or improvement. However, under the terms of the *Maastricht Treaty* of 1987 (implemented in 1993) and the 5th *Environmental Action Plan* of the EU, environmental policy was required to be integrated into all EU policies including the CAP (EC, 1997a).

Finally, by the time Regulation 2078 was approved, a significant number of EU Member States had already embarked upon the establishment of agri-environmental schemes, either as a result of preceding EU legislation (such as Regulation 797/85) or independent of it (EC, 1991b). Regulation 2078 was thereby offered as a harmonising framework for those existing schemes, as well as the basis upon which new programmes and schemes could be elaborated. As such, and as this book will amply illustrate, it covered a far wider set of agri-environmental issues and agendas than the original Regulation, reflecting a broader spectrum of national agri-environmental concerns.

Income support

Regulation 2078 is also a mechanism for delivering income support for farmers who undertake low-income farm practices considered as being environmentally friendly. Here, the Regulation can be seen as responding to two distinct concerns. On the one hand, it is a response to the charge that the financial benefits both of European agriculture in general and of the CAP were being concentrated in the hands of a relatively small number of essentially arable farmers (who were held to be the cause of the bulk of farm-based environmental damage). On the other hand, it is a response to a long standing European policy concern for the maintenance of farming practice and rural communities in marginal regions. As such, the Regulation follows in the tradition of the Less Favoured Areas (LFAs) Directive 268/75.

What does Regulation 2078 do?

Regulation 2078 makes possible the granting of EU co-funding aid for nationally implemented schemes that seek to encourage environmentally friendly forms of farming. Under Article 2 of the Regulation, the types of activity that might be eligible for aid are those that seek:

- to reduce substantially the use of fertilisers and/or plant protection products, or to keep to reductions already made, or to introduce or continue with organic farming methods;
- to change, by means other than those referred to in the previous point to more extensive forms of cropping (including forage production), to maintain extensive production methods introduced in the past, or to convert arable land into extensive grassland;
- to reduce the proportion of sheep and cattle per forage area;
- to use alternative farming practices compatible with the requirements of protection of the environment and natural resource, as well as maintaining the countryside and the landscape, or to rear animals of local breeds in danger of extinction;
- to ensure the upkeep of abandoned farmland or woodlands;
- to set-aside farmland for at least 20 years with a view to its use for purposes connected with the environment, in particular for the establishment of biotope reserves or natural parks or for the protection of hydrological systems;
- to manage land for public access and leisure activities.

In addition, aid may be given to improve the training of farmers with regard to farming or forestry practices compatible with the environment and for the establishment of demonstration projects, although implementation of this part of Regulation 2078 is optional for Member States. Further, Article 4 mentions a support scheme for the cultivation and propagation of useful plants adapted to local conditions and threatened by genetic erosion. Article 6 provides for demonstration projects promoting farming practices compatible with the requirements on environment protection, and in particular the application of a code of good farming practice and organic farming practice.

This list covers a broad spectrum of agricultural activities aimed at promoting or maintaining environmentally friendly farming systems and thereby reducing the environmental impact of either intensification or abandonment of farming. Other issues targeted in the Regulation include landscape management and nature conservation, including conservation of plant and animal genetic resources. A measure to facilitate outdoor recreation completes the catalogue.

Member states were asked to design zonal programmes of at least five-year duration (Article 3). The concept of zonal programmes involves the idea of maximising positive effects of the measures on natural and environmental conditions by relating them to a concrete spatial context. Thus, the programmes should be targeted at sufficiently homogenous areas, they should contain a definition of the geographical area and a description of the natural, environmental and structural characteristics of the area; further, the specific programme objectives should be explained with regard to the characteristics of the targeted area. The agri-environmental programmes had to be submitted to the Commission for notification (Article 7). Once approved, the programmes were co-financed by the EU at 75% in *Objective 1* regions and 50% in all other regions (Article 8).

In the breadth of its remit, Regulation 2078 thereby sought to bring together originally disparate policy measures such as extensification and various landscape management policies (de Putter, 1995; Baldock and Lowe, 1996; Scheele, 1996; Höll and von Meyer, 1996). Unlike Regulation 797/85, it was mandatory. Within one year (by July 1993) all Member States had to submit a national framework for its implementation as well as a detailed set of individual agri-environmental schemes.

A further change compared to previous EC policies relates to the fact that with Regulation 2078 EU-funding for AEP was shifted from the *European Agricultural Guidance and Guarantee Fund* (EAGGF) Guidance section section to the EAGGF Guarantee section, suggesting that there would be access to a larger and more flexible budget for AEP than before (Baldock and Lowe, 1996). Expectations were expressed that agri-environmental policies would lead to a 'greening of the CAP', and that it would have positive side-effects with regard to social conditions in rural regions (Potter and Lobley, 1993; Robinson and Ilbery, 1993; Baldock, 1994; Reus *et al.*, 1995; de Putter, 1995). Whether such a 'greening' process has, in fact, taken place is the subject of this book.

The structure of this book

In its analysis of implementation of Regulation 2078 in the EU, this book adopts both a country-specific focus by investigating the responses of individual EU Member States (and Switzerland) to EU AEP (Chs. 2-11) as well as a transnational focus by comparing and contrasting individual member state responses to Regulation 2078 (Ch. 12).

The order of the country-specific chapters in this book does not follow any preconceived notions about which countries should be treated 'first' or 'last', and we have consciously avoided clustering specific countries together (e.g. north European countries versus Mediterranean countries) in order not to detract the reader from the breadth and variety of approaches towards AEP implementation in individual EU Member States. As this book will highlight, however, 'regional patterns' of implementation can be identified, especially with regard to 'old' Member States versus 'new' ones (essentially emphasising the north-south divide already highlighted by Whitby, 1996b), countries with mountainous areas and/or substantial areas of LFAs versus countries or regions dominated by intensive agriculture, and countries with previous agri-environmental experience versus those with no or only limited experience (in theory, any of these regional patterns could have formed an alternative structure for the chapter sequence presented in this book).

In order to understand current implementation patterns of Regulation 2078 in individual Member States it is important to analyse pre-2078 AEP and conditions, as well as more complex 'cultural' issues related to national attitudes towards the countryside in Member States, and the processes that have led to the drafting and implementation of AEP. To investigate the latter, it is particularly important to identify both the specific actors in charge of implementing AEP within the framework of multi-layered environmental management processes in the European countryside (Wilson and Bryant, 1997), as well as understanding the response of the 'recipients' of agri-environmental policies (i.e. the farmers) towards Regulation 2078 and the role that these farmers may have played in the implementation of AEP across the EU (Morris and Potter, 1995; Wilson,

1997a). Each of the country chapters (Chs. 2-11) follows a loose structure based on these issues, usually with an emphasis on:

- the agricultural and environmental situation in the countryside prior to AEP implementation
- the implementation of pre-2078 AEP and associated policy mechanisms with implications for countryside management (where applicable)
- patterns and processes of implementation of Regulation 2078
- the 'success' of AEP implemented under Regulation 2078 (where information has been available)
- conclusions with regard to possible future trajectories of national AEP within the framework of wider changes in the EU.

Chapter 12 draws together the analyses presented in the individual country chapters by assessing transnational patterns of implementation of Regulation 2078. It focuses specifically on the emergence of national AEP agendas and compares and contrasts the different approaches that have been used in the ten countries under investigation in this book. It also discusses patterns of adoption of Regulation 2078 in Member States, with a specific emphasis on agri-environmental budgets and differential organisation of national agri-environmental programmes, and compares the contents of agri-environmental schemes implemented in different European regions under Regulation 2078 by looking at the range of measures offered in individual countries and the differences in premium rates offered to participating farmers. Chapter 12 concludes with a discussion of the relative 'success' of national agri-environmental programmes with regard to farmer participation figures and contract areas entered into schemes. Brief concluding remarks to the book are provided in Chapter 13 with an emphasis on the implications of future EU agricultural policies (in particular *Agenda 2000*) on the trajectories of AEP in a changing Europe.

We feel that this book should be of interest to students, academics and researchers in any discipline related to European rural and agricultural issues, environmental management (especially those with a focus on countryside management), policy analysis, European studies and political sciences. The book should appeal to both practitioners and theorists as it addresses a multitude of issues that are of increasing relevance in a rapidly changing Europe.

2 France: farm production and rural product as key factors influencing agri-environmental policy

Henry Buller and Hélène Brives

Agriculture and the environment: the classic divide

For many years, France appeared to regard the agri-environmental debate as an almost quaint, essentially British, obsession with wildlife that had little in common with the reality of French farming culture and with French rural environmental concerns. Today, however, France is the fourth highest spender on AEP among the EU Member States. How do we account for this seeming shift? Does it represent a genuine 'sea-change' within the agricultural policy community or rather a pragmatic sense of policy opportunism in the face of inevitable changes both in the nature of the relations between farming and the environment and in direct funding for agriculture within the EU? In this chapter, we examine the emergence of the agri-environmental debate in France and the gradual implementation of a policy that, today, covers some 23% of the French agricultural land surface.

In all European states, the emergence of AEP is fundamentally rooted in national rural and agrarian culture (Buller, 1997a). The French experience is no exception. Indeed, we would argue that the agri-environmental agenda in that country reflects above all a wider and more complex internal debate about the future direction for French farming as a whole and the future role of the agricultural profession in contemporary society (Courtet et al., 1993). The socio-cultural backdrop to AEP can be briefly summarised under three headings: the territorial importance of agriculture, the demographic and economic heritage of the French farming profession, and the relative absence of an alternative non-production related conception of French rurality.

France is one of the largest European states, with an area of 554,000 km² and an overall population density of around 104 persons per km² (which places it between Spain and Greece with around 77 person/km² and

Germany and the UK with 225 and 250 respectively). The relative vastness of the national territory, coupled with the great variety of landscape types, has produced a particular relationship between the natural environment and primary production. On the one hand, agriculture has historically stood for the 'civilisation' of that territory, its appropriation from its natural state and its conversion into something useful both in economic and social terms. On the other hand, it has given rise to the belief that the territory is sufficiently large to accommodate individual instances of pollution and degradation, which has, in turn, led to a long-standing separation (in spatial and policy terms) of the environment to be specifically protected and the environment as it is farmed. Thus, national parks, nature reserves and ecologically sensitive areas have all tended to be located in areas where agricultural activity has not been predominant (Moreux, 1994). Elsewhere, the existence of extensive areas of high amenity and low intensity hill farming (e.g. the Massif Central, central Brittany and the Jura) has had the effect of negating the perception of farming as anything but environmentally friendly, and of reinforcing the importance of maintaining agricultural activities in such areas.

Second, France's long-standing agrarian tradition and the importance of farming in national symbolism, within the national economy and in national socio-professional and political structures, continue to play a significant role in setting attitudes to both agriculture and the rural environment (Hoggart *et al.*, 1995). A large peasant agricultural population, occupying a multitude of small land holdings and selling its surplus produce locally, has been for centuries the dominant model of French farming (Braudel, 1986). Reinforced by, and indeed at the heart of, successive political regimes, the defining role and function of the rural environment has long been agricultural exploitation. Although post-war modernisation has considerably altered the social and economic structure of rural France, it also reinforced the economic and political hegemony of the agricultural policy community within rural areas and rural policy formulation (Buller, 1997b), endowing the nation with a significant and, in political terms, powerful agricultural profession with respect to its immediate north European neighbours (Coulomb *et al.*, 1990; Hervieu and Lagarve, 1992). The active agricultural population, at just over 1.2 million persons, represents 5.6% of the national working population (compared for example with the UK, Belgium or Germany where only 2.1%, 2.7% and 3.2% of the civilian workforce are engaged in agriculture respectively). Yet, in 1954, that population amounted to some 5.1 million persons or 27% of the total civilian workforce. In social, territorial, economic and, latterly, environmental terms, this precipitous decline of the French agricultural profession and the real possibility of a *France sans paysans* are today the dominant preoccupations making the maintenance of agricultural activities a critical element in the protection of rural space.

Third, being an essentially rural nation until the 1950s, France has not developed a tradition of rural preservationism and amenity protectionism that so characterises its historically more urbanised northern neighbours. An explicit social demand for protected landscapes and on-farm environmental management is a relatively recent phenomenon and, even then, is often limited to rural zones that have experienced population growth following urban outmigration. Hence the farming profession has been able to retain, virtually unchallenged, its historic status as the natural guardian of the rural environment; pollution, for example, being, until relatively recently, almost exclusively associated with urban areas. While British farmers might equally claim, with some legitimacy, to be also the traditional guardians of their rural environment, the central difference is that, if in Britain urban pollution is seen in opposition to a rural residential or recreative 'idyll' within which agriculture plays a part (Lowe *et al.*, 1997), in France, the agricultural occupation and exploitation of the countryside remain the critical defining components of that space and its social and political representation.

Reflecting these three considerations, and the implicit linkage between an active agricultural population and a 'healthy' countryside, the agri-environmental debate in France has primarily focused on the sustainability of French agricultural activity, particularly in areas of relatively marginal economic viability. The threat of agricultural retreat, farm abandonment, a declining agricultural population and a shrinking rural economy, all components of a process of *deprise* or *desertification* and the consequent degradation of once productive lands to their 'natural' state, thereby emerge as one of the central agri-environmental concerns within France (Fottorino, 1989). Herein lies a central paradox in French farming (Buller, 1992): France has arguably benefited more than any other single EU state from the CAP and has emerged, during the post-war period, as the largest exporter of foodstuffs within the EU. Yet, the situation of a great number of farmers remains fragile. Although it is common to draw attention to the polarisation in French agriculture either between the major producers (who are also the principal recipients of subsidies) and the other less economically viable agricultural sector (Alphandéry *et al.*, 1990) or between different regional agricultural models (Neveu, 1993), French farming as a whole is facing a series of demographic, economic, social and territorial shifts (Charvet, 1994) that many commentators refer openly to as the 'crisis of French agriculture', the ineluctable and unacceptable consequence of which is rural desertification.

Therefore, while we might acknowledge the importance and the impact of the essentially Community-led farm pollution and agri-environmental agendas in ultimately provoking, coalescing and informing the French debate, the central 'environmental' preoccupation within France remains intrinsically agricultural and territorial; the protection and maintenance not only of farmers and their revenues but also of local production systems and, consequently, of the agricultural landscapes and environments that they sustain.

From heroes to villains

What were once habits are now vices

French concern for rural desertification and the economic marginalisation of upland and mountainous regions had already given rise to a series of initiatives prior to the development of a specific Community-led AEP; the designation of LFAs, the use of management agreements within the Cevennes National Park (Mousset, 1992), the creation of regional nature parks and a succession of state-led rural development programmes. While many of these strategies actively sought to maintain the rural population and to modernise the rural economy, they were also undoubtedly motivated by the need to create more equitable distribution of the agricultural policy inputs and thereby to 'compensate' such regions for the relative decline many suffered as a result of the impact of post-war agricultural modernisation and regional agricultural specialisation. The issue of rural desertification and farm abandonment has become more pertinent as agricultural intensification increased the distance between productive and marginal agricultural regions, especially between highly commercialised cereal and husbandry systems of northern France and the more extensive mixed systems of western and central parts of France, a distance that has been, if anything, reinforced by subsequent AEP.

The 1980s, however, were characterised by the relatively abrupt introduction of a new and very different agri-environmental agenda whose immediate focus was less territorial and culturally defined but notably more normative and environmental (Buller *et al.*, 1992). To a certain degree, this agenda was, initially at least, largely external to French agricultural preoccupations (Buller, 1997b). Nonetheless, concern for pesticide and nitrate levels in drinking water, ground water sources and rivers and the eutrophication of lakes and coastal waters (Ministère de l'Agriculture, 1980; Ollagnon, 1985; Larrue, 1992), stimulated by developing EU legislation in these domains, greatly raised the profile of agricultural pollution and the means, regulatory or otherwise, to combat it (Bodiguel and Buller, 1989), while the extension of cereal production into zones formerly given over to animal husbandry, and the destruction of hedgerows and farm holding reorganisation (*remembrement*), all raised questions over the destructive impact of modern farming methods (Ministère de l'Environnement, 1989). Yet, such concerns emerged at approximately the same time within a number of European States (as the current volume bears witness) and in North America (Thompson, 1995; Potter, 1998). What has, therefore, been distinctive about the impact of these concerns in France?

The answer lies in the unique role and position of the farming profession within the French economy and within France's own view of itself as a nation. Although no longer an agrarian democracy (Barral, 1968), France arguably remains strongly rooted in that tradition. French farmers had been, for 30 years, the heroes of post-war national modernisation, the foot soldiers of the 'second French revolution' and the sole and 'natural' guardians of rural space. For the first time, these emblems both of French modernity and of French post-revolutionary democratic history found not only their never-so-modern practices and their position within national representation openly challenged, but also their very (state encouraged) *raison d'être*, namely to produce, contested.

This critical period, which began in the early 1980s, was marked by a more or less explicit confrontation between the farming and environmental lobbies, the latter increasingly ready to decry the ecological effects of modern farming techniques (Buller, 1992). While it gave rise to a number of early institutional and legislative responses, notably the creation in 1984 of a joint committee for the reduction of nitrate and phosphate pollution of agricultural origin (CORPEN) and the designation of intensive animal units as classified activities, the 1980s largely failed to bring about any major positive changes either in agricultural policy or in the position of the agricultural profession which was left fragmented and defensive by a series of increasingly harsh criticisms (Caillot, 1992) and searching for a new place and identity within the French social and political landscape (Mengin, 1991; Deverre, 1998). Having undergone one 'revolution' in their lives, the post-war generation of French farmers were not about to go through another.

Aided by the relative importance of farming in the national economy, specifically as a source of exports, by the political strength of the farming lobby which had, since the 1930s, enjoyed a strongly corporatist relationship with government, and by the persistent importance accorded to farmers within national identity (Billaud and Pinton, 1996), the strategy of the agricultural profession during this period was to consistently play down the importance of farm-based pollution, when held in comparison to industrial and urban pollution. Where it had undeniably occurred, unfavourable climatic conditions were frequently evoked. Emphasising their 'traditional' role as countryside managers, while stressing, rather paradoxically, their obligation to follow the productivist logic of national and European agricultural policy and their very modernity as polluters, the agricultural policy community sought actively to resist or to contain initial agri-environmental legislation throughout the decade. For many, however, the statement in 1990 of the then Environment Minister, Brice Lalonde, marked both the end of this period of confrontation and marginal adjustment and the beginning of a more realistic position. Specifically identifying farmers as major polluters of water supplies and calling for a stricter application of the polluter-pays-principle (Berlan-Darqué and Kalaora, 1992), Lalonde ultimately created the framework for a more effective political response. While his remarks drew instant and wholly anticipated fire from the agricultural profession, they equally provided farmers' organisations with the opportunity to draw attention to those environmental actions that had already been initiated. In addition, by so openly polarising the debate, Lalonde's statement left little room for anything other than a gradual *rapprochement*. In 1991, for example, the Ministry of Agriculture launched its national labelling programme *Ferti-Mieux* aimed at reducing nitrate pollution through improved fertilisation techniques. Finally, the timing of Lalonde's statement was also significant. Preceding the 1992 CAP reforms, largely anticipating the forthcoming EU *Nitrates Directive* and Lalonde's own *Water Act* of 1992 and coinciding with the albeit late adoption in France of EU Regulation 797/85, it highlighted, above all, the need for a more co-ordinated agri-environmental strategy.

Regulation 797/85

The agricultural policy community had successfully resisted the adoption of EU-inspired agri-environmental measures until 1989 when three, albeit experimental, *Article 19* schemes (the French equivalent of the British ESAs; see Ch. 6) were created. At first at least, Regulation 797/85 was seen both as being irrelevant to wider French agricultural and indeed environmental preoccupations (Briand, 1990) and as being implicitly critical of farmers and their role in countryside management (Alphandéry and Deverre, 1994). However, after this dramatically slow start, and following the repositioning of the agri-environmental debate at the end of the 1980s, the number of schemes did expand, reaching 61 immediately prior to the implementation of Regulation 2078 in 1993. Collectively, these concerned 737,000 ha of which some 205,200 ha were eligible for payments (representing 2.5% and 0.7% of the agricultural area of France). Their objectives reveal, above all, the dominant and territorially distinct concerns of the agricultural policy community (Table 2.1). Schemes aimed at supporting agricultural incomes, combating agricultural withdrawal and the accompanying environmental consequences, covered the largest area and predominated in the Alps, the Jura and the Pyrenees as well as the southern fringe of the Massif Central. A second set of schemes, established to protect wildlife in small and focused sensitive areas, were concentrated in the coastal marshes of western France. In addition, a small number of schemes were established to combat forest fires through the maintenance of extensive woodland grazing systems and to reduce farm-based water pollution through extensification. These later schemes, however, were ruled ineligible for Community co-funding as they were considered contradictory to the polluter-pays principle and contrary to the principle of reducing production respectively.

Table 2.1 *Article 19* **zones under Regulation 797/85 in France**

	Number of ESAs (n)	Number of agreements (n)	Area under agreement (ha)	Average area under agreement per contractant (ha)
Water pollution	4	130	4,622	35.5
Sensitive ecosystems	28	2523	47,265	18.7
Farming retreat	25	781	24,472	31.3
Forest fire Prevention	4	85	5,086	59.8
TOTAL	61	3519	81,445	23.1

Source: CNASEA, 1993

Nonetheless, despite this late expansion, *Article 19* policy was, in terms of national agricultural policy, never more than a marginal exercise. It benefited from a minimal annual budgetary allocation (15 MECU by 1993). It was composed of relatively small schemes whose average size was around 3,350 ha and whose total eligible area fell well below that of other EU states (nearly one million ha in Britain; see Ch. 6). Schemes were frequently established in marginal agricultural regions, thereby perpetuating the long-standing divide between production oriented and non-production oriented agricultural policy. Finally, the first agri-environmental schemes were often met more with bemusement than with enthusiasm by farmers, particularly in upland areas. The relatively low total area under contract (81,445 ha or 0.2% of the French agricultural area) can be chiefly explained by the unease which farmers felt over the implicit challenge that agri-environmental schemes contained to their fundamental 'right to produce' and by their subsequent labelling as 'nature's gardeners'. Ultimately, as we have stated elsewhere, the central reason for the limited implementation of *Article 19* policy in France derives from the agricultural sector's early reluctance to allow agri-environmental measures to develop in any way as a broad challenge, either to pre-existing agricultural policy or to the traditional role of the farmer in countryside management (Boisson and Buller, 1996). If Britain saw Article 19 of Regulation 797/85 as a way of introducing an environmental agenda into agricultural policy (Whitby and Lowe, 1994; see Ch. 6), France sought to implement it above all as a structural measure for aiding agriculturally less-favoured regions; an interpretation that, we would argue, continues to dominate that nation's AEP.

Yet, while it is easy to be dismissive of the French response to *Article 19*, we should nonetheless be careful not to overlook the subtle shifts that accompanied its eventual implementation. There are three such shifts that ultimately served to prepare the political ground for a more comprehensive agri-environmental programme following Regulation 2078. First, it reinforced the role of local actors in the elaboration of agricultural policy by not only providing financial assistance to areas in difficulty, but also by allowing farmers to take a more active role in establishing a territorial policy for agricultural management (Alphandéry and Deverre, 1994). In doing so, it created an increasing distance between, on the one hand, the national agricultural policy community which continued to see such measures as being essentially marginal, and, on the other hand, local farming communities for whom it had a very real pertinence (Rémy, 1997). Second, it introduced the notion of contractualisation hitherto virtually unknown to the French agricultural profession. Accustomed to unconditional agricultural support systems, the idea of voluntarily engaging to respect a set of obligations and thereby receiving premiums linked to compliance was, initially, a difficult concept to get across. It remains, to this day, a controversial issue and one that limits the wider application of agri-environmental measures. Third, the implementation of agri-environmental schemes provided France with an important negotiating position during the discussions over CAP reform and its accompanying measures. The centre piece of the current programme, the *grassland premium*, is thereby an inspired juxtaposition of the classic French agri-environmental preoccupation, rural desertification, and the need to redistribute agricultural support (see below).

Ultimately, French AEP remained, at least until 1994, focused, first, upon land that was essentially marginal to agricultural production and, second, upon agricultural rather than environmental management styles. In this, *Article 19* policy – though it clearly had an important impact within specifically sensitive zones such as the Crau in Provence (Deverre, 1998) or the Marais Poitevin (Billaud, 1994) or in those broader areas where designated zones were integrated into other rural management structures such as national or regional parks – has been perhaps less successful in challenging the long-standing policy separation that has characterised the French approach to agriculture and the environment since the 1960s.

Regulation 2078 and all that

The implementation of Regulation 2078 marked a major departure for French AEP up to that point. Economic circumstances, particularly those linked to agricultural policy evolution and the need to find other forms of direct payments to farmers, environmental concerns prompted by growing awareness not only of the scale of agricultural pollution but also of the image and identity problem it was creating for the farming profession, political considerations, and the need to take an innovative approach, all led the French government to respond far more positively to Regulation 2078 than had ever been the case with Regulation 797/85. Regulation 2078, thereby, marked a turning point in agricultural and environmental policy relations in that it permitted the generalisation of measures rather, as was the case under its predecessor, than their restriction to known and relatively small sensitive areas. Thus, while AEP under 797/85 (*Article 19* zones) and other pre-2078/92 Regulations (extensification and voluntary set-aside) concerned approximately 300,000 ha under contract, amounting to one percent of the UAA, measures adopted under Regulation 2078 currently cover nearly 6 million ha or 20% of the total UAA.

French AEP resulting directly from Regulation 2078 can be divided into three central elements (Table 2.2). The first consists of the national *grassland premium* for the maintenance of extensive husbandry: a 'horizontal' scheme made available to eligible farmers throughout France and for which the contractual obligations, rules and payment levels have been set nationally (Figure 2.1). The second element consists of the 'regional programmes' that include seven standard measures broadly corresponding to the agri-environmental actions identified in Regulation

2078. The contractual obligations, rules and payment levels for these are set nationally through the definition of target zones (where appropriate), and the setting of budget allocations are undertaken by the regional level administrations in consultation with local actors. The final element of the French policy are the 'local operations' which, though they in fact form part of the regional programmes, may be considered separately because of their fundamentally different structure (Figure 2.2). Following on directly from *Article 19* under Regulation 797/85 (the bulk of former *Article 19* schemes becoming local operations under Regulation 2078), these specifically targeted or 'zonal' schemes are established locally or regionally; the territories concerned, the contractual obligations, rules and payment levels being decided by local actors prior to submission for approval to the Ministry at the European Commission.

Table 2.2   Agri-environmental schemes adopted in France under Regulation 2078

Type of measure		Schemes
National Measures		Maintenance of extensive grassland-based husbandry systems
Regional programmes	1	Protection of water resources through the reduction of entrants
	2	Conversion of arable land to extensive grassland
	3	20-year set-aside for water protection
	4	Extensification through the reduction in stocking rate or by enlarging grazing area
	5	Preservation of threatened breeds
	6	20-year set-aside for wildlife protection
	7	Conversion to organic farming
Local operations		Landscape and wildlife protection, the maintenance of traditional farming practices and countryside management

Source: authors

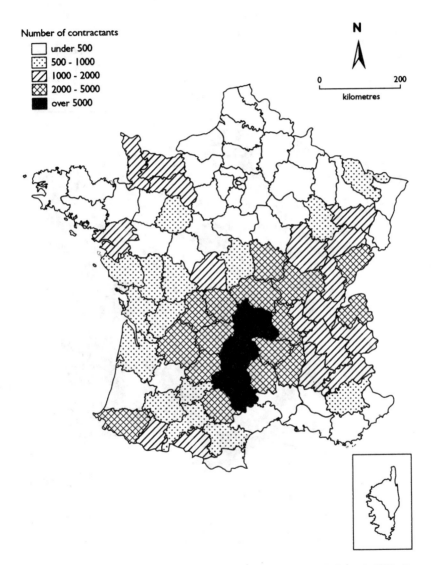

**Figure 2.1   Numbers of contractants to the French *Prime à l'Herbe*
(by Départment 1996)**

Source: From unpublished Ministry figures

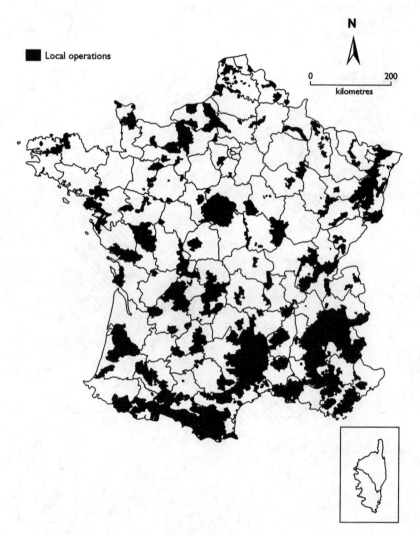

Figure 2.2   Local operations in France

Source: authors

The grassland premium

From the outset, the emphasis, both in terms of budgetary allocation and targeted agricultural area, has been placed upon the major 'horizontal' scheme: the maintenance of extensive husbandry or *grassland premium*. This single scheme, introduced in 1993, currently accounts for 70% of the annual agri-environmental budget (200 MECU out of a total of 290 MECU), despite the fact that the premium payment (46 ECU/ha/year) is one of the lowest agri-environmental payments available. As an agri-environmental scheme, the premium is revealing both of the French agenda and of the French position *vis-à-vis* EU AEP as a whole. The stated objective of the scheme was to maintain low density permanent pasture-based husbandry systems, the bulk of which are located in the LFAs of France, and thereby protect the landscape and associated habitats either from the consequences of abandonment, conifer planting or conversion to arable crops. Thus, it responded to the classic preoccupation for the sustainability of agriculture within marginal regions, as well as to a growing environmental concern for the decline of permanent pasture land within France. However, the *grassland premium* was also adopted in response to growing criticism of the inequalities of CAP direct aid schemes. Not only did beef and milk farmers complain that CAP reforms favoured cereal growers, but also that forage crops were favoured over permanent grassland. The decision to adopt a grassland premium was announced by the French Minister of Agriculture in anticipation of Regulation 2078. Subsequently, and after much negotiation, the Commission agreed to accept it as part of the Regulation and, thus, co-finance the measure, though this has been, in many ways, a reluctant acceptance (Boisson and Buller, 1996).

During its first year of operation, the *grassland premium* was made available to farmers over the entire national territory, provided they had a minimum UAA of 3 ha on which to apply the scheme and a stock density not exceeding 1.4 LU/ha. Contractants currently receive 46 ECU per ha of grassland per year, with an annual ceiling of 4,545 ECU per farm, for which they engage to maintain stock densities, not to reduce their grassland area, retain at least 75% of the UAA as grassland for the five-year period, to undertake basic grassland management (including hedgerows and water courses) and not to apply more than 70 kg/ha of nitrogen fertiliser.

As a broad and shallow agri-environmental measure, the *grassland premium* has been an undoubted success. Currently (1997), some 102,000 contracts have been established, covering a total area of 5.5 million ha (nearly 20% of the French UAA). Though this figure is unlikely to rise further, as the vast bulk of contracts were established in the first year of operation, it comes very close to early Ministry estimates of the potential surface concerned (around 5.7 million ha). In spatial terms, the *grassland premium* has had the most successful take-up rates in the Massif Central (Auvergne and Limousin regions). Closely linked to areas of husbandry and particularly upland farming (with 45% of the surface area currently under contract being in mountain zones and 36% in other LFAs), the scheme has had little, if any, impact in the lowland regions of northern and north-eastern France where the bulk of farms fall outside the eligibility criteria (18% only of contracts in these regions) (see Figure 2.1).

For the beef sector, threatened by falling prices, a crisis in consumer confidence, and a fragile aid system, the grassland subsidy has been a welcome support. Likewise, it has been generally considered as a viable contribution to rural support in LFAs. Certainly, representing as it does 2.8% of all French direct aids to farmers, it is a significant complement to LFA policy (around 5% of all direct aids) and specific cattle subsidies (13% of all aids although not all of these concern LFAs). While combined these fall a long way behind the proportion of direct aid given over to arable area payments (65%), they can be seen as an attempt to achieve a more equitable distribution of agricultural funding, both in territorial terms and in terms of farm systems. Where the *grassland premium* has seemed less immediately convincing, is as an agri-environmental scheme. Yet, criticisms based upon the absence of a perceived threat of possible environmental degradation, the relative stability of extensive grass-based production systems, and the minimal obligations linked to contractualisation, have obfuscated the central 'environmental' goal of the scheme; to maintain what is intrinsically a relatively environmentally friendly farming practice in areas that are not only valued for their agricultural landscapes but are also heavily dependent upon the maintenance of agricultural activities. The *grassland premium* does not actively seek changes in farm management practices. In a nation where the active loss of permanent pasture land is still regarded as significant (Institut Francais pour l'Environnement, 1997), and in regions where rural depopulation and agricultural land abandonment are common, a scheme that maintains as farmed grassland some 20% of the agricultural area is of clear value.

The regional programmes

Under the terms of France's implementation of Regulation 2078, each of the 22 French regions was required to submit, during 1993, a regional agri-environmental programme comprising proposals and desired budgetary allocations for the seven standard schemes (see Table 2.2 above) and for any intended 'local operations'. The total budget set-aside for the regional and local schemes was initially set at around 80 MECU/year or 400 MECU for the whole five-year period of contractualisation, compared with an average of 210 MECU/year or 1050 MECU over five years being allocated to the *grassland premium*.

The distribution of allocated annual funds by scheme (Table 2.3) reveals the clear domination of the 'local operations' (including the former *Article 19* schemes) within the regional programmes (see also Figure 2.2 above). Beyond these, those schemes aimed at reducing agricultural pollution (the reduction of entrants and the conversion of arable land to grassland) account for nearly 20% of the allocated budget, while the schemes implying a longer term commitment to environmental protection (long-term set-aside and conversion to organic farming) account for only a relatively small percentage of total budgetary allocations (at 11%).

Table 2.3 Budgetary allocations of regional agri-environmental programmes by measure for 1995

Scheme	% of total budget	Annual budget (MECU)	Target (LU or ha)
Reduction of entrants	9.8	7.8	43,265 ha
Organic farming	8.6	6.9	45,692 ha
Conversion of arable land to extensive grassland	9.6	7.7	20,424 ha
Extensification	11.9	9.4	41,725 LU
Protection of threatened species	1.8	1.4	23,766 LU
Long term set-aside for water protection and nature conservation	1.6	1.2	2,416 ha
Local operations	56.7	45.6	609,427 ha
Total	100	80.0	–

Source: Ministère de l'Agriculture, various years; CNASEA, various years

Three years on from the establishment of the regional programmes, these broad intentions have been confirmed by highly differential rates of farmer engagement. Of the 29,120 contracts currently established, 8,887

(30.5%) concern the seven standard schemes and 20,233 (69.5%) the local operations. Among the former, the experimental reduction of entrants measure, which seeks a 20% reduction in the application of nitrogen fertilisers within regionally designated nitrate sensitive areas and offers participating farmers up to 182 ECU/ha, has recorded some success with 2,452 contracts concerning 58,106 ha. Of all the standard measures, it is the only one to have had any impact in the cereal areas of Picardie and Centre. However, it has proved largely ineffectual with respect to its central objective of combating water pollution on any significant or long term scale: the areas under contract are often too isolated or too small to have a major impact upon water quality, while farmers frequently perceive the premiums paid less as an encouragement to adopt an alternative management style than as a temporary compensation for profits momentarily foregone (Barbut, 1997). The measure aiding farmers to convert to organic farming has, by way of contrast, had an arguably more significant impact, despite the fact that the number of contractants is inferior (1189 contracts concerning 28,381 ha). Not only does conversion to organic production imply a far more radical change to farm practices, and hence a longer term commitment, but the scheme is having the effect of breaking the long-held taboo regarding organic farming as a marginal activity carried out by an essentially non-agricultural neo-rural population.

In general, the standard schemes of the regional programmes have met with limited success when held in comparison both with the *grassland premium* and the 'local operations'. Three principal reasons for this might be advanced. First, they reflect an essentially 'environmental' agenda (pollution reduction) which continues to remain external to dominant French agricultural concerns. Extensification, farm expansion and the taking of land out of production are difficult to advocate in a nation that is rather seeking to protect its agricultural area and to replace its ageing agricultural population by the installation of young farmers. It is notable, for example, that the standard schemes have a significantly greater success in the northern regions than in the south where the agri-environmental debate, focusing upon abandonment and land degradation, is fundamentally different. A second reason is that the standard schemes offer little room for local negotiation, the contractual obligations and the remunerations being established nationally. Finally, and linked to the second point, the standard schemes have not proved attractive to local authorities who are increasingly emerging as important financial and political actors in the support of agri-environmental schemes. Where local authority finance is forthcoming, 81% of it is directed towards 'local operations' (CNASEA, 1997).

The local operations

Arising from *Article 19* policy prior to Regulation 2078, the local operations might be seen both as a continuation and as an extension of the *Article 19* approach. First, in being zonal, they have a distinct spatial focus (see Figure 2.2 above), second, they are drawn up locally with contractual obligations that are tailored to meet local criteria and, third, they frequently form part of a broader concern that embraces not only ecologically sensitive rural territories but also the farming systems that are integral to them. Where the local operations differ from the preceding *Article 19* schemes is, first, in their budgetary status, second, in their numbers and third, in the range of agri-environmental situations they address.

For 1995, the local operations had an allocated annual budget of 45 MECU (57% of the total agri-environmental budget to that time excluding the *grassland premium*). This might be compared to the *Article 19* budget which never rose beyond 15 MECU. By the end of 1997 that had risen to 57 MECU or 60% of the total, with some 250 operations approved by the Star Committee. The total surface contracted under these schemes amounted to 551,603 ha by the end of 1997. Once again, this needs to be seen against the 61 approved *Article 19* schemes under Regulation 797/85 whose total contracted area amounted to 80,445 ha.

The local operations address a wide range of agri-environmental issues and conditions and, in doing so, vary considerably in their size and financial envelopes. Although the Ministry of Agriculture offers a broad six-point grouping (Table 2.4), in reality local operations can differ significantly even within one group. By 1997, some 67% (11,952) of established contracts concerned wildlife and ecosystem protection schemes, the bulk falling in the west and north of the country (Pays de la Loire, Poitou Charentes, Haute Normandie) and 26% (7,663 contracts) concerning the maintenance of low intensive farming practices in regions threatened by land abandonment, notably the southern regions of Languedoc Roussillon, Midi-Pyrénées, Rhône Alpes and Provence-Alpes-Côte d'Azur. By contrast, the intensive agricultural regions of the north (Picardie, Champagne-Ardenne and Ile de France) contain only 12 schemes in total, representing 3.6% of the total area and 5.7% of the total national local operations budget (see Figure 2.2).

Table 2.4 Types of approved local operations (January 1996)

Type of operation	N° of schemes	Allocated budget (MECU)	Potentially contractable surface (ha)
Landscape protection	78	15.4	251,879
Wildlife and species diversity	98	21.7	280,931
Water protection	14	4.6	28,837
Prevention of forest fires	11	2.2	26,673
Public access	2	0.06	12
Experimental zones	1	0.0003	2,050
Total	**204[1]**	**43.9**	**590,382**

(1) Since 1996 an additional 46 schemes have been approved.

Source: Ministère de l'Agriculture, 1996

The French response to Regulation 2078 has been unquestionably significant. France now ranks fourth among Member States in its agri-environmental budget and among the highest states in terms of the proportion of its UAA given over to some form of agri-environmental management. The agricultural policy community has come to accept, firstly, that increasing productivity is not the sole means by which agricultural activities need to be assessed and rewarded and, secondly, that there is an outstanding need to address modern farming's contribution to, and impact upon, environmental quality. Here agri-environmental schemes, as defined by Regulation 2078, have not emerged in isolation. Indeed, the *grassland premium* and the regional programmes constitute one aspect of an increasingly important range of measures, schemes and programmes that are, for the most part, both voluntary and operated by actors within the profession. The *sustainable farm development plans* (PDD) were introduced as an experimental scheme in 1995 on 1,200 farms. Although there is little financial premium associated with the scheme for participating farmers, it has nonetheless paved the way for a new approach to whole-farm management planning, in a way that recalls the Irish REPS scheme, that is fundamentally different from the long-running *farm modernisation plans* that the PDD might ultimately replace (Buller, 1997a). Similarly, the *farm pollution scheme* (PMPOA), though not part of statutory AEP, shares many of its broad approaches. It is also voluntary, offering financial incentives to farmers agreeing to improve pollution control techniques on their holdings. Its high take-up rate (90% of eligible farmers) and extended budget (92 MECU) bear witness to its strategic importance as a means of gaining an advance on inevitable and mandatory legislative control, particularly that anticipated with respect to EU Directive 676/91 whose implementation, France, like many of its neighbours, has successfully delayed. Significantly, as France prepares its next five-year agri-environmental programme, the relationship between the 2078 schemes and the non-2078 schemes becomes more blurred. The PDD will, it is intended, become incorporated in the new programme, while the regional standard scheme for the reduction of entrants will be abandoned, as will a number of others. Recognising the agricultural profession's clear preference for the *grassland premium* and the 'local operations' these will be strengthened and simplified.

A new role, a new divide?

If France's response to Regulation 2078 represents a major advance, that advance cannot be dissociated from that state's own particular internal agenda. AEP in France is essentially about maintenance: the maintenance of extensive, often family farm structures operating in low density rural areas where structural disadvantages remain significant; the maintenance of 'traditional' practices that have not undergone substantive intensification during the *Trente Glorieuses* that so marked the agricultural landscapes of the Ile de France, Picardie and the Marne; the maintenance of farming's role in rural communities. Second, the French experience has been about the environment as *territory* rather than the environment as *nature* – the environment as a product of agricultural activity and as a critical element in that activity rather than something external to and affected by that activity. Third, AEP has been about farm policy and the achievement of a more equitable distribution of farm support. In many upland regions, the *grassland premium*, LFA schemes, and *male and suckler cow premiums* combine to form a set of aids that are as much about a type of farming as a type of environment or landscape. What conclusions can we then draw about French AEP? Has it really changed anything or has France been able, in characteristic style, to turn a largely Anglo-Saxon and north European agenda into a particularly French form of farm subsidy?

AEP has had little impact upon the broad geography of farming-environment relations. The areas most concerned are those that have remained largely marginal to French agricultural intensification: the extensive upland regions often still touched by rural depopulation or the wetlands and other sensitive ecosystems that have, for the most part, escaped intensification for economic reasons. The geographical correlation between, on the one hand, the *grassland premium* and 'local operations' aimed at combating desertification and, on the other hand, the designated LFAs and Objective 5b regions is quite evident (Buller, 1998c). Thus, just as an 'extensive-husbandry-France' has long been distinguished from an 'arable-France', so an 'agri-environmental-France' might now be distinguished from a 'compensatory-payments-France'. However, at a more local level, AEP is perhaps having a more significant geographical impact. Often linked to attempts to stimulate or to reinforce the development of regionally specific products, agri-environmental schemes are, we would argue, helping to promote a new territorialisation of agricultural systems. It is notable, for example, that many 'local operations', particularly those that seek to maintain traditional farming practices, have been set up within the framework of regional nature parks (themselves as much oriented towards rural development as to landscape protection) and, as such, have been implicitly linked to regional product labelling schemes. As rural France seeks to display its diversity and richness to an increasingly selective non-agricultural population, agri-environmental schemes become important elements in the de-specialisation of regional agricultural models (Buller, 1998c) and in the promotion of rural development.

Has AEP changed the way in which agricultural policy is made and implemented? Although it is far too early to hazard a response to this critical question, we can offer a number of tentative observations. First, there is little doubt that if AEP has not, in itself, been a force for policy decentralisation, it has clearly reinforced the current trend towards an increasingly sub-central input into agricultural policy-making. The adopted methodology of the regional programmes has given the regional state bureaux and the elected regional councils a significant input not only into the elaboration of policy, but also its implementation and monitoring. The 'local operations' have undoubtedly been as important for their form as for their content. The bringing together of farmers' organisations, environmental groups, local elected leaders, agricultural advisory services and state administrators within the individual scheme 'pilot committees' has been, for many local actors, a fundamental breakthrough permitting a redefining of the classic 'positions' of the various interests involved (Mormont, 1996; Jauneau and Rémy, 1997) and leading to an albeit gradual construction of what can become alternative forms of social relation between farmer and non-farmer within the territorial context of the schemes.

Second, many traditional roles and positions have shifted as the environmental agenda has assumed a greater importance. In part, this has been in response to the need to contain the debate. The agricultural profession has consistently sought to demonstrate its 'hands on' response, achieving important concessions with respect to mandatory controls and monitoring, in exchange for voluntary adhesion to schemes and codes of good practice. The agricultural advisory services of the *Chambres d'Agriculture* have played a central role in this shift, emerging as key proselytisers of local AEP (Brives, 1998).

Third, AEP has, if anything, confused a formerly straightforward corporatist model of agricultural representation. Clearly, it has not been the only element in this confusion. Arguably, the traditional hegemony of the national farmers' union was in any case bound to come under threat as European policy gradually rendered national corporatist structures less powerful. Nevertheless, the growing dissimilarity between the interests of the intensive cereal producers and the extensive beef producers, one that AEP is strengthening, has led to a pronounced division not only in terms of strategy and demands but also in terms of representation. While the former interests see AEP as wholly marginal to their principal concerns and essentially a means of aiding regions suffering from structural disadvantage, the latter increasingly see it both as vital to their survival and as recognition of the inherent legitimacy of their particular production systems.

Finally, AEP has, as one would have every reason to hope, brought the agricultural and environmental policy communities closer together. Hitherto, environmental considerations are part of environmental policy and a set of specific interministerial structures exist to facilitate the interchange. The environmental lobby has declared itself to be, for the present, both encouraged by the progress on 2078 implementation and, to some extent, astonished that it has happened at all. Ten years ago, the commitment of 252 MECU/year of the farm budget to environmental schemes, the placing of 20% of the French agricultural area under agreement and the engagement of some 140,000 farmers would have been unthinkable (Metais, 1997). That having been said, the difficulties encountered with respect to the implementation of the EU Habitats Directive reveal how far these two policy communities still have to go in achieving a genuine balance between agricultural and environmental objectives. Ultimately, the French experience with Regulation 2078 demonstrates the fundamental paradox of agri-environmental schemes. Their success (or failure) cannot be ascertained according to purely agricultural or purely environmental criteria. A recent conference in Paris failed to resolve the question as to whether AEP at a national or regional level, or agri-environmental strategies at the farm level, were, in reality, an 'alibi' or a genuine contribution to agricultural sustainability (Société française d'économie rurale, 1997). As the basis for farm payments moves away from food and raw material production, that paradox will perhaps yield to a more territorial notion of farming as one, albeit central component of a rural product.

3 Denmark: implementation of new agri-environmental policy based on Regulation 2078

Erling Andersen, Anita Henningsen and Jørgen Primdahl

Agriculture and environment in the Danish context

Danish landscapes have been largely formed either by glacial processes or, in the northern parts of the country, by subsequent natural uplift. Today, these landscapes are essentially given over to agriculture. A little more than 60% of the Danish land area is agricultural land, of which more than 90% is arable. No other European country has such an intensive agricultural land use structure, a factor which partly explains the relatively limited importance hitherto given to agri-environmental schemes (Whitby, 1996a; EC, 1997a). Forest covers about 12% of the country, and it is a government objective to double the forest area in the next 100 years. Most of the high ecological value landscapes are found either in small patches of forest or within semi-natural grasslands such as salt marshes, bogs, meadows, pastures and heathlands. Undisturbed natural habitats are rare, located only in certain forests and along parts of the Danish coastline.

The agricultural structure in Denmark is characterised by a mixture of large family-owned farms and small part-time farms dependent mainly on supplementary urban incomes. This farm structure polarisation is currently increasing; farms smaller than 5 ha and farms larger than 50 ha are growing in numbers while those in-between are decreasing (Strukturdirektoratet, 1998). Tenant farming is rare, but about one-fourth of the agricultural land is managed by farmers who do not own the land they work (land is usually leased on a short term basis). Danish agricultural production is relatively intensive compared to other EU countries. Although Denmark only accounts for 2% of the UAA of the EU, more than 5% of the total EU cereal production in 1995 came from Denmark and almost 10% of pigs in the EU are on Danish farms (De danske landboforeninger, 1996a). As in most other EU members states, during the last 35 years Danish agriculture has undergone substantial intensification of production, reflected in increased chemical inputs per ha, decreased inputs of person-power, and higher commodity outputs. While in 1960 an average of 40 kg/N/ha was applied on arable land, by 1990 this figure had risen to 117 kg/N/ha. Over the same period, the full-time agricultural workforce declined from 300,000 people to 80,000. Total agricultural production over this period, however, grew by 74% (De danske landboforeninger, 1996b).

The development of Danish agriculture as described above has had a profound impact on landscape and environment. We might identify the following changes: First, small biotopes such as hedges, ponds and small wetlands have almost disappeared in many parts of Eastern Denmark (Agger and Brandt, 1988; Brandt *et al.*, 1994). Second, the area of permanent grassland has been reduced from approximately 345,000 ha in 1960 to about 200,000 ha in 1996, mainly due to reclamation of wet meadows and the ploughing up of pastures (De danske landboforeninger, 1996b). Third, since the mid-1980s, eutrophication and the pollution of groundwater due to leaching of nitrates have become major concerns (Daugbjerg, 1998). In groundwater (which is the dominant source of drinking-water supplies), the content of nitrates has been found to exceed 25 mg/N per litre in 22% of drinking water boreholes and 50 mg/N per litre in 13% of boreholes (Christensen *et al.*, 1993). In watercourses, the concentration of nitrates is at least seven times higher in agricultural areas than in uncultivated natural zones (Miljø- og Energiministeriet, 1995a; Daugbjerg, 1998). Fourth, since 1990, pollution of groundwater by pesticides has received increasing attention in Denmark. Following an extensive monitoring programme of 900 boreholes, pesticide residuals were found in 9% of the boreholes, while maximum standards were exceeded in 3% (Miljø- og Energiministeriet, 1995a). In recent years, the monitoring programme has been enlarged to include a wider range of pesticides. The first results show that in some Danish counties traces of pesticides can be found in 40-75% of boreholes. Finally, the impact of agriculture on biodiversity has also been a cause of concern. The population change of three key species in the agricultural landscape provides some indications about habitat changes. The number of hares (*Lepus capensis*) killed by hunters, for example, has been reduced from more than 400,000/year in the 1950s to less than 250,000/year in the 1980s while that of partridges (*Perdix perdix*) has similarly fallen from more than 300,000/year to less than 100,000/year, both due essentially to a decline in the total population. The total population of lapwings (*Vanellus vanellus*) is estimated to have been reduced by 70% during the period from 1976 to 1994 (Miljø- og Energiministeriet, 1995b).

These factors have prompted increasing popular concern and have led to a growing demand on farmers to act not only as food producers but also as environmental managers. They have also led to the establishment of a comprehensive set of regulations governing the environmental impact of modern farming practices. In addition, an increasing amount of money is being offered to farmers to support them in their role as environmental managers.

Danish environmental and landscape regulations

Environmental regulations

From the early 1980s onwards, the use of fertilisers and pesticides has been regulated and monitored, initially in order to achieve a target reduction of nitrate leaching of 50% by 1993 (later postponed to the year 2000), and to reduce both the use of pesticides and pesticide residuals found in water. The schemes to reduce fertiliser use have focused largely on technical solutions including requirements on storage capacity, stipulations that winter-green fields should cover a minimum of 65% of the agricultural area, restrictions on the number of livestock per ha and obligatory cropping plans and fertiliser balance accounts which also include maximum N-application limits at field level. Similar technical solutions have also been implemented for pesticides. In addition, a tax of up to 37% of the retail price has been introduced in order to reduce pesticide use (Miljøministeriet, 1994).

Landscape regulations

In Denmark, there are no centrally designated protected national landscapes or national parks of the type found in most other European countries. Instead, Danish nature conservation is based on general regulations, including planning regulations and so-called 'conservation orders'. Under conservation orders, specifically designated areas are protected against undesired changes not included by environmental regulations, with landowners receiving one-off compensations for changes in management practices. Conservation orders normally provide for wider recreational access for the public, and include landscape management guidelines that entitle county councils to manage specific areas regardless of the owners' wishes. By 1993, about 5% of the country (190,000 ha), including sites varying from a few ha to several thousand ha, had been placed under conservation orders. While such land is usually privately held, an additional 120,000 ha of forest and natural areas are owned and managed by the Danish *National Forest and Nature Agency* (Primdahl, 1996).

Through various amendments to the *Nature Protection Act*, more and more habitats have been subject to general protection provisions. All bogs, heaths, salt marshes and semi-natural grassland larger than 2,500 m² are protected and no compensations are paid to landowners when applications to make changes are turned down (e.g. draining or reclamation of natural meadows). Barrows, stone- and earthwalls and natural water courses are also included under these provisions. The protection status prevents changes to protected landscape elements. Thus, an established agricultural practice may continue, but no intensification will normally be allowed. Finally, the *Nature Management Act* 1989 (now incorporated in the *Nature Protection Act*) has been an important initiative to ensure financial support for nature conservation, nature restoration, afforestation and recreation. The Act has made funds available for public acquisition of land and associated management projects. It also provides for subsidies to counties, local authorities, other organisations and landowners for the conservation, management and restoration of nature, as well as for recreational access and facilities.

Danish agri-environmental schemes, therefore, should be seen in the context of a well-developed land use and nature conservation legislation that has already ensured the conservation of many ecologically valuable landscape elements.

Danish agri-environmental policies before 1992

AEPs (or policies with similar contents) already existed in Denmark before they were formally incorporated into the European agenda. Danish counties had agreements with farmers concerning the maintenance of ecologically valuable areas through conservation orders (see above), and the *Nature and Forest Agency* had agreements with farmers to manage state-owned farmland. Both these types of agreements focused particularly on environmentally sustainable management of permanent grassland. Further, before it became a part of the agri-environmental programme (see below), support for organic farming was also offered nationally in Denmark in 1987.

Danish legislation concerning agriculture in *Environmentally Sensitive Areas* (ESAs), according to *Article 19* of Regulation 797/85 (EC, 1985b), was approved by the Danish Parliament in 1989, and the first agreements were signed in 1990. The county authorities were placed in charge of implementing the scheme and their responsibilities included the designation of ESAs, the formulation of specific prescriptions for each ESA, and decisions about the content of individual agreements. The Ministry of Agriculture was charged with approving designated ESAs, and was also the main Danish authority responsible for liasing with the EU Commission. Many counties started designating ESAs in 1989 based on guidelines from the Ministry of Agriculture that left considerable scope for individual regional strategies. The counties made optimal use of this discretion. A total of 915 ESAs covering an area of 126,010 ha were designated, corresponding to 4.5% of the Danish UAA. Some counties avoided establishing ESAs on land already covered by other forms of environmental legislation so as to increase the total amount of protected land. Other counties designated ESAs within such areas in order to finance their management costs. Overall, about 25% of the total ESA area was covered, or partly covered, by conservation orders. Further, 35% of the designated area was fully or partly covered by the EC *Bird Protection Directive*. Whether already under protected status or not, the counties generally designated areas with comparatively high landscape and environmental values (Primdahl and Hansen, 1993). Thus, habitat protection emerges as a central objective in nearly all ESAs, while landscape values and the protection of surface waters (water courses, lakes, and coastal areas) are specifically identified in certain, but not all, areas. The protection of groundwater and protection against ochre pollution are limited to a smaller number of specific ESAs.

All the agreements signed under *Article 19* of Regulation 797/85 were five-year agreements, with payments varying from 51 to 114 ECU/ha/year. Five counties used the maximum rate for all agreements, while in the remaining counties payments varied according to the degree of management restrictions. The average payment for all agreements signed in 1990 was 100 ECU/ha/year. Most agreements were concerned with the maintenance of permanent grassland, although restrictions within agreements varied significantly from county to county. For example, two counties out of 14 consistently banned the utilisation of fertiliser/manure and pesticides while other counties permitted the application of fertiliser up to a specified N-level. Overall, 40% of agreements included a ban on fertilisers, 54% established maximum N supply limits, and 6% had no fertiliser or N supply constraints. Further, 41% of agreements included a ban on pesticides, and 61% included a ban on ploughing, levelling and re-seeding (Primdahl and Hansen, 1993). The permitted date for mowing and restrictions on livestock units per ha also varied between counties.

That agreements could include very different restrictions between the counties had advantages and disadvantages. On the one hand, it made them flexible and responsive to local natural conditions and local farming practices. On the other hand, the great variations in payments and restrictions caused confusion and, in some cases, clear injustices between farmers in different counties.

The ESAs were approved by the *Directorate of Agriculture* in early 1990, and over 3,000 agreements had been signed by the end of that year. This large number was made possible by two factors. First, agreements were signed at a decentralised level and, second, most agreements had only a limited impact on current management practices thereby making the conditions relatively attractive to farmers. Between 1990 and the end of 1991, the two-year period during which it was possible to enter agreements, 4,200 agreements were signed covering an area of 31,500 ha or 1.1% of the UAA and 10 to 15% of permanent grassland (Jordbrugsdirektoratet, 1993). The agreement costs amounted to one million ECU in 1990 and reached a maximum of 2.7 MECU in 1992 (Danmarks Statistik, 1993). The uptake of agreements was particularly successful in ESAs where salt marshes were the dominant landscape type. In such ESAs, around one-third of the area had already been placed under agreement by the end of 1990. River valleys (mainly meadows and wet pastures) also had relatively high coverage, while there was relatively poor uptake on farms located on moraines and outwash plains. The latter is somewhat surprising as the predominant soils are sandy and poor, with conditions suited to more extensive forms of farming. There was a significantly higher uptake in ESAs partly or totally covered by conservation orders (see above) or by the *Bird Protection Directive*. Overall, the number of ESA agreements, together with the size of area covered by agreements, varied considerably across the counties.

Research has shown that the preservation of existing permanent grassland was the most significant outcome of ESA agreements (Hansen and Primdahl, 1991). Indeed, 86% of agreements comprised areas for which continued management of permanent grassland was the main objective of the agreement. Of the areas under agreement, 8% were converted from arable land to grassland, and another 6% remained in rotation. This indicates that relatively few agreements were entered for arable land and few agreements led to landscape enhancement in the form of conversion from arable to permanent grassland. It must be asked therefore whether the *ESA scheme* had any genuine effect on the protection of those permanent grasslands threatened by changes in management or by abandonment.

The immediate effects of the initial ESA agreements were studied in detail by Hansen and Primdahl (1991). In a wide-ranging farm survey, farmers were asked, first, if they had changed the actual management practice because of the ESA agreement and, second, whether they would have changed the use of the area, for instance abandoned grazing and mowing, had they not signed an agreement. Of the 93 farmers who had signed an agreement on permanent grassland, 42 had changed their management practices as a consequence of the agreement. Typical changes in management practices were reduced fertiliser application and a cessation of re-seeding. Yet, many (51 of the 93 farmers) said that the agreement did not result in any changes in management practices, and 81 mentioned that they would not have changed the use of the area if no agreement had been offered. In other words, these 81 farmers would have continued grazing or mowing, even without the agreement. Farmers, however, are rarely in a position to predict the future: a change in fodder and crop prices, including subsidy-related changes, as well as unexpected events at the farm level (e.g. a broken leg), could have easily put a stop to grazing on the most outlying or poorest grasslands. Although the detailed study suggested a considerable number of 'free-riders', their actual share is therefore probably lower. No statistics or information on reasons behind free-riding exist, but officials observed that many farmers applied for cancellations of the agreement before the five-year term ended.

Overall, implementation of this first phase of agri-environment policy created new and closer connections between county landscape officials, farmers and agricultural advisers. These contacts have been mentioned by many as the most important outcome of the first Danish schemes.

Implementation of Regulation 2078 in Denmark

The introduction of Regulation 2078 resulted in major changes to those pre-existing agri-environmental schemes offered to farmers under Regulation 797/85. First, there were major changes in institutional competencies and roles, which meant an increased centralisation of scheme administration. Second, the new generation of schemes created the possibility of signing agri-environmental agreements outside designated ESAs. Up to this point, all Danish agri-environmental schemes under Regulation 797/85, with the exception of organic farming, only operated in designated ESAs. Third, several new schemes were introduced and, in general, the payments offered were raised. Further, many of the 2078 schemes themselves have subsequently undergone several changes (involving the content of the agreements, increased targeting towards designated areas and changes in institutional responsibility) since the first agreements were signed. Finally, parallel to the national implementation of Regulation 2078, the *Association of Danish Counties* applied for EU co-financing of four specific county programmes. These were approved by the Commission in 1996 and were offered to farmers for the first time in July 1996.

Implementation of agri-environmental schemes[2]

The Danish agri-environmental programme under Regulation 2078 has three distinctive components: *Environmentally Beneficial Farming and Organic Farming*, the *County Programme* (approved 1996), and *Training and Demonstration Projects* (approved 1996). By 1996, six schemes were in operation under the first programme, four schemes were introduced in a few counties under the *County Programme*, and no schemes have been implemented yet under *Training and Demonstration Projects* (see below). Except for 20-year set-aside, all agreements have so far been signed for five-year periods.

Table 3.1 Agri-environmental measures in Denmark 1996: objectives and targeting

Measures	Objective according to Regulation 2078 (Article 2)	Targeted land
Reduced use of nitrates	A	All agricultural land but with higher payments in ESAs
Ryegrass as groundcover	a,b,d	All agricultural land but with higher payments in ESAs
Maintenance of extensive grassland	a,b,d	ESAs
Spray-free margins	A	ESAs
20-year set-aside	F	ESAs
Organic farming	A	All agricultural land but with higher payments in ESAs
Cultivation-free field margins	A	ESAs (some exceptions outside ESAs)
Reduced drainage/ raised water levels	a,b,d	ESAs (some exceptions outside ESAs)
Management of grassland	a,b,d	ESAs (some exceptions outside ESAs)
Recreational access	G	ESAs (some exceptions outside ESAs)

Source: authors

---

[2] The rapid rate of change in the implementation of Regulation 2078 in Denmark makes it difficult to fully describe the schemes. In the following, we therefore refer to the situation in 1996 (unless other years are specified).

The following six measures have been implemented under the *Scheme for Environmentally Beneficial Farming and Organic Farming*:

Reduced use of nitrates   To obtain payments through this measure, the farmer has to reduce N-inputs to 60% of the official standards set by the Ministry of Agriculture. The whole farm must be covered by the agreement. No grant can be given to set-aside areas, to areas cultivated with non-food crops, and to crops which have no need of N-fertilising. Outside ESAs, payments are 55 ECU/ha/year while inside ESAs the rate varies between 69 to 96 ECU/ha/year depending on the previous yield of the agreement area.

Rye grass ground cover in arable crops   Rye grass must be sown before the 15th of May. Using the grass for seed production in the following year is forbidden, as is re-ploughing before the 15th of February in the following year, or applying fertilisers or pesticides from the harvest of the grain crop until after the 15th of February in the following year. A minimum of 5 ha must be included in the agreement, but the area with rye grass may change with the rotation of crops. Outside ESAs the payment is 34 ECU/ha/year, while inside ESAs the rate is 55 ECU/ha/year. At least 50% of the farm must be located within an ESA to be eligible for the higher grant level.

Maintenance of extensive grassland outside rotation   This measure is offered at two levels and only within ESAs. At level 1, the maximum fertiliser level is 80 kg N/ha per year. Level 2 does not allow fertiliser use at all and requires a grazing density not exceeding 1.4 LU/ha. For both levels it is not permitted to irrigate, to re-plough, or to apply any pesticides; nor is grass mowing permitted before the 15th of July in order to protect ground nesting birds. The grass must be established before the 1st of October. If the area entered into the agreement is permanent grassland, the farmer is not allowed to re-seed it before entering an agreement. The payments offered depend on former yields, and vary from 112 to 195 ECU/ha/year at level 1 to 179 to 268 ECU/ha/year at level 2.

Spray-free margins   This measure is offered within certain ESAs only. No use of pesticides is permitted within a 12-metre zone along specified landscape features. The measure is offered only on arable land. ESAs designated for this measure are typically located along water courses, lakes, and in some cases along hedgerows. Payments are 0.24 ECU/metre, amounting to around 200 ECU/ha/year.

20-year set-aside   This measure is offered only within certain ESAs (264 ECU/ha/year). Only arable land may be included into the agreement. By the 1st of October the area must have a vegetation cover. No irrigation, fertiliser use, or use of pesticides is permitted. During the phase of plant cover establishment, however, some fertiliser application is allowed. Extensive grazing is permitted in order to avoid overgrowing with shrubs and trees, but not for commercial purposes.

Organic farming   It is possible to obtain grant aid for the conversion of conventional to organic farming, as well as for the continuation of organic farming. To obtain payments for conversion, at least one ha per year must be converted, and after four years the whole farm must be organically farmed. The conversion period is two years. Aid is also given for the continuation of organic farming during the conversion period. In addition, aid can be given for the reduction of fertiliser levels but only for crops with a proven need of fertilisers. Payments offered amount 145 ECU/ha/year during the conversion period, and 117 ECU/ha/year for farms already converted. On top of that, a payment of 30 ECU/ha/year is given inside ESAs. Permanent grassland is not eligible for payments under this measure.

Although four different measures exist under *The County Programme*, not all had been implemented in all counties by 1996. In general, the measures have been offered to farmers within ESAs only. The four measures are as follows:

No cultivation within 12-metre buffer zones   Payments are offered to farmers establishing 12-metre zones without any cultivation adjacent to fields with grain or seed crops in rotation. No tillage or fertilising is allowed and the green cover must be mowed once a year after the 15th of July. Additional conditions such as, for example, the means of establishing vegetation within buffer zones, are negotiated between the county officials and the individual farmer. The maximum payment varies from 138 to 207 ECU/ha/year.

Reduced drainage/raised water levels   Payments are offered to farmers accepting a raised water level as a consequence of modified drainage conditions. The payment is intended to compensate farmers for yield reductions caused by raised water levels and should cover all expenses connected with the modification of drainage systems. Details about the conditions are negotiated between the county and the individual farmer. The maximum payment in all counties is 207 ECU/ha/year.

Grassland management (including clearance of shrubs and trees)
Payments are offered to farmers performing management practices on
permanent grassland. This measure was designed to include certain
protected areas that were excluded from the national grassland scheme. The
measure is offered at three levels and the detailed agreement conditions are
negotiated between the county and the farmer. Payments depend on the level
and vary between the counties, with minimum payment of 69 ECU/ha/year
and maximum payment of 317 ECU/ha/year.

Recreational access   Payments are also offered to farmers accepting
pedestrian public access to an area or a path already established in the area.
It is the farmers' responsibility to look after the path and, to some extent, to
maintain the path and associated facilities. Payments are meant to
compensate farmers for yield reduction and the inconvenience of increased
pedestrian traffic, as well as to cover the expenses of establishing the trail.
The measure is offered at three levels, and the detailed agreement conditions
are negotiated between the county and the individual farmer. Payments vary
from 79 to 138 ECU/ha/year.

Environmentally sensitive areas in Denmark

ESAs have been designated in Denmark with the purpose of targeting 2078
aid schemes. All of the measures identified above are targeted at ESAs,
either through differential premium rates, with higher premiums being
available within designated ESAs, or through the restriction of their eligible
areas to ESAs (see above, Table 3.1). In contrast both to the first generation
of Danish ESAs (see above) and to the British ESAs (see Ch. 6), Danish
ESAs, designated under Regulation 2078, do not constitute an agri-
environmental programme or aid scheme in themselves. They are a
territorial framework for the targeting of agri-environmental measures.
Although most measures are applicable in all ESAs, 20-year set-aside and
spray-free margins are only available in a limited number of areas. The
ESAs were designated in 1994 by the counties based on guidelines from the
Ministry of Agriculture. The total spatial extent of ESAs is 365,000 ha,
equivalent to 13% of the Danish agricultural area. As with the first round of
ESAs established in the 1989/90 (see above), the new ESAs are evenly
distributed across the country, as each of the 14 counties were asked to
designate 13% of their UAA regardless of differences in agricultural,
environmental and natural conditions. The individual counties largely
followed their own objectives which only in some cases corresponded to
national agri-environmental goals. In total 2,500 ESAs have been

designated, with an average size of 146 ha of agricultural land[3] (Figure 3.1). The areas have been designated within four categories, with groundwater areas covering 28% of the UAA in ESAs, coastal areas comprising 11%, existing and former wetlands 52% and drylands with high conservation priority 9%.

The focus in ESA designation has been on soils of relatively poor agricultural value, organic and sandy soils, and on valuable and sensitive landscape types, marshland, river valleys and land reclaimed from the sea (Andersen *et al.*, 1998). In this respect the 1994 ESAs are a continuation and enlargement of the 1990 *ESA scheme* described earlier. To some degree, the designation of the new ESAs is also in line with the objectives of national and supranational conservation policies. For example, areas under conservation orders, as well as areas protected under the *Bird Protection Directive*, include twice the share of land in ESAs as in the rest of the country (Andersen *et al.*, 1998).

Reasons for non-implementation of certain agri-environmental schemes

Regulation 2078 specifies the different options available to Member States concerning the specific content of individual schemes. As Table 3.1 (above) has highlighted, several of the schemes implemented in Denmark address a number of objectives, but a few objectives have not been addressed at all. The latter include, in particular, livestock reduction per unit area (Article 2.1c of the Regulation), the preservation of local breeds (2.1d), and the management of abandoned agricultural land and woodland (2.1e).

One of the reasons for this has been that the leaching of nitrates and the use of pesticides are seen as the most important Danish agri-environmental problems (Daugbjerg, 1998). Consequently, schemes have focused on these problems. Thus, the most widespread scheme, *maintenance of extensive grassland outside rotation,* is primarily aimed at a reduction in the use of fertiliser. Landscape management is not considered as an important issue[4], and many of the most valuable protected habitats have been excluded from the Danish agri-environmental programme, as fertiliser use is already prohibited in these areas. In terms of the stated goals of Regulation 2078, this means that although the Danish programme refers to

---

[3] Although Danish ESAs cover roughly the same percentage of UAA as in the UK (see Ch. 6), the fact that thousands of relatively small ESAs have been established in Denmark highlights the different targeting approaches between the two countries.

[4] The Danish agri-environmental programme, therefore, differs considerably from the Swedish programme (see Ch. 4).

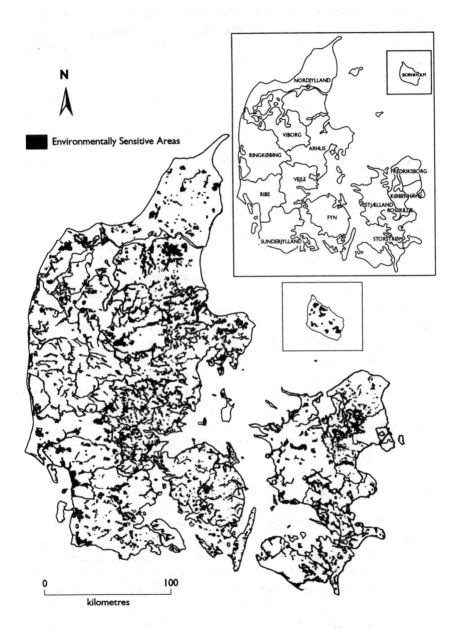

N

Environmentally Sensitive Areas

NORDJYLLAND

BORNHOLM

VIBORG

RINGKØBING

ÅRHUS

VEJLE

RIBE

FREDRIKSBORG

KØBENHAVN

VESTJÆLLAND

ROSSKILDE

FYN

SUNDERJYLLAND

STORSTRØM

0   100
kilometres

Figure 3.1   Environmentally Sensitive Areas in Denmark 1998

Source: authors

the reduction of entrants (2.1a), extensification (2.1b) and landscape and nature protection (2.1d) or the grassland scheme, landscape and nature protection was not a specific agri-environmental objective, at least until the establishment of the *County Programmes* in 1996 (the same applied to the issue of public access under article 2.1g).

The Danish regulatory framework and general trends in land use must also be taken into account when explaining why some schemes have been implemented and others not. In Denmark, the number of animals per ha, for example, is regulated under environmental legislation[5] (article 2.1c in Regulation 2078), while abandonment of agricultural land is not considered to be a problem (article 2.1e in Regulation 2078).

Although training schemes do not form a major part of the current Danish agri-environment programme, Denmark did apply, as early as 1994, for the approval of 'demonstration projects' as specified in article six of the Regulation, and their adoption was suggested in the original Danish agri-environmental programme. Approval of the scheme was delayed until 1996, but following the revision of the Danish programme in 1997, two demonstration projects were finally launched in that year. These projects are aimed at increasing interest for agri-environmental schemes among farmers, and the scheme will pay up to 100% of the costs of the activity. It should, however, be noted that a more 'traditional' form of farmer training has already been incorporated into the Danish agricultural education system, with associated possibilities for financial support. Yet, although several courses have been provided about organic farming in general, so far only one specific course has addressed agri-environmental schemes in particular. Further, none of these have been co-financed by the EU under Regulation 2078, although some courses on organic farming have received co-financing under Regulation 2328/91.

Spatial targeting of Danish agri-environmental schemes

As described above, the Danish agri-environmental programme is partly targeted towards ESAs. This targeting policy has, however, shifted considerably over the last few years and four distinctive 'targeting stages' can be identified. First, before implementation of Regulation 2078, agri-environmental measures under Regulation 797/85 were only available in ESAs. Second, with the introduction of new schemes under Regulation 2078 in 1994, agri-environmental incentives were made available to farmers throughout the country with a top-up payment in ESAs. Only the 20-year set-aside and the spray-free margin measures were restricted to ESAs. Third,

---

[5] Similar regulations apply in Switzerland (see Ch. 10).

in 1995 the grassland measure was limited to ESAs, and, finally, from 1997 onwards all measures, except for organic farming, were made available only in ESAs. Thus, following a short period after 1994 when the Danish programme targeted the entire national territory (as a result of the implementation of Regulation 2078), there has been a move back towards re-concentrating aid schemes towards designated ESAs.

The reasons for this change of targeting strategy are not clear-cut. Indeed, it is blurred by current discussions related to the carving-up of Danish agricultural land. In 1994, schemes were made available throughout the country because the primary goal was to reduce the input of fertilisers; high levels of fertiliser use were considered a problem on all agricultural land (the whole of Denmark is, for instance, designated as 'nitrate-sensitive' under the EU *Nitrate Directive*). However, in January 1996 the Ministry of Agriculture published a White Paper on nature, the environment and EU agriculture policies (Landbrugs- og Fiskeriministeriet, 1996). Commenting on the limited level of scheme participation up to that date (see below), the paper proposed a tightening of targeting towards ESAs, and the transferring of implementation responsibilities to the counties. The reasoning behind this was to enable a more pro-active approach in selected areas, particularly through the combining of different agri-environmental schemes with other types of regulations.

The impact of Regulation 2078 in Denmark: initial observations

The new agri-environmental schemes under Regulation 2078 were first offered to Danish farmers in April 1994. Despite the rather limited information campaign, as well as a very short period for applications (seven weeks), agreements were signed for more than 28,000 ha. However, this area was practically the same as that covered by the first schemes implemented in 1990-1991, though it should be noted that for the latter the time for entering agreements had amounted to eight months. Before signing contracts for the 1997 season, a little more than 93,000 ha was covered by agreements, and of this area about 35,000 ha fell under the organic farming scheme[6]. It is evident from Table 3.2 that grassland schemes – accounting for 85% of the agreement area under the agri-environmental programme – are most attractive to farmers. Possible explanations for this are that the

---

[6] It should be noted, however, that the organic farming scheme was passed by Parliament in a separate act with its own budget. As a result, politically rather different goals are addressed through organic farming compared to the other agri-environmental schemes. In the following, therefore, the organic farming scheme will be discussed separately, while the term 'agri-environmental schemes' will refer to all other schemes.

grasslands in question are relatively marginal to agriculture, and that the agreements do not (or only to a limited extent) affect existing management practices.

Table 3.2 Agreement area under different agri-environmental schemes in Denmark in 1996

Scheme	Agreement area (ha)
Reduced use of nitrates	6,441
Rye grass as groundcover	2,401
Maintenance of extensive grassland[a]	
Level 1: max. 80 kg N/ha	20,282
Level 2: no fertiliser use	28,551
Spray-free margins	79
20-year set-aside	1,001
Organic farming	34,679
County schemes:	
Cultivation-free margins[b]	
Reduced drainage/raised water level[b]	
Management of grassland[b]	
Recreational access[b]	

(a) Including agreements signed in 1993 and 1994 under the schemes *maintenance of grassland outside rotation* and *conversion to grassland outside rotation*.
(b) Uptake figures are not available, but they only cover relatively small areas.

Source: Strukturdirektoratet, 1997

As was the case with the first Danish *ESA scheme* between 1990 and 1992, it appears that the protection of semi-natural grassland against agricultural intensification or abandonment has been the most important effect of the new agri-environmental schemes (Andersen *et al.*, 1998). However, this may change in the coming years as further changes to existing schemes are suggested and as new schemes are implemented. Even though a relatively large number of agreements have been signed in a short time, the stated policy objectives have not been achieved. It was originally anticipated that 150,000 ha would be covered by agri-environmental agreements by 1997. This discrepancy between expectations and results is also reflected in budgets and costs to date. As highlighted in Table 3.3, there have been some difficulties in meeting the anticipated costs of agri-environmental schemes, as the *organic scheme* demonstrates. This scheme has exceeded its original budget expectations largely because the amount of land contracted (35,000 ha by 1996) was considerably higher than originally anticipated (20,000 ha).

Table 3.3 Expenditure and budgets of agri-environmental schemes under Regulation 2078 in Denmark (MECU)

	Expenditure	Initial budget expectations (1993)	Available budget (1994-1996)
Organic farming			
1994	3	3.1	3.9
1995	5.2	2.5	3.6
1996	5.6	26.6	4.7
Other schemes			
1994	1.2	6.2	2.7
1995	2.2	13.9	10.7
1996	5.2	26	24

Source: authors

Clear differences in scheme 'success' exist between the pre- and post-Regulation 2078 periods. Both the *organic farming scheme* and the *grassland scheme* operated in Denmark before the implementation of Regulation 2078. The former has exceeded expectations while the *grassland scheme* has had a satisfactory uptake (although the target uptake was never defined). The success of the Danish *organic scheme* is partly due to its insertion in a much wider set of organic support mechanisms that extend to virtually all parts of the Danish agri-food chain and to which Regulation 2078 aid only contributes a part. In 1995, for instance, additional 'indirect' funding was given to support the development of organic farming and to promote the sale of organic food, rather than using 'direct' support of the *organic scheme* through Regulation 2078. At the same time, the largest Danish dairy company gave premiums to farmers converting to organic milk production on top of 'official' payments, while one of the largest supermarket chains cut the prices of organic products, resulting in a significant increase in public demand. As a result, the success of the *organic scheme* in Denmark has been largely based on the 'Earth-to-Table' marketing concept, which has become an increasingly powerful slogan for Danish agricultural policy over recent years.

The failure of other schemes to meet the anticipated uptake can partly be explained by the fact that they are new. Farmers may not yet be familiar with the schemes, and the authorities still need to adjust the schemes accordingly. In an effort to increase the low uptake of the *20-year set-aside* and the *rye grass as ground-cover* schemes, payments were raised substantially in 1997. However, low payments may not be the only factor explaining low uptake. An additional reason may be that farmers simply do not find the schemes to be the right way to solve environmental problems, or that they do not recognise that such problems exist in the first place. Finally, in some regions the lack of a clear and well-targeted information strategy also partly explains low uptake figures.

Nonetheless, the preliminary results of scheme uptake in 1997 are more positive. New agri-environmental agreements were signed for a further 8,500 ha in 1997 (excluding *organic farming*). Non-grassland schemes have also had a relatively high uptake in 1997 (one third of the area enrolled), although the total agreement area still remains relatively low. It should also be mentioned that schemes under the *County Programme* (now amalgamated with the national agri-environmental programme) have at last been fully implemented (about one-fourth of agreement area in 1997).

Discussion

The introduction of the Danish agri-environmental programme has not led to political controversy within Denmark. Legislation to implement EU agri-environmental programmes was passed by an overwhelming majority in Parliament in 1989, and again in 1993. In 1989, there was no debate surrounding the schemes, and the only discussion in 1993 focused on the size of the payments to organic farmers. Yet, compared to other EU-countries, the anticipated uptake has been rather modest. Only Belgium and the Netherlands had lower expectations of the proportion of their UAA placed under scheme contracts. Figures for 1997 show that the uptake relative to UAA in Denmark is the 5th lowest in the Member States just above Spain, the Netherlands, Belgium and Greece[7] (EC, 1997a).

The national programme under Regulation 2078 in Denmark has been designed by the Ministry of Agriculture within a highly decentralised political and administrative system. There are no nationally designated areas

---

[7] It should, however, be noted that area uptake alone may be a poor indicator of a country's enthusiasm for Regulation 2078. In Denmark, in particular, low area uptake relative to UAA may simply reflect the highly targeted policy trajectory adopted in the country's agri-environmnetal programme (especially ESAs).

referring to landscape or nature conservation priorities as in many other EU countries, and the county councils play a central role in countryside planning. Contrary to the old programme introduced in 1990, the 2078 programme was designed and implemented by the Ministry of Agriculture, with the exception of ESAs which were designated at county council level. This design and implementation of agri-environmental schemes at a central level has caused several problems, as it is the counties – rather than the central government – that generally have the necessary knowledge and experience about the appropriateness of different countryside management mechanisms.

Three general points emerge from the discussion on the implementation of Regulation 2078 in Denmark. First, the implementation process started in a somewhat confusing manner. The signing of agreements began before ESAs were designated, which meant that farmers entering into an agreement during the first round did not know if payments would be low or high (as they did not know whether their farm would eventually be located within or outside an ESA). Further confusion was added through the introduction of a new and more complicated nomenclature for second generation agri-environmental schemes which were different from the first scheme usually known simply as the *ESA scheme*. Many farmers did not understand the connection between the original and the new schemes. In addition, it was also somewhat unclear which policy actors should be responsible for information provision to farmers, as the counties were in charge of designating areas, while the Ministry controlled the signing of agreements. During the whole period, the counties also prepared their own schemes which were finally approved by the EU Commission in 1996. Consequently, many counties were not very active in the process of promoting schemes under the national agri-environmental programme.

Second, measures have not been implemented according to any clear-cut strategy. In fact, individual measures have changed substantially during the implementation period. The first alteration came in 1995, only one year after original implementation, when the two grassland measures were merged into one and the 20-year set-aside scheme became available in all 14 counties instead of only three. Payments were raised, but the grassland measure was now targeted at ESAs only. In 1997, another set of new measures was introduced, payments in some of the existing schemes were further raised, and the targeting towards ESAs was tightened with the result that all measures, with the exception of organic farming, are now only applicable within ESAs. The changes are in part a response to the disappointing uptake, but they also reflect some confusion with regard to general strategy and competence. In particular, it has remained unclear to what degree the Danish agri-environmental programme should be aimed at pollution control, and to what degree nature conservation and landscape management should be included. Nonetheless, in total about 59,000 ha of agricultural land, the majority of which is permanent grassland, were put under agreement between 1994 and 1996. This has to be seen as a success from a nature and conservation point-of-view, particularly if the relative extent of permanent grassland in Denmark is taken into account (and despite the already high uptake of grassland measures under the first generation of agri-environmental schemes). On the other hand, existing schemes have not yet proved to be suitable instruments for new policies aimed at pollution control.

Third, the success of organic farming schemes, particularly as part of a whole package of instruments under the motto from 'Earth-to-Table', shows both the possibilities and the limitations of Danish agri-environmental schemes. This successful framework for organic farming – both psychologically as well as economically – is lacking for other Danish agri-environmental schemes, thereby limiting their success.

Some adjustments have already been made to the Danish agri-environmental programme (implemented in 1997). The main authorities for the administration of the national programme are again the counties, hopefully leading to a more pro-active implementation in ESAs. This includes new measures and the possibility to give top-up payments in ESAs (to attract more farmers). Although some elements of pollution control have also been tightened (i.e. the possibility to use wet meadows and pastures to reduce nitrate leaching), the overall impression is that the latest changes will have their greatest benefits from a nature conservation point-of-view. In the long term, substantial changes are needed if pollution control is to become more effective. It is interesting to note that the ongoing discussion of integrating structural policies and AEPs at a European level will not solve this problem in the Danish case, given the relatively limited importance of structural policies in Denmark. A similarly comprehensive instrument in Denmark would be the integration of arable payments, headage payments for livestock, and agri-environmental schemes which would offer a radical, albeit unrealistic, solution for the future.

4 Sweden: agri-environmental policy and the production of landscape qualities

Helene Carlsen and Knut Per Hasund

Introduction

The initial establishment of the Swedish agri-environmental programme based on Regulation 2078 encountered a number of difficulties, not the least being the design of schemes and the problem of inconsistencies between measures and stated policy goals and principles. However, the programme also has a number of major innovative components that may prove to be good examples for inspiring the development of sound, justified, and efficient support programmes for European agriculture and the environment.

The driving principle of the Swedish agri-environmental programme has been that of paying farmers to produce landscape qualities and services as public goods. Farmers receive payments, for example, to maintain biologically rich pastures and historically important landscape features. Land that is marginal in terms of market conditions is often rich in biodiversity and other such landscape values. In the longer term, payments will thus make the cultivation or grazing of marginal land more viable. Thus, the Swedish agri-environmental programme, albeit with some important exceptions, does not generally pay the agricultural sector for reducing negative environmental impacts – an approach perceived to be inefficient in general as well as being contrary to the PPP. The main objective has been rather to pay for positive externalities. The core of the programme is, thereby, based around landscape and biodiversity schemes which conform with the PPP, though some exceptions do exist, such as payments for ley farming[8], for organic production and (albeit minor) payments for the establishment of wetlands and riparian protection zones. These latter schemes have largely emerged in response either to pressure exerted by both consumer and producer groups or to the recognition of both the

---

[8] Ley is a grass-crop on arable land for hay, silage, or grazing.

high transaction costs necessary for alternative policy solutions and of the central role of ancient property rights in sensitive areas[9].

The emphasis in Sweden on maintaining landscape values comes from two assumptions. First, the landscape (with its associated biodiversity, cultural-historic artefacts and aesthetic qualities) is widely perceived as a public good that normally cannot be efficiently supplied or maintained by the private market. Second, without agri-environmental payments modern agriculture would provide both less 'countryside' (i.e. the agricultural area would shrink) and less environmental quality (particularly on cultivated land and within semi-natural habitats) than what would be considered optimal in terms of social demand. If pre-war agriculture in Sweden delivered a significantly larger amount of landscape quality as a 'free' by-product, this cannot be said to be case for modern agriculture. In addition, given the high proportion of the Swedish territory given over to forest, the loss of open landscapes is considered a serious environmental impact by almost all citizens (Pettursson, 1993). Finally, modern Swedish agriculture has also led to harmful leaching of nitrates and phosphates with resulting hazards to human health and ecosystems. These latter problems, however, are generally controlled by other regulatory and fiscal measures and do not form a core concern of agri-environmental schemes.

This chapter considers the Swedish agri-environmental programme before and after Regulation 2078. The first section briefly sketches the agricultural and environmental background of the country and discusses theoretical and political explanations behind the selection of specific measures in the Swedish agri-environmental programme. The second section then analyses AEPs before 1995 when Sweden joined the EU, while the third describes the Swedish response to Regulation 2078 in terms of objectives, measures and budget allocations. The chapter concludes with some thoughts as to why the 'new' Swedish agri-environmental programme (i.e. since 1995) has its current form.

Agricultural and environmental background

The changing nature of Swedish agriculture

The Swedish agricultural sector has undergone radical changes during the 20th century (Table 4.1). From being a dominant sector influencing the whole of Swedish society, it has become a relatively minor sector among

---

[9] It is argued in Sweden that taking away these property rights would be against the general sense of justice towards the individual.

many others. Rationalisation has been one of the primary means to increase profitability and efficiency of agriculture in the post-war period, and has led to a 70% reduction in the number of farms. There are currently less than 30,000 full-time farms left in Sweden. While the average arable area per holding has increased by 250% (SS, 1955, 1995, 1996), there has been a concomitant and dramatic fall in agricultural labour from initially 19% of the entire national labour force in 1950 to only 1.5% today.

Table 4.1 Primary agricultural data for Sweden 1951 and 1995

	1951	1995
Agricultural land (million ha)	4.3	3.2
Number of holdings[1]	282,000	87,000
Milk cows	1,603,000	482,000
Sheep (including lambs)	229,000	395,000
Cereal production (million tons)	2.4	5.4
Agricultural workforce[2]	540,000	87,000

(1) Only includes holdings > 2 ha.
(2) Excludes employment in fishery and forestry. Employment figures for respective years should be treated with caution due to differences in the definition of 'employment'. The 1995 figure refers to full-time employment, defined as 1,800 hours per year.

Source: SS, 1955, 1996

Agricultural rationalisation has brought three forms of structural change. First, far-reaching specialisation in farm production has led to a decrease in the number of livestock-farms and a sharp increase in average numbers of animals on remaining livestock-farms. Second, a concentration in both geographical and structural terms has taken place. Large-scale livestock production and intensive cereal production are now concentrated in the plains in the south and central parts of Sweden where soils and climate are more favourable, while agriculture in the northern forested areas and in areas with mixed agriculture is to a larger extent based on small-scale extensive farming (although there is still considerable dairy production in some of these areas). Third, mechanisation has led to major changes in Swedish agricultural structures. For most of the post-war period, new technologies, plus rising costs of labour relative to machinery, were powerful forces for the substitution of traditional farm practices with less labour-intensive forms of farming. In the long run, chemical fertilisers, machinery and other industrial inputs have been substituting labour as well as land (Pettursson, 1993).

Lost landscape values and nutrient leaching

Many of the agricultural changes that have occurred since World War Two have adversely affected the landscape. One effect has been a decrease in landscape variation. As a result, the Swedish countryside has become more uniform. Wetlands have been drained, ditches filled in, landscape elements removed and considerable areas of land have been abandoned. As Figure 4.1 highlights, arable land has decreased by 20%, and the area of semi-natural grazings and meadows has been reduced by 60% between 1945 and 1990 (SS, 1990c). The decrease has mainly taken place in forest regions. When land is abandoned, the rich mosaic of open landscape elements disappears and a more uniform and biologically less diverse spruce forest returns. Such changes have not only resulted in a significant reduction of biodiversity, but also in losses of cultural-historical values and aesthetic landscape qualities. The diversity of biotopes in agricultural landscapes is, therefore, a critical prerequisite for the broader diversity of Sweden's plants and animals, as nearly 70% of Sweden's vascular species, 25% of other plants, and 35% of endangered animal species (or species that demand special consideration) are found in agricultural landscapes (Ingelög *et al.*, 1993).

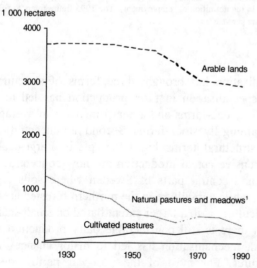

(1)   Changes in definitions through time make an exact comparison impossible. The figures for semi-natural pastures between 1961-1966 do not include holdings with less than 0.3 ha.

Figure 4.1 Arable land and pastures in Sweden 1930-1990

Source: SS, 1990b, 1990c

The main reason for the loss of agricultural landscapes has been the reduced demand for semi-natural grazing lands. Agricultural structural change, together with increased ley production and fertiliser applications, have made most semi-natural grazings superfluous to production needs. Further, the number of grazing animals has decreased while the geography of grazing has generally shifted from semi-natural pastures to higher yielding arable lands. Changing relative prices of labour, land and machinery, plus technological development, have resulted in large-scale removal of landscape elements such as stone walls, remnant habitats, ditches and ponds. To facilitate cultivation, fields have been amalgamated to larger units and 'obstacles' to cultivation have usually been removed in the process.

Associated with these processes have been increased leaching of nitrates and phosphates and the resultant environmental degradation (including algal blooms and the destruction of habitats for pelagic fish). The leaching of nutrients from agricultural fields into watercourses now contributes 30% of the total nitrate load and 10% of the total phosphate load (SS, 1990a). The average leaching is estimated at 17 kg N/year/ha and 0.5 kg phosphate/year/ha (SBA, 1996b). However, regional variations are large, and leaching in southern Sweden is considerably higher than in northern parts, mainly due to the milder climate, higher farming intensities and different soil properties.

The emergence of the agri-environmental debate

Awareness of environmental impacts of farming activities is not a new phenomenon in Sweden, although the foci have shifted over time. In the 1960s the issues of farmland abandonment, resulting from extensive rural depopulation, and forest encroachment were already a major issue within public and political debate. As in other states undergoing agricultural intensification, serious concern was also expressed over the increasing use of biocides, leading eventually to the banning of mercury-based fungicides and later DDT (Vail *et al.*, 1994). It was this 'mercury debate' that raised the profile of environmental issues relating to agriculture within the political agenda (Lundgren, 1990), and in the light of this debate an alternative agricultural movement began to take shape.

Environmental and natural resource concern shifted, however, during the 1970s. Inspired by the doom-and-gloom scenarios of global overpopulation by the *Club of Rome*, global food scarcity became the predominant concern of Swedish agricultural politics. The debate focused on issues of soil-conservation and domestic food self-sufficiency – the latter having been a central agricultural policy objective since World War Two. The loss of farmland to urban expansion and infrastructure was taken most seriously during the 1970s (Vail *et al.*, 1994). The dominant rationale of agricultural productivity was further re-confirmed by the *Act for the Management of Agricultural Land* which stated that farmland should be maintained not for landscape values or biodiversity reasons but for the sake of national food security (Drake, 1984). Agricultural interests exploited this and managed to obtain favourable and wide-reaching price regulations and subsidies, including those for rationalisation with detrimental environmental effects. Yet, the 1970s also saw a worsening of the problem of nitrate leaching, which little by little became perceived as a serious problem by the wider public. Some initial policy measures were introduced to alleviate the problem. In addition, a landscape policy was introduced that was largely aimed at the removal of second-growth vegetation from pastures, often accomplished through work programmes for unemployed people. Although lacking overall coherence, these initial programmes nonetheless generated useful experiences for subsequent landscape management policies.

In the 1980s, the negative environmental consequences of industrialised agriculture, aggravated by productivist agricultural policies, became more widely recognised. It was not, however, until the middle of the decade that environmental protection actually emerged as a specific goal of Swedish agricultural policy, along with the more 'traditional' objectives of food security, distributional equity, and reasonable consumer prices. Although the nascent agri-environmental schemes that emerged at the time were essentially annexes to a far larger productivist policy that continued to aggravate several environmental problems, the first schemes, though they did alleviate some of the inherent and policy-induced damage to the environment, served chiefly to highlight the fundamental economic and environmental downside of the hitherto dominant productivist agenda and, in doing so, heralded the beginning of a more radical and far-reaching reform process (Vail *et al.*, 1994).

In 1990, an agricultural policy reform was forced through which deregulated price and market regulations and put environmental aspects into new focus, in addition to strengthening environmental objectives contained within earlier policies of the 1980s. Before 1990, the main mechanism used to achieve agricultural policy goals had been through the regulation of farm prices, both through import protection and through internal market regulation involving relatively high state guaranteed prices. In distinct contrast to this former approach, the 1990 reform sought to subject agriculture to the same market conditions as other sectors, though it acknowledged that import protection had to be continued in the short-term until mutually reduced by GATT and other international agreements (MOA, 1989).

Through a set of new policy mechanisms, producers were to be compensated for goods and services that were in demand. Subsidies were considered justified only in the case of demand for specific public goods, or in the case of market forces otherwise failing to satisfactorily meet consumer requirements. In this way, the radical reform of 1990 attempted to reconcile consumer demands for low commodity prices with an environmentally friendly and efficient agriculture. As the deregulation of agriculture was also expected to deliver negative side-effects, such as provoking the loss of an estimated 500,000 ha of arable land (MOA, 1989), direct payments for the production of public goods in the form of landscape and environmental quality were introduced on a relatively large scale.

The radical agenda introduced by the domestic agricultural policy reforms of 1990 (and implemented from 1991) was, however, severely interrupted and ultimately greatly weakened by Sweden's application for membership of the EU. Only some of the 1990 reforms were enforced through their first transition stages. Even these were eventually halted and then replaced by the CAP. Consequently, the expected side-effects of Sweden's 1990 deregulation policies (notably the abandonment of arable land and forest encroachment) never materialised (MOA, 1995). As they stood at the time, the EU's CAP mechanisms closely resembled those operating in Sweden before the 1990 reforms. EU membership thus led to a partial re-regulation of Swedish agriculture.

Swedish agri-environmental policies before 1995

The effects of modern agriculture on the environment are widely influenced by general policy measures such as tax and infrastructure policies, by general agricultural policy measures such as the price regulations, and by directed agri-environmental measures. Within the latter category, Sweden had a broad set of regulations to control the negative effects but also provided grants to support the agricultural provision of environmental public goods. In spite of the pervasive effects of the general policy measures (Hasund, 1991), this section will deal only with the grants in order to reflect the focus of the current Swedish agri-environmental programme under Regulation 2078. Pre-1995 schemes can be divided into targeted measures for landscape preservation, and untargeted measures.

Targeted measures for landscape preservation

One type of targeted measures are management agreements. Two agri-environmental schemes – the *scheme for nature conservation measures in the agricultural landscape* (NOLA) and the *scheme for landscape conservation* (MLC) – were introduced in 1986 and 1990 respectively. Both involved agreements between farmers and the state, but they differed slightly in their aims. MLC was introduced to preserve valuable landscapes arising from specific types of agricultural production. The scheme was directed towards larger landscape areas and aimed at preserving the entire agricultural landscape intact. NOLA, on the other hand, was directed towards more specific or isolated habitats, such as traditionally mowed meadows or semi-natural grazing areas with high ecological values. For both schemes, the contract period was normally five years. Compensation was mostly based on estimates of the necessary management costs incurred by the farmer to comply with the management agreements. Payments consequently varied depending on the circumstances of individual holdings.

By 1994, 4,400 NOLA contracts had been signed, and the total area contracted reached 50,000 ha, of which a major part was semi-natural grazing land. For the MLC, approximately 15,000 contracts had been signed by 1995 (comprising 377,000 ha), half of which covered arable land (SBA, 1996a, 1996b). Although amounts paid per contract in both schemes were relatively low, farmers expressed support for the schemes and felt encouraged to continue with traditional management practices. In this sense, the schemes were judged to be successful. While they also attracted criticism for favouring protection of the ground-level flora at the expense of other environmental interests, for being unevenly distributed among farmers, and for being inefficient with regard to incentives and control, large areas of unique and highly valued farmland were nonetheless preserved. For the first time, Swedish farmers were being given clear signals that society valued these types of agricultural landscape because of their high environmental qualities (Hasund, 1991; Vail *et al.*, 1994).

The two schemes were stopped after Swedish accession to the EU in 1995, and replaced by the new Swedish agri-environmental programme under Regulation 2078. Under that transition, some 66,000 ha of the areas previously covered by NOLA and MLC were not contracted in the new agri-environmental programme (Table 4.2). This is partly because they did not fulfil the requirements for compensation through schemes established under Regulation 2078, but other reasons such as cumbersome application procedures also played a role. Whatever the reasons, conservationists have seen the reduction as worrying.

Table 4.2 Area of meadows and semi-natural grazing land covered by agri-environmental schemes in 1995 (before EU-membership) and 1996

NOLA/MLC contract area	Eligible area under Regulation 2078	Contracted area under Regulation 2078	Previous NOLA/MLC area with Regulation 2078 contracts
(before 1995)	(1996)	(1996)	(1996)
165,000 ha	373,000 ha	174,200 ha	98,900 ha

Source: SBA, 1997

The second type of targeted measure is mandatory, legislative regulation. The *Act for the Management of Agricultural Land* was amended in 1984 with *The Clause of Consideration*. The clause states that for all agricultural activities farmers have an obligation to take into consideration the natural and cultural heritage values of the landscape. The main purpose of the clause is to restrict the negative environmental effects of agricultural structural change (SBA, 1984). It therefore restricts the removal of stonewalls, individual trees, marl pits, and similar elements of high ecological or cultural value on arable land. The *Natural Resources Act*, meanwhile, sought to limit urban and infrastructural expansion on arable land. In addition, national parks were established to protect particularly valuable ecosystems, with 200 parks covering 20,000 ha now located in cultivated areas (National Environmental Protection Agency, 1990). However, since this policy instrument is both administratively cumbersome and costly, national parks have, in latter years, only been established in cases of unique environmental values or in areas threatened by severe environmental degradation (Hasund, 1991).

Untargeted measures

Several untargeted policy instruments have had significant impacts on how agriculture has affected the environment. Some of the most important instruments before the policy reform of 1990 were the tax system and general agricultural price and market regulations. These helped maintain a positive rent on land that would otherwise have been economically submarginal, and price and market regulations guaranteed prices that were considerably higher than world market prices. Consequently, the profitability of production was increased and marginal farmland remained cultivated. Further, through the tax system farmers could offset losses from income sources such as agriculture from their total taxable income. On the whole, tax instruments and the price regulation system had a positive influence on landscape preservation, particularly for marginal areas (Hasund, 1991). Yet, while some cultivated land and open landscapes might have been maintained through fiscal and price policies, many of these untargeted measures also had clear negative effects on landscape quality, particularly with regard to disincentives for the conservation of ecologically valuable landscape elements. As a result, environmentally and aesthetically beneficial features, such as irregularly shaped fields, open ditches, or stonewalls, have often been replaced by monotonous fields (Hasund, 1991).

The new Swedish agri-environmental programme under Regulation 2078

Programme implementation

Sweden became a member of the EU on the 1st of January 1995 and thus became included into the CAP and its accompanying measures (Rabinowicz and Bolin, 1998). The responsible authorities only had little time to draw up a new Swedish agri-environmental programme that had to be introduced within a year. As Table 4.3 highlights, the new programme was based on three main objectives: to maintain a naturally and culturally valuable and varied agricultural landscape, to conserve biodiversity, and to minimise the negative environmental effects caused by nutrient leaching and pesticide use. The programme is divided into three schemes, with each scheme consisting of several measures with different objectives.

Scheme for the protection of the agricultural landscape and biodiversity Semi-natural grazing lands, their biodiversity, and other values are supported by a set of measures under this scheme. A similar set of measures exists for traditional meadows. Compensation is paid through differentiated payments per ha according to farmer compliance with specified standards. The land is classified into two and four classes respectively, according to its environmental and cultural value. Scheme prescriptions include, for example, the prohibition of fertiliser and biocide use and incentives for annual mowing and intensive grazing. With the aim of preserving cultural historic values, compensation is further paid for the management of landscape features, such as stonewalls and ditches on arable land. A fourth scheme also exists for the maintenance of open landscape in areas threatened by land abandonment, which specifically targets leys and grazing

Table 4.3 Agri-environmental schemes in Sweden established under Regulation 2078

Cluster of schemes under Reg. 2078	Conversion to, or continuation of, organic farming	Extensification of arable land and/or permanent crops		Extensification of grassland	Local breeds	Protection of environment, natural resources, countryside and landscape		Public access and leisure activities	Education and training
Swedish agri-environmental schemes	Promotion of organic farming	Environmentally sensitive areas				Protection of the agricultural landscape and biodiversity			
Specific measures	Organic farming	Establishment of wet-lands	Catch crops	Establishment of permanent grassland	Local breeds	Environmental and landscape protection	Upkeep of agricultural landscape		
Horizontal									
Vertical									

Scheme implemented, horizontal or vertical
Scheme not included in the Swedish 2078-programme
Included in all schemes

Source: Compiled by authors after SBA, 1997

lands within the heavily forested parts of northern Sweden[10]. The conditions are similar to the measures for biodiversity on semi-natural grazing lands. Figure 4.2 shows that the *scheme for the protection of the agricultural landscape and biodiversity* (as well as the *organic farming scheme*; see below) is targeted at the entire country, while the *scheme for the maintenance of open landscapes* targets most of Sweden but excludes intensively farmed 'open' areas in the south and centre.

Environmentally sensitive areas scheme This scheme includes measures to reduce the negative effects on the environment caused by agriculture in environmentally sensitive areas[11], to restore the biodiversity in these areas, and to protect local breeds under threat of extinction. Payments are primarily linked to the extent of management changes required, such as abandonment of fertiliser and biocide use in riparian areas, restricted use of manure, and promotion of catch-crops.

Scheme for the promotion of organic farming An annual premium per ha is paid for arable land (independent of crop type) that has been either converted to organic farming, or where organic farming practices are maintained. Additional compensation is paid for livestock production complying with the standards for 'chemical-free' farming in accordance with EU Regulation 2092/91 for organic production. As Figure 4.2 shows, this scheme is available in the whole country.

Information, education and demonstration

The effectiveness of the above-mentioned schemes for environmental protection depends foremost on farmers' willingness to participate. If farmers seek to maximise their profits and compensations are high enough, it is economically rational for them to participate. However, if profit-maximisation is not their dominant objective, the effect on the environment is to a large extent dependent on whether farmers are willing to implement the measures for other reasons (e.g. environmental conservation). In that instance, the key to successful environmental management lies in increasing the understanding of the benefits and problems that different land

---

[10] The latter highlights how different the Swedish programme is from most other EU agri-environmental schemes, as it encourages the farming of agricultural land in order to prevent forest encroachment.

[11] These environmentally sensitive areas are not dissimilar to those in the UK, for example (see Ch. 6).

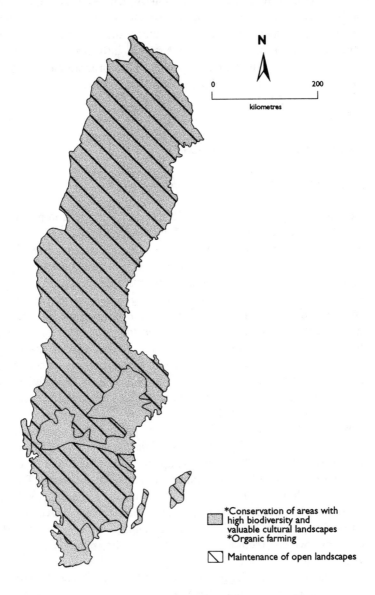

Figure 4.2 Agri-environmental schemes in Sweden under Regulation 2078

Source: authors

management practices may cause. Education of farmers is expected to increase their willingness to participate in agri-environmental schemes. The probability of preserving biodiversity and other landscape values is, thus, increased by changing farmers' attitudes and also by improving farmers' landscape management skills. As a result, information and education have become essential components of the Swedish programme. A relatively large proportion[12] of the financial resources of the Swedish agri-environmental programme (12.5 MECU/year; about 4% of total budget) was allocated to information, education and demonstration projects in 1996 (SBA, 1997). These are piloted by the *County Administrative Boards* following a plan approved by the *Swedish Board of Agriculture*.

Programme budget and participation

The total budget for the post-1995 Swedish agri-environmental programme is 350 MECU/year, of which 50% is financed by the EU. However, and as Table 4.4 indicates, only about half of this budget was used in 1996 (only about 163 MECU). This was mainly due to the increasingly precarious national financial situation and the over-stretched state budget. The initial savings in the budget, however, have given Sweden the opportunity to subsequently extend its agri-environmental programme in order to fully use the allocated amount. The *scheme for the protection of the agricultural landscape and biodiversity* receives the largest part of the budget (up to 77%), while the third scheme (organic farming) receives about 16% of the funds. The smallest amount of resources, 7%, is allocated to the second scheme aimed at reducing the negative effects of agriculture (SBA, 1997).

By the end of 1996, a total of 71,500 applications had been approved (SBA, 1996b, 1997), of which around 85% concerned the *scheme for the protection of the agricultural landscape and biodiversity*. However, within this scheme, the relationship of contracted areas to targeted areas varies from 50 to 320% depending on individual measures. Two of the four measures have thus been considerably oversubscribed and have subsequently been closed to new participants. Oversubscription is particularly high for the measure *conservation of cultural-historical remains*, which includes payments for the maintenance of tree-lined avenues, stone walls and similar landscape elements. The measure has attracted more large farms than was initially anticipated, especially in the central plains of Sweden (SBA, 1997).

---

[12] Particularly when compared with other EU Member States (see other chapters in this book).

Table 4.4 Contracted area and payments 1997 for measures[1] in the Swedish agri-environmental programme

Schemes	Measures	Targeted area (ha)	Contracted area (ha)	Total payments MECU[2]
Conservation of biodiversity and cultural heritage values in the agricultural landscape	Promotion of biodiversity on semi-natural grazing lands and meadows	444,500[3]	176,560	25,1
	Maintenance of open landscape in forest and northern regions	956,000[4]	731,550	65,9
	Conservation of cultural-historical remains	167,000	618,580[3]	21,2
Protection of environmentally sensitive areas	Catch crops, wetland establishment and grassland extensification	57,000	7,650	1,3
Organic farming	Promotion of organic farming	280,000	194,800	27,4
Perennial ley farming	Promotion of ley production	1000,000	720,850	47,8

(1) The measures *conservation of local breeds* and *traditional brown beans cultivation* are excluded.
(2) The currency rate refers to the 1997 average (1 ECU = 8.62 SEK).
(3) Includes both semi-natural grazing lands and cultivated pastures.
(4) Deductions should be made since this compensation overlaps with the measure for *conservation of biodiversity in semi-natural grazing lands*.

Source: SBA, 1997

It is not clear why this should be so, as it was not initially expected that as many large farms of the central Swedish plains would participate, since the scheme entails extra labour demand and in many cases opportunity costs of labour are high. The number of landscape features was also largely underestimated by the authorities. By way of contrast, participation in the *environmentally sensitive areas scheme* has been much lower, with only 13% of the targeted area contracted overall (with the exception of the promotion of local breeds where 77% of the target has been achieved). In the *organic farming scheme*, 58% of the targeted area has been contracted (by 1996). The question whether high participation in the landscape scheme reflects genuine interest among farmers in the scheme, or whether it is just a matter of more favourable payments, is as yet unresolved.

Satisfaction with the programme after one year

The *Swedish Board of Agriculture* conducted an evaluation of the agri-environmental programme after its first year of implementation (SBA, 1997). The evaluation focused on the achievement of the stated quantitative goals in terms of area under contract, leaving an assessment of the qualitative environmental goals for future investigations. Participation rates and the amount of agreement land were considered 'satisfactory' for the *scheme for the protection of the agricultural landscape and biodiversity*, as well as for the *scheme for promotion of organic farming*. Although participation in the *environmentally sensitive areas scheme* has been relatively limited, only some minor changes were considered necessary to obtain a larger contracted area in the future. No radical changes were suggested, and only some minor adjustments and supplements to the existing programme were put forward. However, more radical changes are expected for the next five-year programme period (to start in 2001).

The *Swedish Board of Agriculture* invited several institutions, authorities, and organisations involved in agri-environmental issues to contribute towards the evaluation, asking for opinions and suggestions for improvements. Some of the most common observations and suggestions included:

- Subsidies for cereal production have had a larger impact, although not always positive, on the Swedish environment than any of the schemes under Regulation 2078 due to their financial importance for the farmers compared to agri-environmental payments[13].
- Increased regional and local adaptation of the Swedish agri-environmental programme is recommended. Detailed environmental requirements and management terms have to be based on local conditions rather than on broad-based national guidelines.

---

[13] This criticism is similar to comments made by researchers in other EU Member States (see other chapters in this book).

- Increased flexibility and simplification of the application procedure, management terms, and criteria for eligibility are needed to make the schemes more transparent (and thereby more attractive) for farmers.
- A decrease in the length of the contract period is suggested. Five-year contracts result in heavy administration loads and discourage farmers to participate.
- Changes to the land-use classification system used as a basis for identifying contract areas are recommended.

Some alterations that would benefit the Swedish agri-environmental programme have to be considered at the EU-level, since they would demand a reform of Regulation 2078. However, much could still be improved at the national level. Most of these comments and suggestions, however, could not be taken into account during the first five-year programme, but are expected to influence its successor programmes. It is already widely assumed that the subsequent programme will be simplified and less cumbersome, and some changes and additions have already been enforced within the first five-year period. One of the most important revisions in 1997 was the introduction of a new measure for the cultivation of ley. The grant is eligible over the whole country, provided farmers comply with some modest management demands. Further, the measure for the conservation of biodiversity on semi-natural grazing lands has already been simplified by reducing the number of criteria used to specify management changes. In addition, all types of pastures (both semi-natural grazing lands and cultivated pastures) are now eligible for compensation. This means that the area of pasture eligible for support now covers 440,000 ha (instead of 373,000 ha; see Table 4.2). Finally, it has also been agreed that Sweden should ensure that its entire yearly agri-environmental budget of 350 MECU is spent (from 1998 onwards), and not just a fraction as was the case for 1996 (MOA, 1998).

Why has the new Swedish agri-environmental programme been implemented in its current form?

The Swedish agri-environmental programme based on Regulation 2078 has been adapted for national environmental conditions, and its main focus has been on the provision of public goods in terms of landscape values. Relatively few resources have been allocated to schemes aimed at reducing negative externalities (e.g. nitrate leaching). In this concluding section, which aims at discussing why the new Swedish agri-environmental programme has been implemented in its current form, issues related to historical factors, the political agenda, and the policy background of the programme will be analysed in more detail.

The historical factors that help explain the current emphasis of the Swedish agri-environmental programme include both the prior experience of policy-makers with regard to previous agri-environmental schemes and the legacy of problems resulting from previous agricultural policies. A vital lesson learnt from preceding schemes has been that landscape management is best performed by the farmers themselves. The main reason for placing landscape management largely into the hands of the farmers has been that this strategy has improved landscape quality at lesser cost. Indeed, previous landscape management policies conducted by the public administration turned out to have short-lived effects, to be geographically fragmented, administratively cumbersome, and inefficient (Hasund, 1991). Consequently, there has been an almost unanimous agreement among decision-makers to support new schemes that would provide payments to farmers for landscape management. These new programme objectives were launched just after the drastic 1990 agricultural policy reform with its innovative re-orientation of Swedish agricultural policy (see above), and its basic philosophy was continued with the new Swedish agri-environmental programme. A main guiding principle, laid down by the Government and later confirmed by Parliament, was that each economic sector should bear its own environmental costs, and that state appropriations were only justified for the provision of public goods (Swedish Government, 1994). These decisions, therefore, further consolidated the PPP and PPG principles in Swedish AEP.

A critical political factor in explaining the current trajectory of the Swedish agri-environmental programme was that Sweden had a Social Democratic government at the time of implementation of Regulation 2078. Over the last decades, strong factions within the Social Democratic Party opposed economic favouritism towards the agrarian sector. Together with the heritage of the 1990 reforms, this opposition to a certain extent explains the resistance by some policy-makers to the payment of large sums of money to agriculture when that was not seen as being justified by societal demands. Since 1994, however, the minority Social Democratic Government has had to rely upon the support of the pro-agrarian Centre Party, an informal coalition that explains many of the subsequent 'farmer-friendly' modifications to the agri-environmental programme. As a result, the new programme budget has involved almost a doubling of the payments to farmers for relatively modest services in return, and for some schemes (such as the grants for leys) has, therefore, contradicted the PPP principle.

Neither can the current Swedish agri-environmental programme be fully understood without reference to the contemporary Swedish policy context. Any policy is conditioned by, and has to be accepted by, the national policy framework and its accompanying institutions. Before the implementation of Regulation 2078, the predominant opinion was that the problems of biocides and nutrient leaching were reasonably well controlled through existing national policy measures (see above), while earlier schemes to preserve biodiversity and landscape values (NOLA and MLC) were seen as having been largely insufficient (e.g. MOA, 1994). Organic farming was another issue that was not particularly well addressed before 1995, leading to demands from certain producer and consumer groups for more support for this type of farming. Further, while a few smaller policy options to reduce harmful emissions existed, they had not yet been fully used. The new agri-environmental programme addressed some of these shortcomings, for example through the establishment of riparian buffer zones to reduce leaching, although enforcement has been condemned by landholders and other groups as a violation of ancient property rights. To use payments to encourage the voluntary withdrawal of land from cultivation was nevertheless acceptable, and these mechanisms have now been incorporated into the new Swedish agri-environmental programme.

After Sweden had been incorporated into the EU and the CAP, domestic critics soon argued that something had to be done in order to plug the distorting gaps between different support levels for different land uses (Rabinowicz and Bolin, 1998). This criticism arose, in particular, as CAP subsidies disfavoured leys and semi-natural grazing lands that did not comply with the standards set in the *scheme for the protection of the agricultural landscape and biodiversity* under Regulation 2078 (see Table 4.2). Income compensation paid to Swedish farmers for the cultivation of grain or oilseeds, for example, provides financial support to almost all agricultural land uses, except for the two uses that are ecologically most valuable and environmentally least damaging (i.e. leys and semi-natural grazing lands). Leys, in particular, improve soil quality and generate much less pollution than grain and other annual crops. Although it would be against the PPP to subsidise leys just because they are less polluting, it was argued that because subsidies exist for the cultivation of more environmentally damaging crops, it would also be sensible to introduce payments under Regulation 2078 to counteract this harmful distortion. Further, all cultivated land contributes to the enhancement of open landscape amenities, and it would be in line with the PPG to provide grants to maintain these landscapes. Indeed, such grants should, from a welfare-economics point-of-view, embrace leys, semi-natural areas, and any other land uses in a uniform way (Persson and Westholm, 1993). In addition to the maintenance of open landscapes, semi-natural pastures also support biodiversity and provide recreational and other values, which are all public goods. Although these values vary from site to site, they are considered to be generally high compared to other land uses. It was, therefore, highly unsatisfactory that most pasture land was not eligible for payments in the new agri-environmental programme, especially when arable farming – which provides fewer public goods – was generously subsidised through the CAP. As a result, a revision of the Swedish agri-environmental programme in 1997 made all pastures eligible for a basic payment (see above), which could also be supplemented with higher payments to those pastures that already comply with the stricter standards.

The discussion has highlighted that, overall, the Swedish agri-environmental programme is not optimal, whether it be from an environmental or a welfare-economics perspective. This can partly be explained through conflicts of interest between the various Swedish interest groups, some of which have advocated less stringent environmental standards, relaxed guiding principles, and the adoption of a more pragmatic approach for payments under Regulation 2078. Another, and arguably more important, reason for the relative failure of the Swedish agri-environmental programme lies in conflicting approaches to the programme *per se*. The programme reflects a compromise between the ambitions of Swedish decision-makers to develop an efficient and strictly environmentally oriented programme on the one hand, and specific elements in Regulation 2078 on the other. Conflicts arise since the Regulation states, first, that grants should contribute to farmers' incomes, second, that grants should only compensate programme-induced costs or loss of income foregone (and not in relation to the production of landscape values), and, third, that payments should be provided to farmers for the reduction of cultivation intensity as a goal *per se*. As has been outlined throughout this chapter, the latter point, in particular, highlights that extensification of production specified in Regulation 2078 contradicts one of the key landscape management goals in Sweden, namely the maintenance of farming in areas threatened by forest encroachment. In this respect, Sweden shares some of the problems that Mediterranean countries have faced with the notion of extensification embedded in Regulation 2078 (see Chs. 5 and 8) – albeit from a different perspective. Bearing these difficulties in mind, the Swedish programme has, nonetheless, to be judged as an important step towards an efficient and successful policy framework for an environmentally more beneficial agriculture.

5 Greece: late implementation of agri-environmental policies

Leonidas Louloudis, Nicos Beopoulos and George Vlahos[14]

Introduction

In Greece, environmental problems related to agriculture differ in nature and intensity from those encountered in northern European countries. In addition, they are less apparent, as extensive types of farming, usually compatible with environmental conservation, are still practised in many areas. Further, intensification of agricultural production occurred relatively late in Greece compared to northern European countries. Many environmental problems in Greece are, therefore, linked to the rugged terrain (prone to erosion) and the climate. Currently, Greece is characterised by a high agricultural workforce (20% or 670,000 people in 1991) with high levels of pluriactivity. It is also a country that has, until relatively recently, been marked by relatively high levels of rural poverty. Finally, a large proportion of the urban population are former inhabitants of rural areas who have only recently settled in towns and, consequently, have maintained close links with the countryside and farming; most of them still owning, albeit often symbolically, rural property. For all these reasons, the environmental impacts of agriculture have only recently become the target of public concern – much later than in most northern European countries.

Nonetheless, since the late 1980s there has been growing recognition that Greek agriculture is not entirely compatible with nature conservation, and today it is acknowledged that it can be the cause of environmental degradation, particularly through the use of modern agricultural technology (Hondraki-Birbili and Lucas, 1997). This change in attitudes was initiated by the special attention paid to wetland protection, as the country's most important wetlands became the targets of international protection initiatives through the *RAMSAR Treaty* (ratified in 1974) and EEC Directive 79/409 for the protection of birds (implemented in Greece in 1985). Parallel to this, the EEC began to finance a substantial number of

[14] The authors wish to thank Evi Arahoviti and Dimitris Papadopoulos for their valuable contributions.

projects related to wetland management. Studies linked to these projects highlighted the relationship between certain agricultural practices and wetland degradation (Gerakis, 1990), and as a result NGOs (such as the *Ornithological Society*) rallied to the protection of wetlands. For the first time, farming practices were extensively questioned and the resulting criticism reached the mass media (Beopoulos and Louloudis, 1997).

Any discussion of Greek policy implementation also needs to take into account problems related to the prevailing bureaucratic and administrative culture. It has been argued, for example, that the Greek public administration, along with other southern European national administrations (see also Ch. 8), suffers in terms of efficiency, effectiveness, flexibility and meritocracy. It is, therefore, often regarded as an over-sized and intensely compartmentalised bureaucratic apparatus inhibiting the modernisation process (Primdham, 1994). The established network of clientelism within Greek public administration inhibits the evolution towards. a rationally functioning modern state apparatus. Even when collective interests exist, problems often tend to be addressed through state corporatism. With regard to environmental policy, for example, Greece may be described as a case of bureaucratic fragmentation, whereby the responsibilities for environmental protection are dispersed among different ministries. Although the country's relatively good record with regard to its degree of harmonisation with EU environmental legislation suggests that there has been no lack of relevant legislation, implementation delays – coupled with serious problems of co-ordination among different ministries and directorates – reveal an absence of political will and strategic thinking concerning the environment as a unique and holistic entity. For all these reasons, although the necessity for sound environmental policies has been widely accepted, implementation of such policies has not been realised in any consistent manner.

Prior to the introduction of Regulation 2078 in Greece, no special provisions were made for the protection of the environment from agricultural activities. As will be discussed in detail below, Regulation 797/85, for example, was more a structural policy than an AEP in Greece, and was mainly used as a tool to increase agricultural production capacity. During the past decade, however, pressure from the EU has increasingly triggered the implementation of environmental legislation, although most of these policies only marginally affected the agricultural sector that continued to be dominated by productivist thinking. Consequently, the implementation of AEP in Greece has been greatly delayed, although the country has been a full member of the EEC since 1981. As the case of the Greek response to Regulation 797/85 (*Article 19*) will aptly demonstrate (see below), the main problem rests with the actual implementation of agri-environmental regulations rather than with their initial incorporation into national legislation. Thus, *Article 19* was never implemented in Greece and was considered as inappropriate for the Greek context by the relevant administrative authorities.

The productivist approach to rural development, which is still dominant among Greek agricultural decision-makers, left no room for the development of different and alternative environmental considerations that could have formed the basis for the successful application of *Article 19*. The main concern of state agricultural officials, representatives of farmers' interests, and even of most individual farmers (with few exceptions), has been to increase the volume of agricultural production, especially of those products heavily subsidised by EU funds. Moreover, new codes of 'good agricultural practice' suggested only recently by the Ministry (1995) clash with policies implemented by other departments of the same Ministry which aim at promoting the intensification of agricultural production. Thus, the paradox of farmers being simultaneously eligible for support for both improving and degrading the environment is still a common feature of Greek agricultural policy.

The state of the Greek rural environment

In Greece, there is a lack of continuous and consistent information concerning the impacts of agricultural practices on the environment. Even when data are available, they refer to specific areas and, therefore, do not allow extrapolation to the national level or aggregate assessments of specific environmental issues. Likewise, the infrastructure for the monitoring of ecological parameters is either non-existent or has only been very recently installed, and therefore does not allow for the drawing of conclusions regarding possible scenarios of the impacts that current farming practices have on environmental quality. Thus, a description of the state of the environment as influenced by agricultural activities becomes extremely difficult. Nonetheless, a possible alternative assessment can be attempted by referring to practices and procedures of agricultural production that have threatened the environment in a wider European context (Beopoulos and Skouras, 1997).

Chemical fertilisers Average application rates of fertilisers in Greece stood at 113.8 kg/ha for N-fertilisers (EU 121.8 kg/ha), 49.7 kg/ha for phosphate-based fertilisers (EU 56.6 kg/ha), and 19.3 kg/ha for potassium-based fertilisers (EU 61.5 kg/ha)[15]. This means that as far as applications of N and P fertilisers are concerned, Greece has slightly lower figures than the EU average, while the application of potassium-based fertilisers is much lower than the average EU amount. Further, in recent years total consumption of fertilisers has been reduced, largely due to changes in the marketing of fertiliser[16]. Nevertheless, in a country such as Greece which is characterised by significant differences between agricultural areas, the above mentioned average figures are not always representative. Thus, at NUTS III level, the region of Imathia (on the plains of Macedonia in northern Greece; see Figure 5.1 below) had the highest fertiliser consumption with 204 kg N-fertiliser per ha, while the region of Fokida (a mountainous area in central Greece) had the lowest with 14 kg/ha (data for 1990).

Pesticides The average quantity of pesticides per ha of cultivated land in Greece (arable, vegetables and permanent crops) amounts to 'only' 2.45 kg/ha, while the average figure for the EU is 4.5 kg/ha (both figures for 1993; Beopoulos, 1996). Although the Greek figure is still relatively low, pesticide applications are causing increasing public concern. The example of olive oil production illustrates the complexity of pesticide issues in the Greek context. On the one hand, pesticide spraying by air has been used for many years in order to fight crop damage caused by the olive fly (*Dacus oleae*). Although this practice covers almost two thirds of the entire area planted in olive trees, many regard spraying by air as unreasonable and ineffective from an agronomic point-of-view. This practice, therefore, is being increasingly contested by pressure groups (e.g. environmental groups, tourist lobby), and this pressure is expected to increase substantially in the near future. On the other hand, pesticide residues in olive oil have been found to be relatively small. Results of an extensive study about residues of organophosphate pesticides in olive oil, where samples from all olive oil producing areas of Greece were analysed between 1988 and 1990, revealed that only 4 to 6% of the samples included residues in concentrations higher than FAO/WHO limits (Beopoulos and Skouras, 1997).

Water wastage During the last 30 years, irrigation of agricultural land in Greece has been expanded significantly. During the period between 1963 and 1993, the proportion of irrigated land increased from 15% to 38%. While during the 1960s irrigation was predominantly concentrated on horticultural land and tree plantations, today irrigated areas mainly comprise

---

[15] Data for 1989.

[16] The market for fertilisers was deregulated in 1992, and the removal of state support led to rapid price increases, resulting in a reduction in demand.

arable land (especially maize and cotton), but irrigation of horticultural areas and tree plantations has also further increased (in total 1.3 million ha were irrigated in 1993). This continuous expansion of irrigation, coupled with a lack of studies related to sensible use of water resources, has led to both a severe lowering of groundwater levels and a reduction of river water (particularly during the hot and dry summer period) with severe repercussions for wildlife and ecosystems. Further problems have been caused in recent years in coastal areas where intrusion of sea water into fresh water zones has led to salinisation, largely due to over-pumping for irrigation purposes. Clear evidence of this problem can be found on the irrigated plains of Argolis in the Peloponnese in southern Greece.

Wastes from intensive animal production As a result of small farm sizes and the geographical dispersal of livestock holdings in Greece, animal wastes do not appear to pose an immediate threat to the environment. However, wastes from intensive pig farms (and to a lesser extent from poultry farms) have caused local pollution problems. This is partly due to the high pollution potential of these animal wastes (i.e. concentrated liquid waste with a heavy biological load), although the problem has also been exacerbated by the recent tendency for a concentration of pig-breeding installations in certain areas. A case in point is the high concentration of pig-breeding farms in the Louros Basin adjacent to the sensitive wetlands of Amvrakikos in central/western Greece.

Loss of biodiversity The disappearance, contraction or degradation of wetlands – phenomena for which agriculture has been largely responsible – pose a direct threat to many wild species. According to the *Red Data Book of Threatened Vertebrates of Greece* (Hellenic Zoological Society, 1992), about a quarter of all bird species are endangered, and six have already become extinct. Nonetheless, since 1975 many Greek wetlands have been declared *Internationally Protected Wetlands* under the RAMSAR Treaty, and *Special Protected Areas* under Directive EEC/79/409. So far, however, the necessary legislation for the designation of these areas is incomplete, which means that their protection is far from guaranteed.

Soil erosion As a result of Greece's geography (characterised by rugged relief and steep slopes) and its Mediterranean climate, soil erosion is a frequent occurrence. Naturally high rates of erosion have been further accelerated by human activity, particularly in mountainous and hilly areas. The cultivation of steep land without proper protective anti-erosion measures has been one of the major problems in this respect. Although there are no officially available data concerning the extent of erosion on agricultural land, data provided by the CORINE programme estimates that about 40,000 km², or   30% of the country's terrain, are seriously eroded (Ministry of Agriculture, 1993).

Forest fires   Forest fires are a very important cause of soil erosion in Greece. Fires are destroying 30,000-50,000 ha of forest every year, particularly during the hot and dry summer months. Burnt areas are often illegally occupied by land developers, especially in peri-urban and coastal areas where land prices are high. This is mainly a result of the specific ownership status of Greek forests, often characterised by multiple and complex forms of ownership. This is further aggravated by the absence of a *National Forest Land Register*, which leads to largely ineffective controls over changes in land use in forested areas.

Structural policies and the Greek environment

Regulation 797/85 in Greece: structural rather than agri-environmental policy

Regulation 797/85, which aimed at improving the efficiency of agricultural structures, was implemented in Greece in April 1986. The funds allocated during the period 1986-1990 included 54% allocated to compensatory payments (absorbed mainly by LFAs), 36% as investment aid to farmers and 7% for the improvement of pastures. From an environmental point-of-view, subsidies provided under the scheme *investment aid for farmers* further intensified the already existing imbalance between crop and livestock production (with 73% and 21% respectively of all funds allocated). As far as livestock production was concerned, however, the implementation of this scheme contributed considerably to the improvement of sheep and goat farms (50% of investments were directed towards these farms; Table 5.1). These types of farms are mostly located in mountainous areas and are based on extensive use of natural pastures[17]. The scheme offered incentives for the enlargement of herds without paying attention to existing environmental constraints and, consequently, without providing an appropriate framework for protective restrictions. It, therefore, reinforced the already present trend towards sedentary forms of livestock farming, leading to abandonment of marginal and remote grazing areas while at the same time encouraging overexploitation of easily accessible pastures.

---

[17] Pastures occupy 5.2 million ha, or 40% of the total area of Greece, and are mainly located in semi-mountainous or mountainous areas.

Table 5.1 Investment aid for farmers by sectors between 1986 and 1990 under Regulation 797/85 (in MECU)

Year	Livestock	%	Crops	%	Others	%
1986	6.2	37	10.1	60	0.5	3
1987	17.0	31	36.4	65	2.3	4
1988	17.3	22	56.0	71	5.5	7
1989	20.2	19	77.0	74	6.8	7
1990	13.6	14	77.1	80	6.0	6
Total 1986-1990	74.4	21	256.7	73	21.1	6

Source: authors

The distribution of investment aids within the crop sector (30% for tractors and 21% for irrigation) further reinforced the specialisation of Greek agriculture towards intensively irrigated and heavily mechanised farms. Not only did such specialisation lead to a worsening of regional inequalities (Louloudis and Maraveyas, 1997), but it also resulted in the accumulation of surpluses related to certain commodities (e.g. peaches and oranges). Further, investment aids were also an indirect incentive for increased use of fertilisers and other agro-chemicals in areas already threatened by environmental degradation, but these artificial inputs were often used in vain due to the need to destroy surplus production from these areas. From a socio-economic perspective, implications of compensatory payments were generally positive. Compensations were given to Greek farmers to offset natural handicaps, to improve lagging agricultural structures, and to conserve rural communities in LFAs. The latter has been particularly important as a basis for successful implementation of conservation policies in marginal areas, as viable agricultural communities are necessary to maintain the countryside. Compensatory payments were often the *sine qua non* prerequisite for the survival of small scale holdings in mountainous areas, as well as for rural communities that depend on these productive activities.

Article 19 of Council Regulation 797/85 authorised Member States to introduce national schemes in ESAs and to subsidise the maintenance or adoption of farming practices favourable to the environment. However, the article was never implemented in Greece[18]. Even when ESA payments

---

[18] Initially, Article 19 was implemented only by the UK, Germany, the Netherlands and Denmark, but was subsequently implemented by most Member States (see other chapters in this book).

became eligible for reimbursement from EAGGF in 1987 under Regulation 1760/87 (with maximum payments of 100 ECU/ha), Greece did not take any steps towards implementation of the article.

There are three possible explanations for the Greek position on this issue. First, the Greek Ministry of Agriculture had no experience with implementation of agri-environmental schemes. In part, this can be explained by the fact that Regulation 797/85 had been launched only four years after Greek accession to the EEC, which left only little time for policy officials to adjust to the new EEC AEP framework. Second, the inertia (and in some cases even the reluctance) of the Greek public administration towards the application of such schemes was a major hindrance for the implementation of ESA schemes. This was particularly apparent as no potential ESA areas had been designated in Greece, although such designation was a vital prerequisite for implementing *Article 19*. Third, non-implementation of *Article 19* was also partly due to the fact that environmental concerns were not treated as matters of priority by the Greek government (similar to other southern European governments; see Ch. 8, for example). Greece saw the intensification of agriculture as a more important priority in order to 'catch up' with its northern European counterparts in terms of agricultural productivity. In Greece, therefore, national priority was to secure higher agricultural incomes by directing agricultural production towards heavily subsidised crops (i.e. cotton, tobacco) and to improve agricultural structures by promoting investments for farm holdings. The latter point, in particular, was used repeatedly by Greek policy-makers to justify criticisms of *Article 19*, emphasising that the article suffered from a northern European bias. By overemphasising extensification of agricultural production, *Article 19* was thought to be of little relevance to the rural problems of southern Europe (Baldock and Lowe, 1996). Overall, therefore, although the demographic and socio-economic impacts of compensatory payments under Regulation 797/85 were relatively positive for Greek farmers, the regulation did little to improve environmental management in the Greek countryside.

Regulation 2328/91

Subsidies were also given to Greek farmers under Regulation 2328/91, which encouraged the payment of investment aid for farmers. These subsidies further increased the disparities between crop and livestock areas (Table 5.2; see also Table 5.1 above). From 1991 to 1995, the amount spent on livestock farms amounted to only 13% of the total budget, while the money devoted to crop production was raised to 74%. The most important measures were payments for the purchase of tractors (36% of total amount), irrigation (>20%) and greenhouses (>13%). This uneven allocation of resources, therefore, has further perpetuated the structural deficiencies of Greek agriculture.

Table 5.2 Investment aid for farmers by measure between 1991 and 1995 under Regulation 2328/91 (MECU)

Measure	Invested amount	% of sector
Livestock production	82.2	100
	(13.1%)	
Sheep and goats	44.8	55
Cattle	26.5	32
Pigs	0.9	1
Bees	5.9	7
Others	4.1	5
Crop production	464.1	100
	(74.2%)	
Green-houses	62.4	13
Irrigation	95.4	21
Land reclamation	32.5	7
Tractors	167.3	36
Machinery	47.4	10
Buildings	39.8	9
Tree planting	8.5	2
Others	10.8	2
Other activities	79.1	100
	(12.7%)	
Fencing	19.6	25
Rural tourism	56.1	71
Rural handicraft	0.7	1
Others	2.8	4

Source: authors

With regard to aid for new farmers provided under Regulation 2328/91, the number of applications increased substantially from 897 in 1991 to 1,315 in 1993 (Ministry of Agriculture, 1993). It should, however, be noted that the number of rejected applications also considerably increased over this time period. Nonetheless, there are some important indirect environmental impacts resulting from this measure, as it has influenced the demographic balance between upland and lowland areas in

Greece. Particularly in mountain areas and LFAs, this measure has provided additional aid and has helped maintain farming populations in areas threatened by depopulation. As a result, it has helped encourage the continuation of traditional and environmentally friendly farming methods.

Implementation of Regulation 2078 in Greece

Compared to many other EU Member States, Regulation 2078 was implemented relatively late in Greece. In theory, the Greek agri-environmental programme makes provision for the implementation of four horizontal agri-environmental schemes and five zonal schemes (only applying within specifically targeted areas; Table 5.3). However, designing these nine schemes has been a lengthy process. Only three schemes approved by the European Commission have so far been implemented: the horizontal *scheme for organic farming* implemented in 1995 (scheme A1 in the table), the zonal scheme for the *reduction of nitrate-pollution related to farming in the plains of Thessaly* implemented in 1995 (scheme B1), and the horizontal scheme providing for the *long-term set-aside of agricultural land* implemented in 1996 (scheme A2). Three zonal schemes aimed at the *preservation of animal breeds*, the *preservation of species diversity (animals and cultivars)* and the *conservation of biotopes of special importance* have not yet been approved by the Commission (by 1998), despite the fact that they were submitted for approval in 1995. Two other horizontal schemes for the *protection of soil against erosion, extensification of stock breeding, restoration of burned agricultural land, and management of abandoned farmland* and *training, education and public awareness*, together with another zonal scheme for the *conservation of rural landscapes*, are still being drafted and have not yet been submitted to the Commission.

   Elaboration of all schemes under Regulation 2078 has occurred in a typical top-down manner, with the *Directorate of Spatial Planning and Environmental Protection* (DSPEP) of the Greek Ministry of Agriculture as the responsible institution for implementation. The top-down policy-making structures can be linked to several factors. Possibly most importantly, the pressure of time has been an important factor influencing the pattern of implementation of the Greek agri-environmental programme. The Greek state administration had no previous experience with the design and implementation of agri-environmental schemes, which are generally more complicated than structural measures implemented during the 1980s (see above). This has meant that state policy-makers were the first to be enrolled

Table 5.3 Implementation of Regulation 2078 in Greece

Schemes	Reg. 2078 (article no.)	Stated objectives	Area (ha) or Livestock Units (LU)	Budget (1000 ECU)	% of total expend-iture
A National schemes (horizontal)					
1 Conversion to or continuation of organic farming practices	a 3.1	• Reduction of pollution • Preservation of wild flora and fauna • Preservation of public health	6,000	6,480	4
2 Long-term set-aside of agricultural land	f 1, f 2	• Increase of biodiversity • Protection of water against pollution	30,000	16,800	11
3 Protection of soil against erosion/extensification of stock breeding/ restoration of burned agricultural land/ management of abandoned farmland	d 4, c 1, c 2, e 1	• Protection of soil against erosion • Protection of flora and fauna against fire	380,000 ha (LU not defined)	102,000	64
4 Training/education/ public awareness	2			2,850	2
B Targeted schemes (zonal)					
1 Reduction of nitrate-pollution related to farming in the plains of Thessaly	a 1.1	• Reduction of nitrate pollution of surface and groundwater	25,000	9,860	6
2 Preservation of animal breeds	d 5	• Protection of biodiversity	11,435 LU	1,435	1
3 Preservation of species diversity (animals and cultivars)	d 4	• Protection of biodiversity	2,500	733	0.5
4 Conservation of rural landscapes	d 3	• Preservation of cultural inheritance • Preservation of flora and fauna and soil	35,000	17,500	11
5 Conservation of biotopes of special importance (RAMSAR sites, National Parks, scenic forests, etc.)	d 2	• Preservation of flora and fauna • Preservation of biodiversity	Not defined; reduction of LU	2,325	1.5

Source: authors

in the policy formulation and implementation process, rather than intermediate authorities or grassroots actors. However, from the start, there was also a need for some involvement of regional authorities in the process, but rather than helping implementation of the schemes this has further complicated the situation due to poor co-ordination between central decision-making authorities and regional/local actors. The pressure of time has also meant that new implementation mechanisms had to be put into place very quickly – a problem which was already largely solved in most other EU Member States by 1992 (see other chapters in this book) – and only the state (as opposed to non-state actors) had the means to put into place a workable policy framework in the limited space of time available. Further, implementation of the Greek agri-environmental programme was not helped by the reluctance, or even resistance, of the agricultural policy community to adopt the new agri-environmental schemes.

Nonetheless, there was some (albeit limited) collaboration between state policy-makers, intermediate actors and street-level bureaucrats (e.g. agricultural extension officers) during the initial stages of programme establishment. For example, before adoption of the Regulation based on the original initiative of the DSPEP, a scientific committee was established to evaluate how the Greek environment was affected by farming practices. Apart from representatives of the Ministry of Agriculture, this committee also included representatives from the *Agricultural University of Athens*, the *National Foundation for Agricultural Research*, and the *Panhellenic Confederation of Agricultural Co-operatives* (PASEGES). During the elaboration of the agri-environmental programme, information meetings and consultations were also held with environmental NGOs (e.g. *Ornithological Society*, *WWF Greek Division*, and representatives of the *Organic Farmers Union*), in order for the Ministry to get familiar with outside views. Yet, Greek AEP has continued to be largely formulated in a hierarchical manner at ministerial level, and the final elaboration of the schemes is still entirely in the hands of the DSPEP in collaboration with regional departments of agriculture at the NUTS III level.

The provision of information about agri-environmental schemes to regional agricultural departments takes place through implementation circulars and regular meetings with street-level bureaucrats. In addition, the provision of information to farmers takes place through the regional agricultural departments in charge of scheme implementation, farmers' professional and co-operative organisations, local authorities and the mass media. It should, however, be emphasised that the private sector has also played an important role in the Greek AEP implementation process. Private agronomists and companies have often replaced state extension services with regard to information diffusion to farmers. This can be partly explained by the above-mentioned reluctance of the state and regional administration to commit themselves to implementing a large-scale agri-environmental programme. However, the relatively innovative character of the schemes, together with the already well established role of the private sector in terms of farm extension work, are also important in understanding the specific role of non-state actors within the implementation process. Although the funds devoted to AEP were very small compared to total CAP transfers, they were significant enough at the local level to attract interest of the private sector (agronomists, consultants, input providers, etc.) which, at least initially, offered services of dubious quality from an environmental point-of-view.

Contracts signed by agri-environmental scheme participants have included prescriptions about agricultural practices and the elaboration of an *Environmental Management Plan* (EMP). This has had implications with regard to additional financial costs of scheme participation for the farmers. Thus, the EMP has to be drafted with the help of an expert (e.g. agronomist) and must be submitted together with the application. In addition, farmers are asked to keep a diary of their activities for the whole period of the agreement. These terms, therefore, imply an increased transaction cost for participants that usually are incorporated in the overall consultancy costs to be paid by participants. Scheme monitoring, which is performed either by state or private agencies, also creates additional costs to participants as monitoring activities also have to be paid by the farmers.

As mentioned above, only three agri-environmental schemes have so far been implemented in Greece (out of nine proposed schemes). Table 5.4 outlines in more detail the specific characteristics of these three schemes, and Figure 5.1 shows that the schemes *conversion to, or continuation of, organic farming* and *long-term set-aside of agricultural land* target the entire country, while the scheme for the *reduction of nitrate pollution in the plains of Thessaly* is only available in that specific region. It should be emphasised that tangible results about scheme effectiveness are currently only available for the two schemes *organic farming* and *reduction of nitrate pollution in the plains of Thessaly*, both implemented since 1995. In the scheme *long-term set-aside of agricultural land* (implemented 1996) application procedures are not yet completed, which means that any evaluation of scheme effectiveness is not yet possible.

With regard to the *organic farming scheme*, preliminary results suggest that the modest objectives concerning target areas have been fulfilled. Most of the land entered (46%) is located in mountainous or semi-mountainous areas, while only 35% is located in the lowlands, and 19% within *Natura 2000* areas. Many participants are farmers who already followed organic production methods defined in Regulation 2092/91,

Table 5.4   Characteristics of the three agri-environmental schemes implemented in Greece by 1996

Scheme	Prescriptions	Targeting and participation	Other requirements	Compatibility with other 2078 measures
Conversion to, or continuation of, organic farming (5 years) *Implemented 1995*	• Practices have to conform with Regulation 2092/91	*Horizontal (6,000 ha)* 837 participants Target area partly achieved • Farmers already farming under Reg. 2092/91 • ESAs (applications pending) • Other valuable habitats (e.g. riversides, coast, islands, mountain areas)	Compulsory environmental management plan Diary/cost statement compulsory for some measures	Interlinkages with schemes: • Conservation of breeds in danger of extinction • Protection from erosion • Rural landscape conservation
Reduction of nitrate pollution in the Plains of Thessaly (5 years) *Implemented 1995*	• Reduction of N-fertilisers by 40% (ca. 110 kg/N/ha) • Use of fertiliser in crystal form	*Zonal (25,000 ha)* Target area achieved, but scheme only covers 1/8 of cotton area in Thessaly	Compulsory environmental management plan	Applicants are not eligible for any other scheme under Regulation 2078

• Six fertiliser applications/year • Crop rotation with wheat after max. 3 years • Wheat fertilisation <150 kg/N/ha	• Cotton farms (entire holding targeted if > 5 ha)	Diary compulsory for some measures
Long-term set-aside (20 years) *Implemented 1996* • Maintenance of natural and cultural landscape features • Prevention of grazing of vulnerable habitats • Prevention of removal of biomass and disturbance to fauna • No sewage applications • Scrub clearance only with management plan	*Horizontal (30,000 ha)* No information yet about targeting success • Only farms of 20-850 ha • Farms within *Natura 2000* areas	Compulsory environmental management plan Diary/cost statement/ yearly reports for some measures	n/a

Source: authors

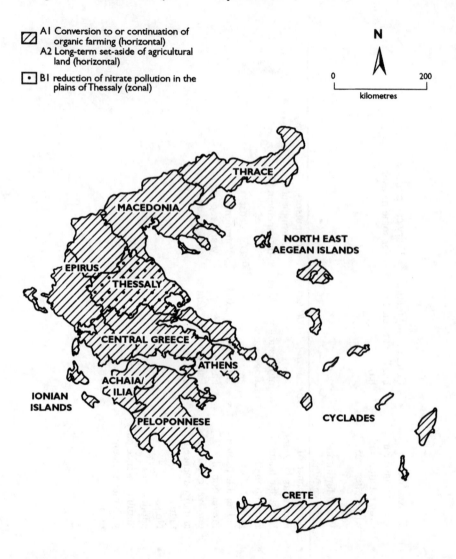

Figure 5.1 Agri-environmental schemes implemented in Greece under Regulation 2078

Source: authors

suggesting strong inter-scheme continuity. Olive plantations are the most important crop targeted by the organic scheme, covering almost 60% of the total area under this scheme[19]. Although there are two different types of payments available under the *organic scheme* (conversion to organic farming and maintenance of organic practices), the total amount paid over a five-year period is the same for both types. This arrangement has been important because of the technical difficulties related to the differentiation of payments (e.g. the biennial harvest of olives). Payments are, therefore, based on the assumption that a fixed amount of aid per year for the whole five year period will encourage more farmers to participate – whether for conversion to, or maintenance of, organic farming. This has also simplified administrative procedures, thereby reducing administrative costs.

The second agri-environmental scheme for which preliminary information is available is the *scheme for the reduction of nitrate pollution in the plains of Thessaly*. This scheme is still in its pilot phase and is targeted at the districts of Larisa, Karditsa, Magnisia and Trikala in central Greece (see Figure 5.1). The target area intended to be covered was achieved, although the target area (25,000 ha) was quite modest. Cotton areas are the main land use targeted (which are also the most important irrigated areas in the region), but only one-eighth of the region's cotton land has so far been targeted (and cotton itself only covers about half the available arable land in Thessaly).

Agri-environmental policy implementation in Greece: a critical assessment

The political dimension

The above discussion has highlighted that implementation of AEP in Greece has been very recent compared to other EU Member States, especially those of the north which preceded Greece by at least a decade (Potter, 1998). One reason for this was that in Greece the contribution of the agricultural sector to the degradation of the natural environment was recognised relatively late (at least at the national level). This has meant that other priorities prevailed in agricultural policy objectives, that productivist thinking has been favoured over post-productivism, and that environmental considerations have been subordinate to commodity production. A variety of factors can be

---

[19] Other organic crops include vines (13%); permanent crops other than vines, olives and citrus trees (8%); cereals (8%); citrus trees (6%); and vegetables (5%).

identified that have influenced this specific line of thinking among the Greek policy-making network.

First, the high contribution of the agricultural sector to national GDP has been a major driving force of productivist thinking, combined with a relatively high proportion of agricultural population which still forms an important part of the electoral body. Based on their political power, people in rural areas have demanded the convergence of rural and urban incomes (especially after the restoration of Greek democracy in 1974) through short-term solutions including price increases, direct income subsidies and credit facilities. Second, the stride towards high productivity rates through intensive use of production inputs (fertilisers, pesticides, energy, water) has also been important – particularly for cereals, tobacco, cotton, maize, fruit and vegetables – in order to support agricultural incomes (Louloudis and Maraveyas, 1997). Third, the failure of the agricultural policy network to promote structural changes (e.g. farm size increases), which would have permitted increases in productivity, has been an important driving force for continued productivist thinking (Collins and Louloudis, 1995). This has been exacerbated by the failure to increase the competitiveness of Greek agriculture through the improvement of production/marketing structures, through the organisation of co-operatives or through the modernisation of marketing and agricultural extension and education services.

Greek agri-environmental policy in a changing Europe

After Greek accession to the EEC in 1981, the problems highlighted above were further exacerbated by the implementation of the CAP. Problems were created, first, through guaranteed prices which used Community as well as national resources to maximum levels in the intensive crop sector and, second, through insufficient support of structural changes which would have been required for the modernisation of Greek agriculture (especially for livestock production which suffered most from Community competition). Although the production of crops which were already facing strong international competition (especially tobacco, olive oil and durum wheat) was encouraged, no additional measures were put in place to help Greek competitiveness in these markets. Concurrently, the security of their disposal, or their withdrawal through intervention mechanisms of the CAP (coupled with national subvention policy through the exchange rate mechanism), led to continued production of crops such as tobacco or citrus fruit, even though they could not be absorbed in the European or world market. During this period regional discrepancies were aggravated, since the favoured sectors of intensive crop production (arable crops, fruit plantations) in irrigated areas (mainly in the lowlands) outcompeted agricultural production in marginal areas. Yet, it was in the latter areas that extensive and more environmentally friendly forms of agriculture had prevailed (e.g. semi-transhumant livestock production, traditional vine cultivation, traditional orchards and plantations), and these areas were now increasingly at risk from rural depopulation and land abandonment. As a result, mountainous areas and LFAs continued to lose population, with direct and indirect consequences for agricultural production and countryside management.

Further, developments within the CAP since the mid 1980s – which led to restrictions on guarantee thresholds, price stabilisation and production quotas for certain products – put additional pressure on Greek agriculture at a time when national budgets were cut dramatically in the wake of demands for convergence of the Greek economy with other EU Member States. This forced Greek agriculture into a period of difficult structural adaptation, as these restrictions also affected protection hitherto offered through the Common Market for basic agricultural products (in particular cereals, tobacco and cotton). This resulted in massive farmer protests against CAP reform between 1995 and 1997 – the most vociferous expression of discontent among organised agricultural interests since the country's accession to the EEC. The main area of agricultural protest was the region of Thessaly, the centre of cotton cultivation in Greece and (not coincidentally) also one of the key target areas of Greek AEP (Louloudis and Maraveyas, 1997; see Figure 5.1 above).

This meant that while the Greek government had to adopt the new CAP orientation to please its European partners, it continued to stress the need to accelerate the delayed structural changes in order to reinforce the competitiveness of Greek agriculture. Simultaneously, however, policy-makers began to acknowledge that the natural environment was an important policy sector towards which agri-environmental resources could be directed to both protect the countryside and provide income support to farmers willing to participate in agri-environmental schemes (Hondraki-Birbili and Lucas, 1997). Yet, despite changing attitudes of Greek policy-makers, most of the decisions concerning AEP implementation in Greece continued to be influenced by external factors. Thus, while the voluntary approach with regard to national implementation of *Article 19* of Regulation 797/85 resulted in the fact that the agri-environmental elements of this Regulation were almost completely ignored by Greek policy makers (see above), by 1992 the compulsory framework provided by Regulation 2078 forced Greece to implement AEPs.

There was, however, some internal political pressure to implement AEPs. These developments were also accompanied by wider changes in thinking among Greek policy-makers in the early 1990s with regard to the nature and purpose of farming overall. For example, there was a recognition that extensive forms of agriculture (e.g. semi-transhumant livestock farming or traditional vine growing in mountainous areas and LFAs) could yield high quality products, while at the same time preserving the environment. It was also recognised that other farming practices in Greece have caused severe environmental problems through pollution, water wastage, abandonment of marginal agricultural lands (also resulting in increased risks of fire) and overgrazing. For the first time, these issues have been included in recent policy discourses of agricultural policy decision-makers. Yet, as Billaud *et al.* (1997) have rightly argued, there is no doubt that agri-environmental schemes implemented on the basis of Regulation 2078 have largely been a response to agri-environmental priorities established by northern Member States pressing for the extensification of agricultural production, rather than being based on the need to address either specific environmental problems or the problems of rural depopulation and poverty in marginal agricultural areas in the south.

The inertia of Greek policy-makers with regard to the introduction of AEP has been the main reason for the long delay of implementation of agri-environmental schemes – a factor which curtails significantly the likely positive impact of Regulation 2078 in Greece (at least at this point in time). Another dimension of this delay is the inefficiency of the Greek public administration. The Ministry of Agriculture, for example, has lacked a clear strategy for rural development and has an over-centralised bureaucratic structure. In addition, Greek agricultural extension services are loaded with the burden of administering EU funds and can, therefore, not fulfil their potentially very important educational role for farmers. Yet, it is the educational element of Regulation 2078 (not yet implemented in Greece) which could be particularly beneficial in a country which has lacked previous experience in implementing schemes about environmentally friendly farming practices. What is likely to remain a matter of discussion and debate in the near future, therefore, are the priorities of decision-makers with regard to policy formulation and implementation. Making the right choices with regard to policy objectives will be decisive for the future success of Greek AEP.

How effective are Greek agri-environmental schemes?

Unfortunately, and as highlighted earlier in this chapter, AEP in Greece is in such an early stage of implementation (i.e. only since 1995) that no relevant evaluation mechanisms have so far been put in place. Yet, judging from other more 'conventional' policy arenas[20], where the Greek administration has been relatively reluctant to implement evaluation and monitoring mechanisms, it remains to be seen whether AEP evaluation mechanisms will provide a suitable framework for the assessment of the effectiveness of the Greek agri-environmental programme. The preliminary overview of Greek agri-environmental schemes discussed in this chapter suggests a variety of shortfalls relating to the nature of schemes implemented, budgetary allocations, and the timing of implementation.

First, an analysis of the nature of schemes implemented in Greece indicates that while some of the most serious environmental threats to the Greek countryside have been addressed, a wide range of serious environmental problems related to agriculture still need to be tackled in an expanded Greek agri-environmental programme. For example, the issue of poor water resources management has only been partly addressed so far. While the problem of water quality has been reasonably well tackled, the wasteful use of water through poor irrigation management (a major problem not only in Greece but also in other Mediterranean countries) has not been sufficiently addressed through current agri-environmental schemes. Further, hardly any provision has been made for the preservation and maintenance of existing extensive systems, although extensive production systems account for more than 60% of the total Greek agricultural area (Beaufoy *et al.*, 1994). A possible exception will be the scheme for the *conservation of the rural landscape* once it is implemented (see Table 5.3). However, it is planned that budgets for this scheme will only account for 11% of the total allocated agri-environmental budget, and the scheme is, therefore, unlikely to have a major impact.

Second, the analysis of budgetary priorities within the Greek agri-environmental programme reveals some important patterns. Budgetary priorities reflect largely the hierarchy of environmental problems, with the exception of water resources use highlighted above. As a result, the planned scheme *protection of soil against erosion/extensification of stock breeding/restoration of burned agricultural land/management of abandoned farmland* (not yet implemented; see Table 5.3) will take the lion's share of the budget (64%), followed by schemes aimed at the protection of water against pollution and the preservation of biodiversity.

Third, the timing of AEP implementation has severely restricted scheme effectiveness in Greece. As mentioned above, there has been a considerable delay in the implementation of Regulation 2078, and factors that probably played an important role in that delay were the constraints imposed by organisational and institutional deficiencies of the Greek

---

[20] For example, Regulation 797/85, Regulation 2328/91 and Regulation 2079/92.

bureaucracy. Further, that the most costly scheme (*protection of soil against erosion*) was still not approved by the end of 1998 contradicts the stated priority given to this environmental issue. In addition to this, no mechanisms have yet been put into place for in-service training of agricultural extension officers or for the training of farmers about the aims and objectives of agri-environmental schemes, despite the fact that there have been many instances where a lack of information has proven to be a severe hindrance for effective policy implementation. A key justification for improved information provision to farmers, for example, relates to the fact that implementation of Regulation 2078 in Greece has coincided with massive protests and road blockades by farmers challenging both national and EU agricultural policies in the 1990s (Louloudis and Maraveyas, 1997). Increased radicalisation of farmers and resulting frictions between farmers and state officials, coupled with increasing scepticism and even mistrust by farmers of EU intentions and the widespread belief that the new agri-environmental schemes aim at reducing production and agricultural incomes under the auspices of environmental protection, are most likely to remain impediments for the long-term success of Greek AEP – problems that could easily be overcome with more and better targeted information campaigns.

The discussion in this chapter has highlighted that the success of Greek AEP will be mainly judged from the quality of control and evaluation of environmental benefits expected from implementation of Regulation 2078. So far, monitoring and evaluation mechanisms have only been put in place for the zonal scheme in the plains of Thessaly. The aim is to assess the impact of the scheme in the reduction of nitrate levels in groundwater and heavy metals in the soil. As far as the programme for organic farming is concerned, the DSPEP anticipates that the environmental diary, which participants are obliged to compile, would offer useful data on the environmental impact of the scheme (farming practices, technical details, innovations, etc.). Especially in cases where participants are located in ecologically sensitive areas, this diary should also include farmers' environmental observations about wildlife changes on their farms. It is, of course, obvious that the successful compilation of environmental data by farmers relies to a large extent on farmers' individual interest and initiative, and that this type of information is, therefore, likely to be highly variable in its accuracy and reliability. However, work elsewhere has suggested that farmers' environmental knowledge can provide important additional information with regard to the effectiveness of agri-environmental schemes (see, for example, Wilson, 1997c, for the UK context).

Research conducted before implementation of Regulation 2078 suggests that it is unlikely that farmers will enthusiastically adopt the new Greek agri-environmental schemes (Beopoulos and Louloudis, 1997).

However, and as argued above, this problem is mainly linked to institutional inertia and delays, rather than to a specific reluctance of Greek farmers to adopt innovative countryside protection mechanisms. Yet, the situation is changing rapidly and changes are likely to accelerate with implementation of *Agenda 2000*. For Greek policy-makers, these developments may also lead to more favourable institutional frameworks and the creation of more satisfactory policy instruments.

6 United Kingdom: from agri-environmental policy shaper to policy receiver?

Kaley Hart and Geoff A. Wilson

Agriculture and the environment in the UK

In the United Kingdom (UK), severe environmental degradation has occurred due to agricultural change over the last 50 years. Subsidies and grants alongside technological development accelerated the growth of agri-businesses which encouraged intensification and specialisation throughout the agricultural sector. In turn, this led to a reduction in the quantity, quality, diversity and consistency of habitats and landscapes (Adams *et al.*, 1992, 1994; Dwyer and Hodge, 1996). Environmental destruction and degradation has been particularly pronounced in the more intensively farmed lowlands (Green, 1985; Robinson, 1991). Yet, contrary to intensively farmed EU Member States such as the Netherlands or Denmark, many upland areas in the UK have until recently maintained relatively rich wildlife habitats whose diversity has been dependent on the maintenance of traditional low-intensity environmental management practices (Bignal and McCracken, 1992; Baldock, 1995). In this respect, the UK shares with other EU countries such as Spain and France the need for a complex set of AEPs addressing both highly modified lowlands and traditionally farmed uplands (Beaufoy *et al.*, 1994; see also Chs. 2 and 8).

Reactions to countryside mismanagement

It was not until the 1970s that the full scale of the impact agriculture was having upon the environment became a political issue (Green, 1985; O'Riordan, 1985). The publication of the *New Agricultural Landscapes* survey by the Countryside Commission (1974), for example, revealed the widespread removal of certain landscape features in lowland Britain, and showed intensification and specialisation of agriculture to be the main causes of this change. A spate of research followed, confirming a concurrent decline in semi-natural vegetation in the lowlands, and pointing to similar effects in the uplands (Sinclair, 1983; NCC, 1984; Bignal and McCracken, 1992). Such research was backed by the publication of various polemics from academic circles (e.g. Shoard, 1980; Body, 1982; Bowers and Cheshire, 1983) where farmers were referred to as 'thieves' (Shoard, 1980) of the countryside – far removed from the hitherto common depiction of farmers as the natural 'stewards of the land' (cf. Newby, 1980). This was followed more recently by many publications from the highly organised UK conservation movement (e.g. RSPB, 1991; FoE, 1992). Due to these increasing criticisms of agricultural impacts on the environment in the early 1980s, countryside management became an issue that could no longer be ignored by the public and policy-makers alike.

Yet, it could be argued that the focus of environmental criticism has taken a slightly different stance in the UK than in many other EU Member States. UK critics of the environmental impacts of productivist agriculture have focused on the underproduction of public goods (e.g. loss of biodiversity, wildlife habitats, diverse rural landscapes and access issues) rather than on externality problems (i.e. pollution, soil erosion). Thus, although the emergence of agricultural pollution issues occurred in the UK at about the same time as in other EU countries (i.e. early 1980s), the emergence of this debate has always been secondary to the more classic environmental issues of access and wildlife protection (Baldock and Bennett, 1991; Hoggart *et al.*, 1995). On the one hand, this can be attributed to the severity of the impact of agriculture on remnant wildlife habitats in a country already characterised by a scarcity of semi-natural ecosystems – especially a lack of natural woodlands, the majority of which had already been destroyed by the Middle Ages (Hoskins, 1955). On the other hand, this may also be due to a historically strong emphasis on wildlife protection (particularly birds), epitomised by some of the earliest established wildlife protection groups in the world (e.g. the *Royal Society for the Protection of Birds* [RSPB] created in the late 19th century).

This may explain some of the patterns of AEP implementation in the UK. For example, although the nitrate pollution of water supplies and the eutrophication of water courses has been recognised as a problem (Robinson, 1991; Abler and Shortle, 1992; Mannion, 1995), it is not as significant an issue in terms of AEP as in many other EU Member States. The UK approach, therefore, differs from countries such as Denmark or Germany where agricultural pollution issues (especially related to drinking water pollution through the leaching of nitrates) have been at the forefront of agri-environmental debates (see Chs. 3 and 7). To some extent, these differences highlight the different cultural approaches to countryside conservation in different EU Member States, often also resulting in different sets of AEPs.

Equally important in the UK context is that the British public still retains its typical preoccupation with the 'rural idyll'. This romantic image of the countryside evolved from the early urbanisation and rural depopulation that took place in the UK in the 19th century, as the open spaces of rural areas grew in importance as amenity resources for a predominantly urban population (Hoggart *et al.*, 1995). This desire to protect rural places led to the creation of a plethora of pressure groups concerned with preserving the countryside and keeping farmers on the land as the 'custodians' of this countryside. This theme, despite taking on a different dimension as a new 'rural' population moved into the countryside from the cities in the last few decades (Marsden *et al.*, 1993), resurfaced in the 1980s as environmental groups became increasingly vociferous and public awareness grew. Groups such as the RSPB, the Wildlife Trusts or the Council for the Protection of Rural England (CPRE) have assumed an important lobbying role in the UK with regard to agri-environmental issues, albeit with less political power than green political parties in other Member States (Lowe and Goyder, 1983; Ruedig, 1992). Due to the UK first-past-the-post voting system, the Green Party in the UK has never obtained any seats in Parliament, and this environmental political vacuum has to a large extent been filled by environmental NGOs who have an important role to play in the UK agri-environmental debate (Hart and Wilson, 1998).

UK farm structures and environmental degradation

Beyond possible differences in cultural perceptions of the environmental impact of agriculture, the UK also stands out in the EU with regard to its agricultural structures – again with important repercussions for the implementation of AEPs. Not only has the UK a high percentage of land area devoted to agriculture (70%) (mainly because almost all upland areas can be used for permanent grazing of livestock), but it is also characterised by a high percentage of grassland (65%) compared to arable land (only 33%). The extensive nature of most of UK farming (with the exception of intensively farmed areas such as East Anglia or the South East), together with historical factors such as the enclosure movement of the 19th century, have resulted in large farm units with a relatively small agricultural workforce. The UK, therefore, has by far the largest average farm size in Europe (>60 ha), with small farms being increasingly uneconomic to run and often becoming amalgamated with larger holdings. Further, the UK agricultural workforce now accounts for only 2.2% of the total working population (a decline of 40% since 1960), the lowest proportion in the EU (DoE, 1992). As a result, many farms are run in a much more business-like way than in many other EU Member States (Buller, 1992; Hoggart *et al.*,

1995) – a factor that has also influenced farmers' adoption of agri-environmental schemes (Morris and Potter, 1995; Wilson, 1997a).

The processes of intensification and specialisation on UK farms since the 1950s have contributed to further losses of valuable remnant wildlife habitats. Arable land has increased at the expense of temporary grassland, rough grazing has declined as a result of afforestation or the improvement of pastures, and a third of UK wetlands have been lost as a direct result of the drainage of agricultural land (Munton, 1983). This loss of habitat, combined with the increased use of chemical fertilisers, pesticides and machinery and changes in management practices and technology, has led to a serious increase in the number of species at threat (especially birds) (Gibbons *et al.*, 1996; Birdlife International, 1996; Pain and Pienowski, 1997). Many plant species once commonly found in the countryside have almost disappeared. It has been estimated that 95% of nutrient-low grasslands, once containing many herb-rich meadows, now lack any significant wildlife interest (Sinclair, 1992). Further, widespread mechanisation, together with the process of land consolidation, have resulted in a demand for larger fields, and hence a loss of traditional landscape features such as hedgerows, ditches and ponds. The loss of hedgerows has been an issue of particular prominence in the UK, being both important wildlife habitats as well as important scenic features in the landscape (Adams *et al.*, 1992, 1994). Between 1984 and 1993, for example, one-third of Britain's hedgerows were destroyed (HMSO, 1996). As such, they have become a symbol representing the loss of an agricultural system compatible with the environment.

The political debate and the emergence of Regulation 797/85

The political debate surrounding agriculture and the environment in the UK began in the 1970s (Shoard, 1980), and rapidly gathered pace during the 1980s. Yet, it could be argued that most UK policy-makers are still caught in a productivist way of thinking (Ilbery and Bowler, 1998; Hart and Wilson, 1998). Although debatable, the UK may differ from other EU countries such as Germany, Denmark or Sweden where post-productivist thinking may already be more deeply embedded within the AEP-making culture (Wilson, 1994; Primdahl, 1996; Rundqvist, 1996; Barnes, 1996). Indeed, until the mid 1980s, the UK government continued to staunchly defend and actively promote its productivist policies, a fact which had been clearly illustrated by its use of the LFA Directive as another way of encouraging increased production and farm amalgamation, rather than making use of the elements of the directive which allowed for more sensitive farming in areas with 'special handicaps' (MacEwan and Sinclair,

1983; Jenkins, 1990)[21]. Even faced with increasing evidence about the effect agriculture was having on the environment (e.g. Countryside Commission, 1974; Sinclair, 1983; NCC, 1984), the UK government remained firm in its belief during the 1980s that environmental and agricultural policy should be kept separate: "if governments wish to introduce schemes for assisting environmental improvement, then it is better that those schemes should be separate from agricultural schemes" (House of Lords, 1984, 16).

Running alongside productivist agricultural policies was the *Wildlife and Countryside Act*. This Act was reformed in 1981 to allow farmers to be paid compensation in return for not carrying out environmentally damaging operations. However, such a system was clearly untenable in the long term, particularly as the Department of the Environment was paying farmers not to carry out practices which the Ministry of Agriculture (MAFF) continued to actively encourage through its 'development' grants. Nowhere was this conflict more apparent than in the case of Halvergate Marshes, where the trend towards increased production and intensification was leading to widespread drainage of ecologically valuable marshes and the conversion of grassland to arable land. The debate that ensued firmly launched the issue of environmental degradation caused by agriculture onto the national political stage. Halvergate became a symbol representing the different values and interests held by the farm lobby on the one hand, and environmentalists on the other. It was to severely dent the carefully nurtured image of the farmer as 'conserver' of the countryside (Newby, 1980; O'Riordan, 1985).

As the debate raged on, however, MAFF did not seize the opportunity to change agricultural policy immediately. It was subsequently criticised by the government for dragging its feet on opportunities for promoting environmentally sensitive forms of farming, and for not paying enough attention to public concern about the way in which farming practices were changing the countryside (House of Lords, 1984). Such criticisms, alongside increasing external pressure and a desire to diffuse costly and increasingly public conflicts between agriculture and the environment, signalled a change of approach by MAFF towards AEP. It led to a turnaround in policy thinking (sparked by the public outcry and further encouraged by environmental NGOs) and led to MAFF's fight for the inclusion of environmental elements and *Article 19* within the revised structures regulation of the CAP in 1984/85. Despite stiff opposition from both the European Commission and other Member States who were concerned that the UK was "seeking some new covert way in which to reward [UK] farmers preferentially" (Waters, 1994, 89), *Article 19* was

---

[21] See also Chapter 8 on Spain where a similar situation occurred.

accepted into Regulation 797/85, and was adopted into British law through the *Agriculture Act* of 1986.

Thus, despite a relatively slow start at recognising the problems in the late 1970s and early 1980s, the UK had played an instrumental role in the establishment of Regulation 797/85. It can be argued, therefore, that the UK had become a 'policy shaper' with regard to early EU agri-environmental regulations. Indeed, Regulation 797/85 became the basis for the establishment of ESA schemes in a variety of EU Member States (see other chapters in this book), and was crucial for the implementation of early AEPs established in the UK before 1992.

UK agri-environmental policy before 1992

National countryside protection mechanisms before 1985

Due to the emphasis on wildlife habitat protection outlined above, UK AEP has traditionally focused on the designation of specific sites of biodiversity importance. Early habitat protection measures were established through the creation of national parks (since 1949) or national nature reserves. However, within these protection mechanisms relatively little emphasis was placed on the protection of remnant wildlife habitats on agricultural land (Brotherton, 1989; Stedman, 1993). Since 1949, it has also been possible to designate wildlife habitats considered to be of significance because of their flora, fauna, geological or physiographical features as *Sites of Special Scientific Interest* (SSSIs). It could be argued that through the SSSI mechanism an innovative approach to countryside conservation had been implemented relatively early, which was meant to counterbalance the accelerating environmental degradation caused by post-war productivist agriculture. Yet, although many SSSIs successfully protected environmental and other features on agricultural land, many were still lost or damaged through agricultural intensification (Adams *et al.*, 1992, 1994). This indicated that the SSSI mechanism, although considerably improved since its inception in 1949, was largely failing to guarantee the survival of ecologically valuable remnant habitats on farms. These concerns gave rise to changes in the *Wildlife and Countryside Act* in 1981, which required farmers to notify the authorities if they intended to carry out a potentially damaging operation. Payments were then made to farmers on the basis of profits foregone for not carrying out the planned changes. In many cases, however, the destruction of SSSIs by farmers could not be prevented. Indeed, during the 1980s agriculture remained the main cause of damage to SSSIs (HMSO, 1996). The SSSI system of site protection, therefore, came under increasing pressure and was criticised for insufficiently ensuring countryside conservation.

The problems with the SSSI scheme came to a head during the case of Halvergate Marshes in 1984/85. This area of wildlife and landscape importance, which was being destroyed by changing agricultural practices, drew widespread attention from conservationists, the media and the public. It led to the setting up of the *Broads Grazing Marsh Scheme*, an experimental scheme which attempted to reverse the pattern of drainage and conversion of grassland to arable land which was taking place by bolstering livestock enterprises in decline (Potter, 1986). While arguably an emergency measure for protecting an area under particular pressure which could not be sufficiently protected through the existing system (Baldock *et al.*, 1990), it nonetheless introduced for the first time the principle of receiving a flat rate hectarage payment for complying with certain management practices, rather than the profits-foregone-system that had been in place previously (e.g. in SSSIs). Farmer uptake was extremely high (89%), and it effectively halted the decline in marshland within the designated area. As a result, the *Broads Grazing Marsh Scheme* became the prototype for the *ESA scheme* in the UK and other EU countries.

EU co-funded schemes before 1992

Although not originally eligible for co-funding, *Article 19* of Regulation 797/85 allowed ESAs to be designated by Member States. MAFF took advantage of this article and, in consultation with other conservation bodies, shortlisted 14 potential ESAs for England and Wales. As with earlier agri-environmental measures (SSSIs, *Broads Grazing Marsh Scheme*), the *ESA scheme* was a targeted agri-environmental scheme that only provided environmental payments for farmers within specifically designated areas (Potter, 1988; Baldock *et al.*, 1990; Wilson, 1997a). The *ESA scheme*, therefore, formed a continuation of the traditional UK emphasis on targeted small-scale habitat protection, criticised by many as neglecting environmental issues in the 'wider' countryside (e.g. Adams *et al.*, 1992, 1994; Wilson, 1997b). The initial ESAs aimed to achieve a broad geographical spread across the country based on the fact that each area had to be of national environmental significance; its conservation had to depend on adopting, maintaining or extending particular farming practices; farming practices in the area had to have changed, or had to be likely to do so in ways that posed a threat to the environment; and each area had to represent a discrete and coherent unit of environmental interest (MAFF, 1989).

The first six ESAs were designated in March 1987 with a budget of approximately ECU 9 million/year, and the remaining eight shortlisted

ESAs were designated in January 1988 with the budget extended to approximately ECU 18 million/year. The latter became possible after modification of *Article 19* in June 1987, allowing 25% reimbursement from the European Commission through EAGGF for payments made under these schemes. At the same time, ESAs were also designated in Scotland and Northern Ireland, covering a total area of 820,000 ha, equivalent to 5% of the utilised agricultural area (UAA) in the UK (Table 6.1).

The *ESA scheme* was set up to be predominantly a landscape protection and biodiversity measure and covered a diverse range of habitats from wetlands to coastal cliffs (Baldock *et al.*, 1990). All ESAs were areas whose landscape and habitats were dependent on extensive, livestock based agricultural systems that were under threat from decline or intensification (see Figure 6.1 below). Requirements were to reduce or maintain low levels of fertilisers/pesticide use and livestock densities in order to counter these trends. The objectives of ESAs were to conserve and enhance the natural beauty, to conserve the flora and fauna and geological and physiographical features, and to protect buildings and other objects of historic interest within the designated areas (HMSO, 1986). Participation in the scheme was voluntary, and farmers were offered a five-year agreement under which they received annual payments for following a prescribed set of farming practices. Management prescriptions and rates of payment were standard within each ESA but differed between ESAs to accommodate local variations in farming practices between regions.

The *ESA scheme* was welcomed by the farming organisations, with the system of management payments seen as a much more positive approach than the previous compensation payments. Farmers responded enthusiastically, with over 1,000 management agreements signed in 1987 alone, representing 103,000 ha of farmland under agreement. By 1991, this figure had risen to approximately 230,000 ha. However, a variety of studies have highlighted that uptake varied significantly between areas (MAFF, 1989; FoE, 1992; Whitby, 1994a), and that participation in the scheme did not necessarily equate with improved environmental conservation (Morris and Potter, 1995; Wilson, 1997b).

The relatively positive response to the scheme was related to a number of different factors. First, and unlike previous schemes such as SSSIs or national parks, the scheme was voluntary in nature. Second, it was generally less restrictive than former schemes, in many cases allowing the continuation of traditional management practices rather than requiring any substantial changes. Third, it was administered by MAFF through its

Table 6.1 ESAs designated in the UK under Regulation 797/85

ESA	Year designated	Designated Area (ha)	Eligible Area (ha)
ENGLAND			
The Broads	1987	29,870	23,900
Somerset Levels and Moors	1987	26,970	23,500
Pennine Dales	1987	15,960	11,640
West Penwith	1987	7,210	6,377
South Downs	1987/88	53,343	*
North Peak	1988	50,250	45,962
Clun (Shropshire Borders)	1988	21,000	16,722
Suffolk River Valleys	1988	32,149	*
Breckland	1988	94,032	46,177
Test Valley	1988	2,690	2,500
WALES			
Cambrian Mountains	1987/88	153,000	92,600
Lleyn Peninsula	1988	40,200	*
SCOTLAND			
Breadalbane	1987	120,000	90,000
Loch Lomond	1987	42,000	30,600
Machair of the Uists	1988	7,000	*
Stewartry	1988	42,000	
Eildon/Whitlaw	1988	8,000	6,000
NORTHERN IRELAND			
Mourne and Slieve Croob	1987	33,000	29,000
Glens of Antrim	1989	38,400	34,600
TOTAL		**817,074**	

* Data not available

Note: Many of these areas have now been revised and extended (see Figure 6.1 below)

Source: Potter, 1988; MAFF, 1989; Baldock *et al.*, 1990; Whitby, 1994a

■ Environmentally Sensitive Areas (ESAs)

N

0   100
kilometres

Scotland
ESAs
Countryside Premium Scheme

England
ESAs
Countryside Stewardship Scheme
Organic Aid Scheme
Countryside Access Scheme
Nitrate Sensitive Areas
Habitat Scheme
Moorland Scheme

Northern Ireland
ESAs
Organic Aid Scheme
Countryside access Scheme
Habitat Scheme

Wales
ESAs
Tyr Cymen
Organic Aid Scheme
Countryside Access Scheme
Habitat Scheme

**Figure 6.1 Agri-environmental schemes implemented in the UK
under Regulation 2078**

Source: MAFF, 1995, 1996a; EC, 1997a; Potter, 1998

Agricultural Development Advisory Service[22] with which farmers were familiar and which farmers trusted (Cooper, 1999). This was also the first time that an 'environmental' scheme had been run through MAFF and not the Department of the Environment, which meant that farmers felt more 'at home' with a scheme run by an agricultural rather than an environmental ministry (Whitby, 1994a).

However, the *ESA scheme* was not without its weaknesses, and criticisms were also levelled at the design of the scheme itself (Wilson, 1998b). With entry being voluntary, there was no guarantee that these areas would be safeguarded through the scheme. Further, with farmers able to enter as much or as little land as they wished, a 'halo' effect began to appear: farmers would extensify production on some of their land and receive ESA payments, while compensating for loss of production by intensifying on the rest of the farm. This led to calls for whole farm participation to be made compulsory (Potter, 1988; Whitby, 1994a). It also became evident that in some areas small farms tended to be less likely to participate in the scheme, creating some tensions within farming communities by increasing income disparities, as well as neglecting the protection of smaller and more dispersed remnant wildlife habitats (FoE, 1992; Wilson, 1997b, 1997c).

MAFF was undoubtedly under a lot of pressure to portray the relative 'success' of the *ESA scheme* – particularly as the UK had been the original implementer of the ESA idea. Evidence from a variety of studies suggests that MAFF tended to target larger farms to enter the scheme first, in order to obtain relatively large uptake figures (e.g. FoE, 1992; Morris and Potter, 1995; Wilson, 1997b; Cooper, 1999). This was epitomised by MAFF's 'eligibility criteria', which in many ESAs neglected small farms with only small and dispersed eligible wildlife habitats who were not provided with adequate information about the scheme. The result of this 'selective targeting' (Wilson, 1997b) was that small farms often felt by-passed by officials, and often did not even know that their farms were located within an ESA. It comes as no surprise, therefore, that the *National Farmers' Union* and the *Country Landowners Association* – representing the interests of larger and economically more buoyant farms – were very favourable of the scheme, as it guaranteed large incomes to large farms often without substantial changes in farm management.

Despite these shortfalls, the implementation of ESAs undoubtedly marked a watershed in UK AEP (Baldock *et al.*, 1990; Whitby and Lowe, 1994). It acknowledged for the first time that there was a link between

---

22 Now called the *Farming and Rural Conservation Agency* (FRCA).

agricultural expansion and environmental degradation. However, the government's true commitment to incorporating environmental concerns within agriculture still remained in question since "all too often ... the Ministry [of Agriculture] uses conservation arguments to justify policy change but the details of policy pay little heed to ensuring tangible and enduring conservation benefits" (Whitby and Lowe, 1994, 10). In particular, the introduction of the *ESA scheme* was criticised for its failure to challenge the existing system of farm support measures, bearing, as Baldock *et al.* (1990, 157) commented, "the familiar stamp of British incrementalism [representing] neither a radical shift nor a new institution but, rather, yet another addition to the already lengthy list of designated areas in the countryside". Without a change to the farm support mechanisms, therefore, any attempt to introduce environmentally sensitive farming practices in the UK was to be seriously limited.

Implementation of Regulation 2078 in the UK

Unlike the UK's relatively progressive position as a 'policy shaper' during implementation of Regulation 797/85 in 1985, implementation of Regulation 2078 has been more problematic. It can be argued that, as the UK was a crucial partner in the formulation of Regulation 797/85, the specificities of that regulation – with an emphasis on targeted agri-environmental schemes – suited the traditional UK approach to AEP (see below). Regulation 2078, however, had a different remit and was 'imposed' onto UK policy-makers rather than being shaped by British interests, thereby putting the UK in a role of 'policy receiver' (cf. Clark *et al.*, 1997). As a result, implementation of AEPs under Regulation 2078 has been a much more selective and hesitant process than under Regulation 797/85.

The UK approach to Regulation 2078

Implementation of Regulation 2078 in the UK represented an opportunity for both the continuation and expansion of existing agri-environmental schemes (particularly the *ESA scheme*) and the introduction of new experimental schemes in order to cover the breadth of the regulation (Figure 6.1). Yet, rather than integrating the additional requirements of the new Regulation into existing schemes to produce an improved and more effective programme, a plethora of new schemes were designed with respect to the individual articles of the regulation. This was, however, done with relatively less enthusiasm than mechanisms put in place during the 1980s, as many parts of the Regulation contravened the prevailing UK emphasis on relatively small-scale targeted countryside protection. In particular, Regulation 2078 forced the UK to address environmental problems in the hitherto neglected wider countryside (Table 6.2).

As with Regulation 797/85, the formulation of agri-environmental schemes under Regulation 2078 is the responsibility of central government, with advice and technical support from the statutory agencies[23]. MAFF takes the lead for the whole of the UK, although the equivalent agricultural authorities in Wales, Scotland and Northern Ireland also put forward their own proposals, resulting in broadly similar, but still distinct, schemes for each region (see Figure 6.1). Variations between the schemes in each region are generally confined to the finer detail with the following exceptions: *Nitrate Sensitive Areas* and *Countryside Stewardship* are restricted to England, *Tir Cymen* to Wales, and the *Habitat Scheme* has different target areas depending on the region.

The *ESA scheme*, as the largest scheme in the UK, has continued to be the government's 'flagship scheme' with regard to agri-environment policy (Whitby and Lowe, 1994). In England, the *Countryside Stewardship Scheme* (CSS), which came under MAFF's jurisdiction in April 1996 (after a pilot phase since 1991), runs parallel to the *ESA scheme* and aims to address agri-environmental issues in the wider countryside. Yet, it is planned that the range of 'other' schemes offered at present will be incorporated into the CSS when their pilot phase comes to an end in 1998. The ultimate aim is to create a twin-track approach to conservation with targeted conservation in ESAs, and protection of wildlife habitats in the wider countryside through the CSS. As Table 6.3 shows, these two schemes accounted for 79% of the agri-environmental budget for 1997/98, highlighting that the other five schemes established under 2078/92 are of relatively minor importance.

Yet, despite being advocated as 'nation-wide' schemes, most of the schemes currently in place in the UK are vertical schemes, applicable only within a designated geographical area targeted for its environmental sensitivity (e.g. ESAs, *Nitrate Sensitive Areas, Moorland Scheme, Habitat Scheme, Tir Cymen*). Only some schemes are available to farmers across the country (*Organic Aid Scheme*, CSS in England, *Countryside Access*). Indeed, only the *Organic Aid Scheme* could be termed truly horizontal, as the CSS targets only particular habitats of wildlife or landscape interest, and the *Countryside Access Scheme* is only applicable to farmers with set-aside.

---

[23] These comprise the *Countryside Commission* and *English Nature* in England, the *Countryside Council for Wales* in Wales, the *Scottish Natural Heritage* in Scotland, and the *Department of the Environment* in Northern Ireland.

Table 6.2 UK agri-environmental schemes implemented under Regulation 2078

Cluster of 2078 measures	Conversion to, or continuation of organic farming	Extensification of arable land and/or permanent crops		Extensification of grassland		Local breeds	Protection of the environment, natural resources, countryside and landscape			Public access and leisure activities	Education and training
Single measures	Organic farming[1]	Fertiliser/ pesticide reductions[2]	Maintenance or introduction of extensive production[3]	Livestock reductions[4]	Local breeds	Environmental and landscape protection[5]	Upkeep of abandoned farmland or woodland	20-year set-aside[6]	Public access and leisure activities[7]	Education and training
	Reg. 2078 Art. 2 (1.a)	Reg. 2078 Art. 2 (1.a)	Reg. 2078 Art. 2 (1.b)	Reg. 2078 Art. 2 (1.c)	Reg. 2078 Art. 2 (1.d)	Reg. 2078 Art. 2 (1.d)	Reg. 2078 Art. 2 (1.e)	Reg. 2078 Art. 2 (1.f)	Reg. 2078 Art. 2 (1.g)	Reg. 2078 Art. 2 (2.)
England										
Northern Ireland										
Scotland										
Wales										

■ Measures for which payments have already begun

▥ Measures already implemented, but for which payments have still not begun

□ Measures not considered

1 Organic Aid Scheme
2 NSAs, ESAs, Moorland Scheme
3 Countryside Stewardship, Tir Cymen, Habitat Scheme, ESAs, NSAs, Moorland Scheme
4 Countryside Stewardship, Tir Cymen, ESAs, NSAs, Moorland Scheme
5 Countryside Stewardship, Tir Cymen, ESAs, Moorland Scheme
6 Habitat Scheme
7 Countryside Stewardship, Tir Cymen, Countr. Access Scheme, ESAs

Source: Hart, 1997

Table 6.3   Uptake and budgetary allocation for UK agri-environment schemes (March 1998)

Scheme	Budget allocation 1997/8 (1000 ECU)	% of total budget allocation	Area under agreement (ha or LU) (March 98)	% of total area under agreement (ha or LU)
ESA	78,264	58.4	1,307,015	74.4
Countryside Stewardship	27,783	20.8	127,225	7.3
Nitrate Sensitive Areas	8,234	6.1	24,917	1.5
Habitat Scheme	4,525	3.4	14,172	0.8
Countryside Access	239	0.2	1,650	0.1
Moorland Scheme	744	0.6	Ewes 17,785	
Organic Aid Scheme	1,253	0.9	35,249	2.0
Tir Cymen	9,236	6.9	82,377	4.7
Countryside Premium	3,625	2.7	162,488	9.2
Total	**133,903**	**100.0**	**1,755,093 ha**	**100.0**

Source: DANI, 1998; MAFF, 1998; SOAEFD, 1998; WOAD,1998

Yet, applications for the *Organic Aid Scheme* have been disappointingly low (see Table 6.3), and the above-mentioned planned incorporation of minor schemes into the CSS will, yet again, change the targeting strategies adopted by UK policy-makers.

As it currently operates, the CSS differs from all the other schemes in that it adopts a discretionary approach towards entering the scheme, whereby farmers have to compete for the available funds with the aim of achieving high environmental value for money. This approach has proved popular, not only with farmers, but also with environmental and farming organisations (Morris and Young, 1997; Hart and Wilson, 1998). However, the budgetary ceiling placed on the scheme has meant that many good quality applications have to be turned down (MAFF, 1996b). Yet, turning away applicants due to lack of funding could severely dent the goodwill of farmers, and is indicative of the government's failure to recognise the need to increase budgets for agri-environmental schemes, if they are to succeed and impact upon the wider countryside.

The convoluted process of AEP implementation under Regulation 2078 in the UK highlights the initial uncertainty of policy-makers with regard to fulfilling the objectives of the Regulation. Only after a lengthy process (six years after formulation of the Regulation!) has the UK government finally decided on a long-term strategy at comprehensive countryside protection. This strategy envisages the continuation and expansion of the two large agri-environmental schemes (ESAs and the CSS), rather than through the plethora of existing schemes which have all targeted slightly different conservation concerns. It should be emphasised that a similar process has already taken place in Scotland where agri-environment schemes have been rationalised into a set of management options under the *Countryside Premium Scheme*. This scheme now covers all land outside designated ESAs in order to make the schemes more streamlined and accessible to landowners (see Figure 6.1 above). The government has also recently committed itself to the introduction of a single scheme covering the whole of Wales, and consultation on what form this might take are currently in progress.

Despite being a significant step in the direction of addressing some of the harmful effects that agriculture has on the environment, UK agri-environmental schemes are still not fully integrated into agricultural policy. This is also reflected in the budget allocation to these schemes which, despite having increased substantially since 1992, still only accounts for approximately 3% of the total agricultural budget in the UK (MAFF, 1998). In addition, CPRE (1996), among others, has pointed out that this increase in expenditure on agri-environmental schemes does not consist of new resources, but represents a reduction in environmental expenditure elsewhere. For example, the increase in the ESA budget in England between 1994 and 1996 was achieved by a pound for pound reduction in the *Farm and Conservation Grant Scheme* (FCGS), and the increased budget allocation for the CSS between 1996 and 1998 is the equivalent of the saving from the abolishing of the FCGS in 1996 (CPRE, 1996).

As a result, the UK government has come under repeated criticism from the EU for not spending sufficient amounts on agri-environmental schemes. Expenditure for the UK in 1996 represented only 1.8% of total agri-environment expenditure in the EU, despite receiving 9% of the total Guarantee budget (House of Commons, 1997). Consequently, the UK has one of the lowest agri-environmental payments per ha UAA in Europe, amounting to only 12 ECU/ha/UAA for the period between 1993 and 1997, compared to, for example, 450 ECU/ha/UAA in Austria and 306 ECU/ha/UAA in Finland (EC, 1997a; Hart and Wilson, 1998). Further, the area of land under agreement only represents 9.8% of the UAA and 6.6% of all UK farms. In addition, the 1996 *Public Expenditure Survey* revealed reductions in MAFF's budgetary provisions for agri-environmental schemes (except for the CSS), reducing the planned budget from ECU 79.8 million to ECU 68.7 million (House of Commons, 1997, xxv).

Some reasons for the relatively unenthusiastic UK response to Regulation 2078

How can this reluctance of financial commitment to AEP budgets be explained in a country that prides itself for its long-term countryside conservation record? There are four possible reasons that may help explain the UK position. First, UK AEP-makers may still be caught in the productivist ethos. It was already highlighted that a productivist emphasis of UK agricultural policies remained the dominant ethos during the 1980s (see above), and there is little evidence that such thinking has changed greatly during the 1990s (Ilbery and Bowler, 1998; Hart and Wilson, 1998; Potter, 1998). Indeed, UK policy-makers still seem to place greater emphasis on the role of AEP as an income support mechanism, rather than as an instrument for countryside conservation. As Tables 6.1 and 6.2 have highlighted, there is an evident discrepancy between the aims and objectives of Regulation 2078 (which could be interpreted as post-productivist with its emphasis on environmental conservation; cf. Clark *et al.*, 1997; see also Ch. 12) and the UK agri-environmental programme that places little emphasis on organic farming or schemes aiming at environmentally friendly farming in the wider countryside outside targeted areas[24] (cf. Clunies-Ross and Cox, 1994). The continuing dominance of productivist thinking is possibly best highlighted

---

[24] It was argued above that the CSS – although hailed as a broad-based horizontal scheme – is effectively another targeted measure that only provides protection for limited habitats (e.g. culm grassland habitats).

by the relatively pitiful budgets allocated to the UK agri-environmental programme (see previous section and Table 6.2). Although this reflects partly the targeted approach of UK AEP through ESAs (deep and narrow schemes are generally cheaper than horizontal schemes) and constraints imposed by the 1982 *Fontainebleau Agreement*[25], it also highlights the failure so far to expand the CSS into a large-scale and well-financed agri-environmental scheme counter-balancing the UK's well established ESA programme (Hart and Wilson, 1998). Productivist thinking is also epitomised by the failure to implement any substantial measures to improve the environmental education of UK farmers, thereby suggesting that there is no real interest in changing the attitudes and behaviour of the farmers involved in agri-environmental schemes beyond mere reimbursement of financial losses incurred to the farmers by the schemes[26] (Wilson, 1996, 1997c; Potter, 1998). Thus, if attitudes of both policy-makers and policy-receivers (i.e. farmers) do not change from a predominantly productivist ethos, then the UK agri-environmental programme is likely to remain a short-term mechanism to appease pressure exerted from Brussels.

Second, top-down policy-making structures prevalent in UK AEP implementation may have hindered an active dialogue between policy-makers and grassroots actors, and may have thereby resulted in misunderstandings between what state policy-makers have perceived to be the most 'appropriate' AEP mechanisms and what farmers, as the recipients of such policies, would have liked to see. It could be argued that the UK agri-environmental programme has been largely formulated by policy-makers in MAFF's head office in London (to some extent in conjunction with the farmers' lobby), rather than resulting from a bargaining process between the various actors (especially the farmers) affected by AEP decisions (Cloke and Little, 1990; Marsden *et al.*, 1993; Jordan *et al.*, 1994; Murdoch, 1995).

Third, the reluctance of UK policy-makers to use the full scope provided by Regulation 2078 can also be explained by the specific British approach towards the 'rural' environment and the management of the countryside (Hoggart *et al.*, 1995). While the targeted agri-environmental programme established in the UK through the *ESA scheme* in the mid-1980s

---

[25] The 1982 *Fontainebleau Agreement* gave the UK concessions with regard to the budgeting of EAGGF payments. As a result, the UK does not receive the full share of EU co-financing for AEP, receiving only about 15% in real terms (Whitby, 1996b; Hart and Wilson, 1998).

[26] It should be noted, however, that the article in Regulation 2078 relating to farmers' education was not part of the compulsory implementation requirements and that, as a result, implementation of mechanisms helping to promote farmers' environmental education has varied considerably between EU Member States (see also Ch. 12).

was ideally suited to Regulation 797/85 (which was largely shaped by the UK), Regulation 2078 had a broader remit that required countries to establish more holistic schemes also aimed at the protection of the wider countryside (Clark *et al.*, 1997). Although this process may highlight a general shift from a UK-dominated agri-environmental agenda at the EU level in the 1980s to one dominated in the 1990s by countries such as Germany with holistic and landscape-based countryside stewardship philosophies (Hart and Wilson, 1998; Wilson *et al.*, 1999), it also highlights the lack of flexibility of UK policy-makers in adjusting their existing programme to the new agri-environmental framework in operation at the EU level during the 1990s.

Fourth, this lack of flexibility and adaptability may also be a result of the changing role of UK pressure groups, in particular environmental NGOs, in the AEP bargaining process. While environmental NGOs operated largely at the fringe of the AEP-making process during the 1980s (Lowe and Goyder, 1983; Cox *et al.*, 1985), they arguably could exert considerable lobbying power in those days through direct challenges of government policy (best highlighted during the above mentioned conflicts surrounding Halvergate Marshes and the establishment of the early *ESA scheme*). In the 1990s, however, environmental NGOs have been increasingly subsumed into the policy-making process (partly by choice) and have in some ways, therefore, become victims of their own success. This has resulted in a stalemate situation in policy power terms between the government, government agencies, the farmers' unions and environmental NGOs. Although arguably a step in the right direction towards breaking down the long-standing top-down policy-making structures, this process has effectively led to a stagnation of the AEP-making process. Environmental NGOs have become 'accommodators' rather than 'challengers', resulting in the small incremental policy changes since 1992, and hindering a complete overhaul of the UK's agri-environmental programme. It could be argued, therefore, that unless environmental NGOs manage to partly disentangle themselves from this policy-making process, or unless new actors such as consumer groups (especially in the wake of the *bovine spongiform encephalitis* [BSE] crisis) take on the role of AEP challengers, the UK is unlikely to implement a drastically reformed agri-environmental programme in the near future.

The success of UK agri-environmental schemes under Regulation 2078

Not surprisingly, the schemes introduced in 1993 on a pilot basis in response to Regulation 2078 (*Moorland Scheme, Habitat Scheme,*

Countryside Access, Organic Scheme) have not proved to be successful in their current form – a major reason why the government has opted to incorporate these schemes into an extended version of the CSS in the near future (see above). With regard to the *Countryside Access Scheme*, for example, a recent House of Commons Select Committee report stated that the scheme "has been completely shunned by farmers and has so far been a dismal failure in terms of its own objectives" (House of Commons, 1997, para. 79). With reference to the *Moorland Scheme* the same Committee argued that it was "dead in the water" (para. 71). The poor uptake of these schemes has been predominantly due to poor scheme formulation and pitiful scheme budgets, whereby payments offered do not even come close to competing with conventional subsidies.

Other causes for concern have been the lack of support given to the *Organic Aid Scheme* – one of the most disappointing aspects of Regulation 2078 implementation in the UK compared to its EU counterparts (Lampkin, 1996; see other chapters in this book). In the UK, provision has only been made for *conversion* to organic farming, not for its *continuation*, and those payments that are given are the lowest in Europe (Lampkin, 1996; House of Commons, 1997). Organisations are calling for the extension of the scheme to include payments for the continuation of organic production, as well as higher payment levels. However, despite of a current review on the rates and structure of aid for the *Organic Aid Scheme* (MAFF, 1997a), the government remains opposed to any support for the continuation of organic farming. MAFF has been of the opinion that organic farmers should compete in the open market with conventional farmers (House of Commons, 1997) – highlighting the notion that UK AEP is strongly influenced by free market capitalist rhetoric and productivist thinking rather than by the aim to achieve sustainable environmental management in the countryside. As a result, the WWF has questioned the real impact that these schemes can ultimately have on the countryside since they are "not reaching the wider countryside and [are] considerably undermined by the commodity payments" (WWF, 1997). This criticism has been reinforced both by the *Game Conservancy Trust*, who has argued that agri-environmental schemes have played "an insignificant role in ameliorating the environmental problems caused by intensive arable agriculture" (GCT, 1997), and by the *Country Landowners Association* (1997) who has criticised that current budgets are "quite inadequate to secure even the most basic environmental objectives".

In addition to these criticisms, there are also certain articles of Regulation 2078 that have not been implemented at all by the UK government. For example, there are currently no schemes to promote endangered breeds and, possibly most significantly, the UK has failed to put any schemes in place for farmer advice and training. As the RSPB have commented, "part of the success of schemes is in farmers understanding what is being asked of them and therefore being able to tune their farming practices to knowing what is required" (RSPB, 1997). This has rarely been the case as personpower for the advisory services is often overstretched due to the above-mentioned budgetary constraints, and the training of policy officials on environmental issues is also often limited (Ward and Lowe, 1994; Cooper, 1999). Critics rightly argue that there needs to be a simplification of the advice structure in England in form of a one-stop shop (as is already the case in Wales), so that farmers know where to go for advice, and that the advice given is not contradictory.

Further criticism of the 'success' of UK AEP relates to the fact that farmer participation in a scheme does not necessarily entail any significant changes in management practices. Research has shown that the majority of UK farmers enrolled in agri-environmental schemes are in fact receiving payments for undertaking very little change (e.g. Whitby, 1994b; Morris and Potter, 1995; Wilson, 1996, 1997b). Uptake figures show that 85% of ESA agreements are for the lowest tiers, which only promote the 'maintenance' of an agricultural system rather than any additional environmental benefits (MAFF, 1996b). Yet, although little ecological change is apparent within these agreements (Whitby, 1994b; Froud, 1994; Wilson, 1997c), it could nonetheless be argued that the maintenance of habitats in their present form is defensible if the alternative would have been their destruction. Indeed, recent MAFF monitoring reports of the first ten years of the original ESAs have shown the scheme to have succeeded in stalling the process of agricultural degradation to a certain degree (see also Ch. 2).

In addition, the importance of raising the environmental awareness of farmers in involving them in a scheme should not be underestimated. Evidence shows that once in a scheme, few decide to drop out, and many will renew their agreement at the end of their contract (Whitby, 1994a; Wilson, 1997a, 1997c). In the recent monitoring report for the CSS it was concluded that the scheme was "a useful 'carrot' that can help to achieve environmental benefits on other land" (Land Use Consultants, 1995, 68). Yet, as a recent study by Wilson (1996, 1997c) has highlighted for one of the UK's ESAs, only few farmers equate participation in an agri-environmental scheme with 'conservation', and few showed changes in their environmental management practices based on scheme participation – thereby questioning the long-term benefits that UK AEP will have, particularly if schemes were to be discontinued.

So far, therefore, implementation of AEP under Regulation 2078 in the UK has only been partly successful. Although many schemes are theoretically offered, uptake under the 'new' schemes has been particularly disappointing. It appears that the UK has merely responded to Regulation 2078 as a 'receiver' of Brussels policy, rather than acting as an active 'shaper' of the Regulation as was the case earlier for Regulation 797/85.

Prospects for the future of UK agri-environmental policy

Where does this leave UK prospects for the future to address environmental problems in the countryside? The UK has certainly played an important role in shaping EU AEP, particularly during the 1980s. Although this role has arguably been diminishing in the 1990s, the experience and long-standing UK interest in countryside conservation will continue to make it an important partner in EU AEP-making. Other countries can particularly learn from the long British experience with ESAs (over ten years of implementation), and experiences gained from this successful programme are constantly being fed into EU AEP. It is obvious that the ESA programme will continue to be the 'flagship' of UK AEP (Whitby and Lowe, 1994; Whitby, 1996a), but "despite nearly ten years' experience with ESAs, agri-environmental policy is still at an innovative, even experimental stage, and farmers, environmental groups and agencies and the Government themselves are still ascending a learning curve" (House of Commons, 1997, xxiv).

What is less clear, is the future of the newly expanded CSS. This scheme will require substantially larger budgets than the current allocation (see Table 6.2) if it is to become the second major pillar of UK AEP. The next few years will, therefore, be an important test for the UK commitment to its AEP programme. This relates in particular to the question whether the government will be willing to implement articles of Regulation 2078 currently not implemented – in particular advice and training for farmers linked to AEP, schemes to promote endangered breeds, and schemes for abandoned farmland and woodland – crucial ingredients for a sustainable countryside.

Undoubtedly, any enlargement of the agri-environmental programme will require a large increase in budgetary commitment from the government for it to be effective. Yet, the government argues that such increases cannot be made until the CAP is reformed. Through this reform (*Agenda 2000*), it is hoped that commodity payments will be phased out and that a proportion will be re-allocated to agri-environmental payments (EC, 1997d). There are various scenarios being discussed (cf. MAFF, 1995; Buckwell *et al.*, 1998), but some action can and needs to be taken now. For example, a pilot *Arable Incentive Scheme* was announced in April 1997 which will address some of the environmental problems inherent in arable farming – thereby clearly indicating a move away from targeted protection of vulnerable habitats, towards recognition of the importance of tackling agricultural pollution issues in the wider countryside. This will become a new targeted landscape type under the CSS. Again, however, the budget allocated to the scheme is very low (ECU 0.7 million).

There are increasing calls for structural and agricultural issues to be brought together, integrating money from the *Structural Funds* into agri-environmental schemes. There is also concern that *Biodiversity Action Plan* targets should be integrated into the schemes, since the majority of the target habitats and species within the plan are strongly linked to farming. This will require improved communication and co-operation between MAFF and the *Department of the Environment*, as without better integration of aims between the different agencies, the UK approach towards environmental protection in the wider countryside will continue to be piecemeal, and, ultimately, less effective.

7 Germany: complex agri-environmental policy in a federal system

Annegret Grafen and Jörg Schramek

Agriculture and the environment

Germany is a highly industrialised, densely populated, and economically affluent country where conflicts between economic development and environmental quality have a long history, and where environmental degradation has, for many areas, been of a considerable scale. It is hardly surprising, therefore, that environmental protection policy and actions have been given particular prominence in recent decades, both in the public and the private domain. However, while environmental awareness remains high in Germany today, the recent economic recession, rising unemployment and the increasing pressure of business lobby groups have, during the 1990s, tended to side-line environmental protection as a predominant national concern, leading to a discernible shift in environmental policy away from costly legislation towards a more voluntary approach. This general trend has also concerned agricultural policy thinking, with the result that particular attention has been paid in Germany to the adoption and implementation of voluntary agri-environmental schemes.

The development of German AEP also needs to be understood in the broader context of agricultural structural change that has taken place since the Second World War. Dramatic changes in German agriculture began in the middle of the 1950s (Priebe, 1985; Rat von Sachverständigen, 1985; Heißenhuber *et al.*, 1994). Since that period, the agricultural workforce has been considerably reduced; of the 5 million people working in agriculture in the early 1950s, only 600,000 remain in 1998. At the same time, the application of fertilisers and pesticides increased considerably, the number of crops in rotations decreased sharply, and a large proportion of permanent grassland was converted to arable land. The number of farms also declined (from 1.6 million in 1949 to 0.5 million in 1998 on the territory of the former Federal Republic) while their average size increased considerably (from 8 ha in 1949 to 23 ha in 1998). These structural changes coincided with the rapid disappearance of traditional farming systems – a process clearly aided by agricultural support mechanisms aimed at both increasing intensification of farms and raising farm incomes.

Although the effects of these changes on land management had been apparent for a long time, the negative environmental consequences of modern farming practices did not really enter the public debate until the early 1980s. In 1985, a seminal government report on environmental problems caused by agriculture (Rat von Sachverständigen, 1985) immediately gained considerable attention. By quoting various scientific studies, the report described for the first time the threatening effects of modern agriculture on the environment in a comprehensive way. The main conclusions were that modern agriculture had been by far the most important cause for the declining number, and indeed extinction, of certain plant and animal species, mainly due to the destruction of ecosystems and agricultural pollution. The report also found that modern forms of soil cultivation had led to increasing soil erosion and, in particular, water pollution. In the following years, it was this latter concern that dominated the policy response, partly because of the introduction of EU legislation governing drinking water quality, and partly due to the fact that German water suppliers openly tackled the problem and lobbied strongly for changes in German and European policies. A parallel concern also emerged for the effects of modern agriculture on climate change triggered, in part, by the *UN Conference on Environment and Development* in Rio de Janeiro 1992 (Grubb *et al.*, 1993).

From the early 1980s, an intense debate emerged over the best approach to making German agriculture more environmentally friendly (e.g. Priebe, 1985; Scheele *et al.*, 1993). A vehement dispute ensued about the validity and use of the two main conservation principles: the PPP and the PPG (Scheele and Isermeyer, 1989). The PPP was advocated above all by the *Council of Environmental Advisors*, who based their arguments on the fact that agriculture had contributed considerably to environmental degradation while being almost completely exempt from environmental regulation through the special 'agricultural clause' (*Landwirtschaftsklausel*) in the German nature protection law (Weinschenck and Gebhard, 1985). The Council proposed levies or taxes on key production inputs as the key instruments to tackle environmental pollution caused by agriculture. The PPP was also supported by scientists and by several nature protection organisations, but it was strongly opposed by the German farmers union (*Deutscher Bauernverband*, DBV) fearing further restrictions on hitherto sacrosanct agricultural practices.

The PPG, on the other hand, based on the assumption that agriculture produces public goods such as ecologically valuable landscapes or a broad variety of habitats and species which are not paid for by agricultural markets, was suggested as an alternative by a range of actors, including farmers, policy-makers and scientists (e.g. Priebe, 1985; Seibert and von Meyer, 1987). The notion of 'cultural landscape' was used by these actors to suggest that society should pay farmers for the provision of public goods, with payments being made either on a flat-rate hectarage basis or being differentiated for specific 'ecological efforts' (Knauer, 1989). Opponents of the PPG have always suspected, however, that support for this approach was largely motivated by the search for new means of agricultural income support. This criticism has persisted to the present day even though payments for environmentally sound farming have now become a well-established component of agricultural policy.

The PPG approach has also been supported by the DBV who, in general, have fought against policy instruments based on hectarage payments. In the run-up to the CAP reform in 1992, for example, the DBV vehemently refused proposals that would curtail price support and compensate income losses through hectarage payments, arguing that payments which are subject to social or environmental conditions would not be secure in the long term, but would fluctuate in response to changing public demand. German NGOs, meanwhile, concentrated on issues that lay beyond the relative merits of PPP or PPG, arguing that discussions about agri-environmental schemes should also address the 'integration' or 'segregation' of environmental conservation with respect to general farming activities (Haber, 1971; Hampicke, 1988). Most environmental associations pleaded for an integration of environmental protection and agricultural policy and for horizontal extensification, rather than for the establishment of targeted nature reserves which would often lead to an intensification of the remaining areas (Ellenberg *et al.*, 1989). They specifically rejected the British model of designating ESAs (see Ch. 6) and lobbied against an area-specific subdivision of protected areas and areas where pollution would be permitted (*Schutz- und Schmutzgebiete*). Nonetheless, despite these intense internal debates, the general thrust of European agricultural policy and the fact that many German *Länder* had already formulated schemes paying farmers for nature protection efforts (e.g. the *Kulturlandschaftsprogramm* or KULAP scheme in Bayern; see below) have clearly driven German AEP increasingly towards the PPG principle. By way of contrast, the application of the PPP has been relatively poor and is likely to remain weak in a climate of worsening economic recession.

Outside the debates surrounding these two principles, German AEP has also been strongly influenced by the continuous demands of German farmers for higher commodity prices (Kluge, 1989; Hendriks, 1991). In the course of CAP reform, Germany, more than any other Member

State, pleaded for a continuation of an income-oriented price support policy and persistently fought direct income transfers. Instead of decreasing agricultural prices, German policy-makers sought regulatory instruments that restricted production and thus relieved surpluses. The *set-aside* and *extensification schemes* are cases in point and were established with strong support by Germany (Jones, 1994; Führer, 1997). In the context of German resistance to a market-oriented reform of the CAP and growing public awareness of the environmental impacts of intensive farming practices, it became politically advantageous for Germany to argue for the linking of expensive new instruments with environmental arguments. Thus, schemes such as set-aside, which originally aimed at market relief, have been backed up by environmental arguments. In the struggle over CAP reform, the *Länder* also played an important part in pressing the federal government towards schemes that linked the restriction of production with environmental objectives, mainly because most *Länder* (in former West Germany) already had schemes which paid farmers for environmentally sound practices since the mid 1980s.

It is important to emphasise that in Germany, as a federal state, responsibilities for agricultural policy, and therefore also for AEP, are shared between the federal (*Bund*) and the regional level (*Länder*). Market policy and social policy within agriculture are the responsibilities of the *Bund*, whereas the *Länder* are responsible for both regional and structural planning and AEP. Thus, in distinction to most other EU Member States, a considerable amount of implementation power in Germany is delegated to the individual regions. This partly explains the complexity of the German AEP sector (Wilson, 1994, 1995; Plankl, 1996a). Due to its federal system, the 'Common Task for the Improvement of Agricultural Structures and Coastal Protection' (or 'GAK') has been used to co-ordinate *Länder* policies with those of the *Bund*, and to ensure an adequate financial contribution from the federal level[27]. Agri-environmental schemes are also co-ordinated among the *Bund* and the *Länder* under the GAK whose budget is usually split into a federal contribution of 60% and a 40% share financed by each region. Until the implementation of AEP in the 1980s, the term 'agricultural structures' in the GAK was restricted to the structure of holdings, agricultural infrastructures and market structures. As a result, the GAK included farm modernisation schemes (investment aids), land consolidation, village renewal and the German LFA scheme. With the reform of the CAP in 1992, however, the term 'agricultural structures' has been expanded to accommodate agri-environmental aims that include countryside protection

---

[27] The GAK was established in 1969 to co-ordinate the agricultural structural policies of the *Länder* and to make them compatible with European structural policies under the CAP.

and management. In line with this shift, the Federal Ministry for Agriculture (BMELF) took over the competencies of implementing Regulation 2078 from the *Länder*, justifying its action by claiming that the CAP accompanying measures were largely aimed at income and market issues rather than environmental aims. This institutional change in implementation responsibilities was strongly opposed by those *Länder* that had already set up their own agri-environmental schemes (e.g. Baden-Württemberg, Bayern) and who feared that the GAK framework would be too restrictive (Höll and von Meyer, 1996).

Implementation of agri-environmental policy before 1992

By the mid 1980s, and therefore long before the introduction of Regulation 2078 in 1992, most of the 'old' *Länder* had already implemented their own agri-environmental schemes (Table 7.1). These schemes were already partly co-financed by the EC under Regulation 797/85 (*Article 19*) and its subsequent amendments. In most cases, the schemes were initially implemented by the environmental administration of the *Länder* and not by the Federal Agricultural Ministry. The bulk of schemes aimed at promoting environmentally sound farming methods with a strong emphasis on grassland extensification (e.g. the KULAP scheme in Bayern). In all, about 60 MECU/year were spent on grassland extensification, whereas schemes targeting arable land only comprised about 3.2 MECU/year (Heißenhuber *et al.*, 1994). Most schemes were initially targeted at specified regions and their terms ranged from one to five years[28]. With the introduction of co-financing by the EC in 1987, however, responsibility for the majority of actions was transferred to the federal agricultural administration – a transfer which reinforced the importance given to the market, social and structural objectives of AEP. This gave the Federal Ministry a greater direct influence over the AEP implementation process.

Implementation of Regulation 797/85

Germany was one of the few EU Member States to implement Regulation 797/85 on a large scale. Implementation was the exclusive responsibility of the *Länder* who defined the objectives and target regions of the schemes, formulated scheme requirements, and fixed the terms of payments. In

---

[28] See Wilson, 1994, and Plankl, 1996a, for detailed descriptions of available schemes before 1992.

Table 7.1 Agri-environmental schemes of the *Länder* in 1989

	Grassland	Arable Land	Orchards	Landscape protection
Baden-Württemberg	Conversion of intensive to extensive grassland; grassland fallowing; conservation of extensive meadows (partly since 1982)	Conversion of arable to grassland; fallowing of arable land; management of field margins (since 1987)	Conservation of orchards (since 1987)	Model project for biotope networks; management measures in nature reserves
Bayern	Compensation for restricted use of wet meadows; protection of meadow birds; conservation of dry and nutrient poor meadows (partly since 1983)	Conservation of wild flora and faun/a on arable land (since 1985)	Conservation of orchards (since 1988)	Various landscape schemes targeted at ecologically valuable areas (partly since 1983)
Bremen	Protection of meadow birds	Conservation of wild flora on arable land (since 1987)		Planting of new hedgerows (since 1987)
Hamburg	Protection of wet meadows (since 1987)	Conservation of wild flora on arable land (since 1987)		Establishment of wildlife refuges (since 1981)
Hessen	Protection of ecologically valuable meadows (since 1986)	Extensification of field margins (since 1986)	Conservation of orchards (since 1988)	Leasing of land to establish biotope networks (since 1985)
Niedersachsen	Compensation for restricted use of meadows in nature reserve areas (since 1985)	Protection of wild flora on arable land (since 1987)		

Nordrhein-Westfalen	Conservation of wet meadows (since 1985)	Protection of wild flora on arable land (since 1985)		Conservation of traditional landscapes in mountainous areas (since 1987)
Rheinland-Pfalz	Extensification of grassland (since 1986)	Extensification of field margins (since 1986)	Conservation of orchards (since 1986)	
Saarland	Extensification of grassland (since 1987)	Extensification of field margins; management of land prone to erosion (since 1987)	Conservation of orchards (since 1987)	Conversion to environmentally friendly farming systems (since 1987)
Schleswig-Holstein	Various schemes for the protection of wild species on grassland (since 1985)	Protection of wild flora on arable land; arable fallowing (since 1985)		Establishment of biotopes (since 1983)

Source: Landesamt für Naturschutz und Landschaftspflege Schleswig Holstein, 1991

contrast to the later *Extensification Scheme* based on Regulation 4115/88 (see below) and to new schemes based on Regulation 2078, there was, therefore, no federal framework for the implementation or the financing of actions under Regulation 797/85. In total, eight schemes were implemented in six *Länder*[29] and all were co-financed by the regions and the EC. The scheme covering most land was the Bavarian KULAP, which encouraged the extensification of grassland and arable land, the protection of natural resources and various smaller actions within designated areas (see Figure 7.1 for the location of the German *Länder*). By 1988, payments for this single scheme amounted to 23 MECU – the largest budget devoted to any agri-environmental scheme in the EC at the time.

Over ten years after the establishment of the first German agri-environmental schemes under Regulation 797/85, their socio-economic and environmental effects remain difficult to gauge, as indeed they are in most EU states with similar experiences. Research on the KULAP in Bayern, as well as for the former Hessian *Grassland Extensification Scheme*, has revealed that farmers who had managed their land extensively before the scheme, and who did not require significant alterations in farming practices after joining the scheme, were the most likely participants (Knöbl, 1989; HMILFN, 1998). The Hessian evaluation further revealed that only long-term extensification of grassland yielded positive effects on biodiversity. Positive ecological effects were also claimed for the KULAP, particularly its grassland extensification measures. Similarly, there were indications that the *Marktentlastungs- und Kulturlanschaftsausgleich Scheme* (MEKA) in Baden-Württemberg resulted in some socio-economic and environmental benefits (Wilson, 1995; Bronner *et al.*, 1997; see below). Nevertheless, in general, there is little conclusive evidence of positive and long-term environmental gains resulting from these early schemes.

Implementation of the 'extensification' Regulation 4115/88

The *Extensification Scheme* was implemented in Germany in 1989 for all the 'old' *Länder* and in 1991 within former East Germany. Due to their size and importance, both the *Extensification* and the *Set-aside Schemes* (see below) necessitated special administrative arrangements within the GAK, which meant that financing was split between the Federal Government and the *Länder* on a 70/30 basis instead of the usual 60/40. The GAK framework offered two forms of extensification to farmers; the first based upon a

---

[29] Hamburg, Schleswig-Holstein, Niedersachsen, Rheinland-Pfalz, Bayern and Nordrhein-Westfalen.

Figure 7.1   The German *Länder*

straightforward reduction of farm arable production yields by as much as 20%, the second based upon conversion to less intensive forms of production including organic farming. In practice, all *Länder* chose to focus chiefly upon the second approach partly because it required no verification of yield reduction, the assumption being that conversion to organic farming would necessarily entail falls in yields. As such, the *Extensification Scheme* became essentially a vehicle for the promotion of organic farming methods. Uptake was high when compared with most other EU Member States. In the first year alone, 4,500 farms amounting to 53,000 ha participated in the extensification of arable crops (almost 0.5% of UAA). In 1992/1993, the last year when new contracts could be signed, 407,000 ha were supported by the scheme either under organic or other environmentally friendly production methods (the latter negligible), representing around 2.6% of the total UAA (BMELF, 1995).

Conversion to organic farming under extensification was most popular in regions with poorer natural conditions (Schulze-Pals, 1994; Klinkmann and Tremel, 1995; Aldinger, 1997; Führer, 1997). These included areas of extensive grassland, mountain regions and areas of extensive arable farming on poor soils (mainly in the new *Länder*). The scheme was less attractive for holdings located in fertile arable regions, as well as for farms with specialised animal husbandry, mainly because in fertile regions payments were not sufficient to compensate for the loss of income induced by changing farming practices to organic farming (Heißenhuber and Ring, 1991). As a result, the extensification scheme did not contribute significantly to the reduction of polluting inputs such as fertilisers and pesticides in these areas. However, in areas with high participation rates, conversion to organic farming resulted in environmentally beneficial increases in crop rotations and decreases of stocking rates (Nieberg, 1997).

Set-aside

In Germany, the *Set-aside Scheme* of 1988 (aimed chiefly at decreasing surplus production) was also interpreted as an 'agri-environmental' scheme. It was argued that set-aside provided environmental benefits in regions where the environment was strained by intensive farming. Thus, the German set-aside experience differs substantially from that of other Member States (Jones, 1991; Jones *et al.*, 1993). As for Regulation 4115/88 (see above), the *Set-aside Scheme* was implemented through special arrangements within the GAK. Federal bodies attached great importance to the scheme, which meant that the available budget for set-aside was relatively high (Heißenhuber *et al.*, 1994). Payments were dependent on soil quality (e.g. only 126 ECU/ha for very poor soils; 745 ECU/ha for very good soils; cf. König, 1991), which partly explains the highly differentiated nature of uptake in Germany (see Jones *et al.*, 1993). In contrast to the low acceptance elsewhere in Europe, the uptake of the set-aside scheme in Germany was very high (over a third of all set-aside land in the Community), with about 4% of the total arable area in former West Germany coming under agreement and an even higher proportion in the new *Länder*. The ecological effects of set-aside were, nonetheless, debatable. On the one hand, the scheme was perceived as a means of increasing biodiversity (HMLFN, 1990; Rammler and Würflein, 1991), although ecologists saw the almost random scattering of set-aside fields as a big disadvantage from a landscape ecology perspective (Pfadenhauer, 1988). On the other hand, the set-aside scheme did little to solve the problems of aquifer pollution with nitrates (HMLFN, 1990).

Implementation of Regulation 2078 in Germany

National and regional institutions responsible for 2078 implementation

As a result of Germany's federal structure, several tiers of government are concerned with the implementation of Regulation 2078. The Regulation is implemented through agri-environmental programmes at the individual *Länder* level, which usually consist of multi-annual zonal schemes for which each *Land* identifies specific problems and defines schemes and payments. For most schemes, the entire regional territory has been designated as eligible (Plankl, 1996a; see Table 7.2 below). While some *Länder* (especially in the south of Germany) integrated pre-existing and ambitious agri-environmental schemes into the framework of the Regulation, other *Länder* (especially in former East Germany and some *Länder* in northern Germany) only began comprehensive agri-environmental schemes on the basis of this Regulation (Höll and von Meyer, 1996). Several *Länder* have amalgamated various former agri-environmental schemes into one comprehensive scheme, such as the MEKA scheme in Baden-Württemberg, the *Hessisches Kulturlandschaftsprogramm* (HEKUL) in Hessen, or the *Bayerisches Kulturlandschaftsprogramm* (KULAP) in Bayern (Wilson, 1994, 1995; see Figure 7.1). These three horizontal schemes are also the largest agri-environmental schemes in Germany (both with regard to budgets and the number of participating farmers).

In 1993, the government allowed the co-financing of schemes established under Regulation 2078 through the introduction of guidelines into the GAK for the support of farming adapted to market and location-

Table 7.2 Targeting of schemes under Regulation 2078 in the 16 German *Länder*

Cluster of schemes	Conversion to, or continuation of, organic farming	Extensification of arable land and/or permanent crops		Extensification of grassland			Local breeds	Protection of environment, natural resources, countryside and landscape			Public access and leisure activities	Education and training
Type of schemes	Organic farming	Fertiliser/Pesticide reductions	Maintenance or introduction of extensive production	Conversion to grassland	Introduction or maintenance of extensive grassland	Livestock reduction	Local breeds	Environmental and landscape protection	Upkeep of abandoned farmland or woodland	20-year set-aside	Public access and leisure activities	Education and training
	Reg. 2078 Art 2 (1.a)	Reg. 2078 Art 2 (1.a)	Reg. 2078 Art 2 (1.b)	Reg. 2078 Art 2 (1.b)	Reg. 2078 Art 2 (1.b)	Reg. 2078 Art 2 (1.c)	Reg. 2078 Art 2 (1.d)	Reg. 2078 Art 2 (1.d)	Reg. 2078 Art 2 (1.e)	Reg. 2078 Art 2 (1.f)	Reg. 2078 Art 2 (1.g)	Reg. 2078 Art 2 (2)
Schl. Holst.	Entire region	Entire region		Entire region	Entire region	Entire region		Partly targeted				
Hamburg	Entire region	Entire region	Entire region	Entire region	Entire region	Entire region		Entire region	Entire region	Entire region		Entire region
Niedersachsen	Entire region	Entire region	Partly targeted	Entire region	Entire region	Entire region	Entire region	Partly targeted		Targeted		Entire region
Bremen	Entire region			Entire region	Entire region	Entire region		Partly targeted				Entire region
Nordr. Westf.	Entire region	Entire region	Entire region	Entire region	Entire region	Entire region	Entire region	Partly targeted		Entire region		Entire region
Hessen	Entire region			Entire region	Entire region	Entire region	Entire region	Partly targeted	Entire region	Entire region		Entire region
Rheinl. Pfalz	Entire region	Entire region	Entire region	Entire region	Entire region	Entire region		Partly targeted		Targeted		

	Col 1	Col 2	Col 3	Col 4	Col 5	Col 6	Col 7	Col 8	Col 9	Col 10	Col 11
Baden-Württ.	Entire region	Entire region	Entire region		Entire region	Entire region	Entire region	Entire region			
Bayern	Entire region	Entire region	Entire region	Entire region	Entire region	Entire region	Entire region	Entire region		Entire region	Entire region
Saarland	Entire region		Partly targeted	Entire region	Entire region	Entire region	Entire region	Entire region	Entire region		Entire region
Berlin	Entire region	Entire region	Entire region	Entire region	Entire region	Entire region	Entire region	Entire region			
Brandenburg	Entire region	Entire region	Entire region	Entire region	Entire region	Entire region		Partly targeted	Targeted		Entire region
Meckl. Vorp.	Entire region		Entire region	Entire region	Entire region	Entire region		Targeted	Targeted		
Sachsen	Entire region		Entire region	Entire region	Entire region		Entire region	Partly targeted	Entire region	Targeted	Entire region
Sachs.-Anhalt	Entire region	Entire region	Entire region	Entire region	Entire region		Entire region	Partly targeted	Targeted	Entire region	Entire region
Thüringen	Entire region	Entire region	Entire region	Entire region	Entire region	Entire region	Entire region	Entire region	Entire region	Entire region	Entire region

Source: authors

specific conditions. Yet, compared to the range of schemes that can theoretically be implemented under Regulation 2078, the number of schemes part-funded within the framework of the GAK is limited and only includes the *management of extensive grassland systems*, the *conversion to (or the maintenance of) extensive management on arable land*, and the *conversion to (or the maintenance of) organic farming*. For schemes addressing these issues, payments and conditions of participation offered by the *Länder* are fixed by the GAK. However, as the provisions of the GAK are relatively restrictive, not all agri-environmental schemes offered in the *Länder* can be accommodated. In consequence, many *Länder* (e.g. Bayern, Baden-Württemberg, Rheinland-Pfalz, Hessen and Sachsen) offer schemes or parts of schemes beyond the GAK framework. In general, *Länder* that had ambitious agri-environmental schemes before the implementation of Regulation 2078 (e.g. Bayern and Baden-Württemberg; see Figure 7.1), as well as the comparatively wealthy regions (e.g. Hessen, Rheinland-Pfalz), have opted to pursue a policy outside the GAK framework (Mehl and Plankl, 1996).

The different relationships of *Länder* schemes with the GAK have significant repercussions for the financing of regional schemes. While schemes that fall within the framework of the GAK obtain 50% of their funding from the EU, 30% from the federal government and 20% from the *Länder*, schemes outside the GAK do not receive any federal share (i.e. they are co-funded directly between the EU and the *Land*; see also Ch. 8 on Spain for a similar situation). Since the five new German *Länder* (Brandenburg, Mecklenburg-Vorpommern, Sachsen, Sachsen-Anhalt, Thüringen) are Objective 1 regions covered by the EU *Structural Funds*, the EU can co-finance agri-environmental schemes within these regions by up to 75% (with 15% contribution by the federal government and 10% by the *Länder*).

The structure of the schemes in the different *Länder*, as well as the payment levels and issues addressed through the schemes, vary considerably. This is due to different natural conditions and agricultural structures, different agri-environmental requirements and aims, and differing political goals and economic conditions in the different *Länder* (Wilson, 1994; Plankl, 1996a). Partly as a result of this, co-ordination between the *Länder* in establishing their schemes has generally been weak, and in some ecologically homogenous areas divided by regional boundaries (e.g. the Rhön mountains between Bayern, Hessen and Thüringen) completely different schemes with different payment structures and different agri-environmental aims have been implemented (Geier *et al.*, 1996; Wilson, 1998a).

German agri-environmental schemes under Regulation 2078

The GAK framework plan for the period 1994-1999 states that agri-environmental schemes should, above all, aim at the protection of soils and aquifers from pollution with pesticides and fertilisers (Deutscher Bundestag, 1995). At present, however, the schemes presented by the individual *Länder* are not restricted to environmental objectives alone; some also aim at the stabilisation of agricultural incomes and markets through the preservation of traditional farming in LFAs (Geier *et al.*, 1996). While recent reviews have highlighted that the preservation of landscape elements and biotopes are increasingly predominating, the reduction of fertiliser and pesticide pollution is rarely mentioned as a specific scheme objective (Wilson, 1994; Plankl, 1996a). There is, therefore, an obvious contradiction between the agri-environmental goals set by national policy-making actors and what has been implemented by regional policy-makers on the ground.

German agri-environmental schemes according to Regulation 2078 can be divided into two main types:

* *Schemes directed at changing farming practices*   These include the conversion to (or the maintenance of) organic farming and the extensification of arable land, grassland and permanent crops. Schemes of this type are offered in almost all *Länder* and make up the bulk of agreement areas and agri-environmental budgets.
* *Schemes aimed at the preservation of specific environmentally sensitive areas[30], biotopes or species*   These are often summarised under the term 'landscape schemes' including, for example, the preservation of extensively used pastures or meadows, the preservation of wildlife on field margins, meadow bird schemes, or the conservation of orchards and wetlands (see Wilson, 1994, and Plankl, 1996a, for detailed reviews of the schemes). Schemes of this type are small-scale, often targeted at specific regions, and involve much smaller financial expenditures than the schemes directed at changing farming practices. In some *Länder*, schemes of this type operate entirely outside the GAK framework and are the responsibility of regional environment ministries rather than the agricultural administration.

The following paragraphs will investigate in more detail what types of agri-environmental schemes have been implemented in Germany, and will also help illustrate the great diversity of responses to the Regulation between the individual *Länder*.

---

[30] Note that the notion of 'environmentally sensitive areas' in Germany differs from the ESA scheme in the UK and other EU Member States.

Conversion to (or maintenance of) organic farming methods According to the GAK, support can be given for the conversion to (or maintenance of) organic farming methods. The support is conditional on organic farming being practised on the entire farm for at least five years and on the farming methods being in accordance with EU Regulation 2092/91 on organic farming. Although all *Länder* offer organic farming schemes, payments range from 135 to 300 ECU/ha for the conversion of arable and grassland farming to organic production, and between 135 and 1000 ECU/ha for permanent crops. In 1995/96, 6,500 farms covering 158,000 ha were supported through organic farming schemes through Regulation 2078. Although this only covers about 1% of the German UAA, it highlights the emphasis placed on organic farming in Germany in a broader EU context (Lampkin, 1996). However, the percentage of agricultural area under agreement varies significantly among the *Länder*. Regions with the highest rates of acceptance are Hessen and Baden-Württemberg (both with 2.1%), and Bayern (1.7%) (BMELF, 1997). In 1996, a total area of 354,000 ha was managed under organic conditions as identified in Regulation 2092/91 (Jungehülsing and Lotz, 1997). However, many organic farms are still supported through the former extensification scheme (see above), though a large proportion of these are expected to apply for support under Regulation 2078 at the end of their extensification agreements.

Extensification of arable land and permanent crops Under the GAK, support can be provided for the conversion to (or maintenance of) extensive farming on arable land. This includes the renunciation of mineral fertilisers and/or pesticides on arable land or permanent crops. No permanent grassland may be converted to arable land, and livestock density may not exceed 2.0 LU/ha for the entire holding. Again, payments differ considerably between the *Länder*, ranging from 40 to 270 ECU/ha for arable land, and between 120 and 650 ECU/ha for permanent crops. Some *Länder* only recently started support for the extensification of arable land (e.g. Saarland and Mecklenburg-Vorpommern). Further, while some *Länder* implement their extensification schemes completely outside the GAK (e.g. Baden-Württemberg, Bayern, Rheinland-Pfalz and Sachsen), others have provided extensification schemes part-funded through the GAK. Preliminary monitoring has revealed that basic extensification schemes supported through the GAK framework alone have met with relatively low support by farmers, with only 7% of German arable land under any form of extensification – a relatively disappointing figure considering the relatively successful uptake of other 2078 schemes by farmers (see below).

Extensification of grassland   The conversion to (or maintenance of) extensive methods of grassland cultivation is eligible for GAK support, provided that livestock densities per ha of grassland are reduced to 1.4 rough grazing LU. Support is also provided for the maintenance of extensive grassland management and the conversion of arable land to extensive grassland. Many grassland extensification schemes are implemented outside the GAK (e.g. schemes encouraging sound application of liquid manure or restricting reaping dates). Payments vary between 40 and 160 ECU/ha for the maintenance of extensive grassland, between 240 and 300 ECU/LU for livestock reduction, between 110 and 160 ECU/ha for extension of grassland area, and between 260 and 390 ECU/ha for conversion of arable to grassland. Almost all schemes are offered as horizontal schemes in individual *Länder* (see Table 7.2 below). It is interesting to note that measures for the extensification of grassland have the best take-up level of all German schemes implemented under Regulation 2078, partly because payments are relatively high, and partly because the schemes often only require few changes in farm management practices. As a result, over a quarter of the total permanent grassland area in Germany is subject to grassland extensification measures.

Rearing of local breeds in danger of extinction   Germany is one of the few EU countries to have implemented schemes under this article of Regulation 2078, and currently ten *Länder* offer support for the rearing of local breeds. Payments vary between 110 and 160 ECU/rough grazing LU for breeding cattle. In some *Länder*, management practices such as melioration, the conversion of grassland to arable land, or the application of fertilisers on grassland, are prohibited in connection with the payments for local breeds. Again, the schemes are offered as horizontal schemes, but acceptance by farmers has generally been poor.

Landscape schemes   Schemes aiming at the preservation, re-establishment and cultivation of specific landscape elements have been implemented in all *Länder*. Many schemes are directed at ecologically valuable grassland areas, including wet, dry, or nutrient-poor grasslands, meadows on steep slopes, and grasslands with traditional and extensive cultivation systems. However, the upkeep of abandoned land and 20-year set-aside are not supported by most *Länder*. These two schemes are, therefore, a relatively unimportant part of Regulation 2078 implementation in Germany. Further, none of the schemes aiming at specific nature protection issues are contained in the GAK, which means that budgets for these types of schemes are comparatively small. Only extensive grassland measures have shown significant uptake rates, especially in those *Länder* with ambitious agri-environmental schemes (e.g. Bayern, Baden-Württemberg).

Education and training of farmers Again, Germany stands out in terms of implementation of this specific clause in Regulation 2078 in an EU context. Schemes to improve the training of farmers are provided by 11 *Länder*, and subsidies are paid for the organisation of, and participation in, educational courses. Some *Länder* even offer additional payments for transport, accommodation, or the invitation of external experts. However, the acceptance of these schemes is only marginal because of general lack of information concerning the financial support of training courses, and some *Länder* (Schleswig-Holstein, Rheinland-Pfalz, Baden-Württemberg, Berlin and Mecklenburg-Vorpommern) do not offer any training schemes at all.

Special case: MEKA It has been argued by a variety of commentators that the MEKA scheme in Baden-Württemberg (see Figure 7.1 above) is one of the most sophisticated schemes implemented under Regulation 2078 in the EU (e.g. Wilson, 1995; Pretty, 1995; Bronner *et al.*, 1997). MEKA, which provides compensation to farmers for market relief measures and the protection of the countryside, is one of the largest and most expensive agri-environmental schemes implemented in the EU to date. Sixty-thousand farms with over 1.3 million ha agricultural land now participate in the scheme (about 70% of all eligible farms in Baden-Württemberg) at a yearly cost of 85 MECU in 1996, and a total expenditure of over 300 MECU between 1993 and 1996 (Bronner *et al.*, 1997). MEKA alone, therefore, commands a larger budget than many national agri-environmental programmes in the EU (see Ch. 12) – indicating both the wealth and the commitment towards countryside conservation in some of the German *Länder*. MEKA is based on a unique system of 'eco-points' which was developed by a variety of policy actors, including the farmers union of Baden-Württemberg (Wilson, 1995). Most measures within MEKA can be combined, with an aggregate payment ceiling of about 300 ECU/ha (Zeddies and Doluschitz, 1996). This point system allows farmers to choose from a 'menu' which gives them more flexibility than most other schemes in the EU, and which certainly is a major reason for the high participation rates. However, MEKA has been criticised for being relatively difficult to control and monitor because of the very individual nature of each agreement (Wilson, 1995; see below).

Regional implementation of Regulation 2078 and farmer participation

Regulation 2078 is widely implemented, well known and accepted in Germany. In some *Länder*, the total financial volume for agri-environmental schemes has increased considerably since implementation of the Regulation, and all *Länder* have made extensive use of improved possibilities for co-financing through the Regulation since 1992 (Plankl, 1996b). There are, however, some interesting differences in the ways in which the Regulation has been interpreted and implemented by the different *Länder*. Table 7.2 shows that different *Länder* have adopted different targeting strategies. For example, in the southern *Länder* (Bayern and Baden-Württemberg), Regulation 2078 has been perceived as an important means not only to improve the environment but also to stabilise agricultural structures and incomes. Only recently, Bayern substantially increased the scope of its KULAP scheme and, in particular, improved the support for agri-environmental measures on grassland. In contrast, the northern *Länder* (in particular Schleswig-Holstein, Niedersachsen and Nordrhein-Westfalen), which are politically more oriented towards their predominant large-scale and competitive agri-businesses, have tended to interpret Regulation 2078 as an additional nature protection scheme for small and specific environmental problem areas. In the new *Länder*, meanwhile, the fact that co-financing opportunities for Objective 1 regions are more favourable than in former West Germany has offered new opportunities for large-scale agri-environmental schemes. Consequently, while the southern *Länder* Baden-Württemberg and Bayern show the highest spending for agri-environmental schemes (per ha UAA), some of the new *Länder* have also made extensive use of co-financing opportunities and have implemented relatively substantial agri-environmental schemes (i.e. Sachsen and Thüringen; see Table 7.3). The northern *Länder* (e.g. Schleswig-Holstein, Niedersachsen, Nordrhein-Westfalen), have, by way of contrast, only allocated relatively small budgets for their highly targeted schemes.

By 1996, more than 5 million ha were under contract in Germany under Regulation 2078 (Table 7.4). It is important to note, however, that this figure is highly influenced by the fact that almost 70% of this area falls under the basic management tiers offered in Bayern and Sachsen only. Among the remaining schemes, extensification of grassland represents the most important type of measure in terms of area and budgets involved[31]. A further 868,000 ha of arable land are subject to Regulation 2078 schemes,

---

[31] The most important proportions of grassland under agreement are in Thüringen (89%), Saarland (86%) and Sachsen-Anhalt (75%).

Table 7.3 Annual spending of the *Länder* for agri-environmental schemes according to Regulation 2078 in Germany

Region	Total spending for agri-environmental schemes 1993 – 1996 (MECU)	Average annual spending per ha UAA (ECU)
Schleswig-Holstein	7.4	1.8
Niedersachsen	17	1.6
Nordrhein-Westfalen	8.3	1.3
Hessen	58	18.6
Rheinland-Pfalz	37	12.8
Baden-Württemberg	274	46.8
Bayern	401	29.8
Saarland	6.5	22.4
Brandenburg	63	11.8
Mecklenburg Vorp.	16	3.0
Sachsen	112	31.1
Sachsen-Anhalt	45	9.7
Thüringen	83	26.0
Germany	**1,130**	**16.3**

Source: BMELF, 1997

with 50% located in Baden-Württemberg where the MEKA scheme contains a variety of measures targeting arable land. Beyond these areas, support for environmentally sound farming practices on arable land is only of marginal importance in Sachsen, Bayern and Brandenburg. The third most important scheme in terms of area contracted is the conversion to, or maintenance of, organic farming (yearly increases are still considerable). However, many organic farms are still supported under the former extensification scheme. Of some importance is the support of permanent cultures and vineyards, but, again, more than the half of the area is situated in Baden-Württemberg. The remaining measures cover only small areas.

With implementation of Regulation 2078 in Germany being so complex and variable, it is difficult to refer to a single German agri-environmental experience. Although the GAK provides a basic national framework for implementation, the response by the individual *Länder* to the Regulation has been highly differentiated and has depended on various factors including existing *Länder* finances, farming structures, political motivations and differing attitudes in different regions with regard to what should and should not be encapsulated within 2078 schemes.

**Table 7.4 The relative importance of measures under Regulation 2078
in Germany**

Groups of schemes	1994/1995 (ha)	1995/1996 (ha)	change (%)
Grassland schemes (including extensification, conversion of arable to grassland, preservation of specific grassland biotopes)	1,210,000	1,355,000	+12.0
Schemes for arable land (including integrated farming systems, reduction or renunciation of mineral fertiliser or pesticides, preservation of field margins, etc.)	660,500	868,500	+31.5
Stock reductions	3,600	5,900	+64.5
Rearing of local breeds in danger of extinction (LU)	8,400 LU	11,200 LU	+33.0
Schemes for permanent cultures and vineyards	50,200	67,500	+34.4
Upkeep of abandoned land	2,500	2,700	+10.2
20-year set-aside	550	1,200	+117.4
Schemes aiming at the preservation of traditional forms of landuse	26,900	26,100	-2.9
Schemes aiming at the preservation of specific biotopes	14,100	15,600	+10.7
Organic farming	112,900	158,400	+40.4
– arable land	*56,600*	*77,900*	*+37.6*
– grassland	*53,500*	*76,700*	*+43.2*
– permanent cultures	*2,700*	*3,900*	*+41.4*
Environmentally oriented basic payment	3,361,500	3,386,500	+0.7

Source: BMELF, 1997

How effective are German agri-environmental schemes?

Although some German *Länder* already had well-established agri-environmental schemes before 1992, Regulation 2078 provided new opportunities for an integrated approach of agricultural and environmental policy. At one level, the Regulation appears well adapted to German AEP needs, which surely reflects the relatively powerful German role in Brussels during the run-up to negotiations surrounding the CAP reform. The implementation of Regulation 2078 in Germany has provided mechanisms for addressing the reduction of environmental damage caused by intensive farming. It has also provided schemes aimed at protecting and further developing agriculture in disadvantaged regions (usually upland areas). The countryside in these less intensively used agricultural regions has been shaped over centuries by extensive agricultural production practices which have contributed to high ecological and landscape values. Yet, these areas are most at risk from abandonment or intensification as they continue to be less competitive than the more intensively farmed regions. In these areas, Regulation 2078 has clearly been used as an income support mechanism. Consequently, proportionally less agri-environmental money has been spent on economically more competitive lowland farms. For several observers, this represents a potential distortion of the original objectives of the Regulation (cf. Plankl, 1996a; Wilson, 1998a). While specific environmental gains constitute an important goal of most *Länder* schemes, nature protection objectives are often more general than specific. In addition, horizontal schemes (which receive the largest budgets and have the highest participation rates) rarely target specific ecosystems, nor do they necessarily address particular environmentally damaging management practices.

The often vague commitment of schemes to tangible nature protection goals is one of the main reasons why it has been difficult for researchers to evaluate the specific ecological effects of the schemes. That having been said, however, some preliminary results do identify clearly positive effects. There is little doubt, for example, that organic farming schemes – which have been implemented relatively successfully in Germany – are highly advantageous in terms of environmental protection because they encourage a greater variety of field crops, reduce inputs of nutrients, and lead to the renunciation of pesticide use. Studies have shown that biodiversity generally increases in organic farming systems, with concurrent reduction of soil, water, and acquifer pollution (Köpke and Haas, 1997; Nieberg, 1997). Nonetheless, there are problems about the spatial distribution of farms participating in organic schemes, as the majority of participating farms are situated in regions with poorer natural conditions where farmers had managed their land extensively even before participation in the respective schemes (Nieberg, 1997). Environmental gains in these areas are, therefore, restricted to the *maintenance* of extensive land use, rather than the *change* of farmers' management practices. Nonetheless, *conversion* to organic farming can result in a stabilisation of agricultural incomes (and therefore the survival of farming), and the positive effects of a growing number of organic farms on the development of processing and marketing structures for organic products, as well as concurrent changes in public attitudes towards organic farming, should not be underestimated.

The above analysis has also highlighted that many German agri-environmental schemes place great emphasis on the extensification of grassland, with more than a quarter of all permanent grassland subject to agri-environmental schemes. Apart from a few biotope-specific schemes, the bulk of grassland measures aim at the *maintenance* of extensive grassland management in disadvantaged regions. This orientation is justified, first, by the fact that farms with grassland continue to lose their economic competitiveness and are, therefore, in danger of both abandonment or intensification and, second, by the fact that many grassland ecosystems are ecologically very valuable. Participation in grassland schemes is concentrated in poorer, upland regions with high shares of permanent grassland and extensive animal husbandry. Changes in farming practices induced by schemes in these areas are relatively limited, but preliminary monitoring results nevertheless suggest that schemes have helped stabilise the trend of further grassland conversion or abandonment.

The impacts of schemes aimed at extensification of arable land are less clear-cut. Participation is generally high in those *Länder* where these schemes are flexible and allow both a stepwise reduction of fertiliser and pesticide use and the combination of scheme-induced management changes with other measures. The environmental effects of schemes aimed at the reduction of external inputs on arable land are judged 'positive' in the evaluation of the MEKA scheme in Baden-Württemberg. Here, it is estimated that 14% of the total arable land has been managed less intensively through the scheme, leading to a reduction in nitrate leaching by 10% on arable land and a reduction in erosion by 3% (Zeddies and Doluschitz, 1996). There is, however, a pronounced lack of research about the effectiveness of schemes in most other *Länder*.

Overall, agri-environmental scheme acceptance is highest where only small alterations of farming practices are required. As a result, most schemes have failed to alter land uses that have detrimental effects on the environment, although they have helped stabilise environmentally friendly farming systems in most naturally disadvantaged regions. Further, intensively used agricultural regions are rarely targeted by agri-environmental schemes despite the fact that these areas would particularly benefit from environmentally friendly farming practices. Even comprehensive and ambitious schemes such as MEKA (Baden-Württemberg) have not been able to alter the detrimental tendencies induced by the CAP, above all the increasing polarisation between intensive agricultural regions with good financial revenues on the one hand and ecologically sound, but economically weak, regions on the other (Zeddies and Doluschitz, 1996).

This latter point also has important implications for the ways in which agri-environmental payments are structured. It is often argued that flat rate payments in heterogeneous regions, where the costs of participation in agri-environmental schemes vary most for farmers, cause substantial windfall-profits on farms that have to undertake only marginal management changes. Yet, a large share of the agri-environmental budget is often spent for schemes encouraging such windfall profits – a fact which is particularly true for large horizontal schemes (Wilhelm, 1995). This is best illustrated through the MEKA scheme, where the measures achieving the best rates of acceptance require no or little alterations in farming systems (Zeddies and Doluschitz, 1996; Bronner *et al.*, 1997). Flat rate payments, therefore, will not select participants who provide most quality in terms of environmental improvement. To improve the situation it is generally proposed to strengthen the environmental objectives of the schemes and to fine-tune and individualise payments (Streit *et al.*, 1989; Karl and Urfei, 1997). Further, the large payment differences that exist between the *Länder* for similar schemes result in distortions which have caused problems in adjoining regions (e.g. Bayern with organic farming payments of 237 ECU/ha compared to adjoining Hessen with only 132 ECU/ha).

The implementation of large horizontal schemes with flat-rate payments also has implications for the ways in which these schemes are controlled and monitored by the relevant agencies. In schemes that are available to tens of thousands of farmers (e.g. MEKA, KULAP), there is very little evidence available as to how participating farmers comply with the requirements of the schemes. Control of compliance is also particularly difficult for part-farm schemes (e.g. MEKA) or for schemes where stepwise extensification measures are required. The number of contract violations is not insignificant, particularly as sanctions are generally light (Heißenhuber *et al.*, 1994; Wilson, 1995; Zeddies and Doluschitz, 1996; Karl and Urfei, 1997). Nevertheless, the high costs of monitoring mean that any large-scale extension of verification procedures seems unlikely in the near future. There are suggestions that schemes should be altered in such a way that only identifiable ecological gains are supported on each farm, which would ease monitoring provided that accurate baseline data were available for the pre-scheme situation (Karl and Urfei, 1997).

Ultimately, the effectiveness of agri-environmental schemes in Germany depends on how farmers assess the long-term reliability of support. Only if farmers have a positive attitude towards the schemes will the long-term effectiveness of the schemes be guaranteed. Yet, farmers are currently under the impression that agri-environmental support is largely the result of short-term budget decisions (Heißenhuber *et al.*, 1994). This is best illustrated through an example from Hessen where payments have been lowered twice in 1995 and 1996, while the conditions for participation have been further tightened. To make the situation worse, agri-environmental financing in Hessen has remained equally uncertain in 1997/98. Even with the long-established MEKA scheme in Baden-Württemberg, a third of the farmers surveyed by Zeddies and Doluschitz (1996) stated that they did not trust the regional government's promises for long-term financing of the scheme. The current uncertainty faced by German farmers with regard to agri-environmental policy suggests that the long-term effectiveness of schemes may only be guaranteed if farmers succeed in making profits through scheme participation, for example, through specialised marketing of environmentally friendly agricultural products. There is, therefore, a strong case to be made for the CAP accompanying measures to be themselves 'accompanied' by the establishment of suitable processing and market structures for environmentally friendly produce.

8 Spain: first tentative steps towards an agri-environmental programme

Begoña Peco, Francisco Suárez, Juan J. Oñate, Juan E. Malo and Javier Aguirre

The agricultural and environmental background in Spain

While Spain's natural environment has generated many opportunities for farming, it also imposes serious restrictions on the widespread development of a rich, competitive and intensive agriculture. The country's mountainous relief, its peninsular and island character and its geographic location, exposed to both Atlantic and Mediterranean influences, have created a series of climatic gradients that are ideally suited to a wide variety of agricultural practices ranging from market gardening to dry steppe farming. 'Moist Spain' covers a narrow northern belt, while 'dry Spain' covers most of the rest of the country. Only about a quarter of the country receives more than 800 mm of annual rainfall, but the high irregularity of rainfall (both temporally and spatially) means that average rainfall figures are only crude measurements of the real climatic situation in most Spanish regions. The intra- and inter-annual variability in rainfall causes extremely dry summers, torrential autumn and spring rains and pluri-annual periods of drought, some of which are very severe. Water shortfalls are made all the more serious in Mediterranean parts of Spain where the seasonal lack of rainfall coincides with the highest evapotranspiration rates of the country (IGN, 1992). Spain also has a high average altitude (88% of the country lies between 200 and 2000 m), and the relief is irregular with steep altitudinal gradients. These climatic and relief factors accentuate the variability of soil quality. Thus, in northern Spain (moist Spain) the climate and vegetation cover have led to soils that are generally more developed than those of southern Spain (dry Spain) where good agricultural soils are rare outside the main alluvial river valleys. Further, particular soil types and steep slopes create a heavy risk of erosion in most of the country – a problem exacerbated by torrential rainfalls. As a result, about half of Spain has serious or very serious erosion problems, with the average national soil loss for 1989 calculated at 30 t/year

(MOPTMA, 1992).

Although the environmental parameters in Spain differ substantially from most of its European neighbours, Spanish demographic and economic trends have nonetheless followed similar patterns to other EU Member States in recent decades, with a gradually declining farming sector. During the period between 1950 and 1993, the farming population fell by 35%, and the contribution of agriculture to the GDP declined by 37% (Barceló et al., 1995). However, this trend has not been geographically uniform. In some regions such as Andalusia, Extremadura and the two Castillas (see Figure 8.1 below), agriculture is still economically important (8-10% of GDP) and with farming populations still making up between 12 to 14% of the total population (Domingo, 1994). There is also widespread polarisation between farms with high capital investments and few highly qualified employees, and farms in LFAs (covering three quarters of the total UAA) with serious economic and structural problems (Barceló et al., 1995; MAPA, 1995). As will be discussed in detail below, these factors have had a major impact on AEP implementation in Spain.

A further factor to consider when analysing policy implementation processes is Spain's governmental decentralisation. Spain consists of 17 autonomous regions which have full powers over agricultural and environmental matters and which are represented in Brussels by the central government which acts as the transmission link for EU policy decisions to the regions. There are, nonetheless, considerable inter-regional disparities in the effective application of EU regulations as each region is able to modulate the structure and quantity of subsidies on the basis of national legislation and even to offer parallel assistance in accordance with their particular regional characteristics and priorities. Further, in many cases inter-regional co-operation and information flows to and from the Federal Agriculture Ministry have been poor – another factor which might have constrained the optimal implementation of agri-environmental schemes in some of the Spanish regions.

Changing agricultural practices

In an attempt to make the most of the adverse natural conditions, farming practices in Spain have had a dramatic effect on water and soil resources, albeit with extremely varied results in different regions. The end result has been a mosaic of farming landscapes with an uneven production capacity and a complex social and environmental composition. One common result has been, for example, the often poorly defined boundary between arable and grazing land. Natural conditions frequently necessitate crop rotations involving fallow periods, which can vary from one to eight years in length and are subsequently used for low-intensity grazing. Another feature is the striking diversity in land uses and areas covered by extensive uses, with dry cereal farming (47% of all agricultural land), dry grassland (24%), olive groves (8%) and vineyards (5%) accounting for 84% of Spain's UAA, the rest being divided among industrial, fodder, fruit, vegetable and tuber crops (MAPA, 1995). A further characteristic of Spanish agriculture is the relatively low level of productivity in comparison with central and northern European countries. Average cereal yields in Spain, for example, amount to only about 2.5 tons/ha, compared to an average of about 6 tons/ha for the rest of Europe (Tió, 1991).

Although Spanish agriculture has been heavily intensified in the more productive areas, this has been paralleled by a process of farm abandonment in the least favourable regions. Thus, while the overall extensive characteristic of Spanish farming has been maintained, the average farm size has increased by 35% between 1972 and 1989 due to land consolidation and abandonment of the most marginal areas. Traditional fallow areas have declined in the same period by 1.2 million ha to currently 4 million ha (MAPA, 1995; Barceló *et al.* 1995). Structural improvements between 1970 and 1991 have also led to increases in fertiliser use by 60%, with a current mean dosage of 71 kg N/ha of arable land. At the same time, the irrigated area has increased by one million ha to 3.4 million ha, and the mechanisation index has almost tripled to 195 HP/100 ha (Barceló *et al.*, 1995). Yet, farm abandonment has also accelerated in the last 20 years. Over one million ha have ceased to be tilled, resulting in the fact that the total arable land area is now barely 20 million ha – only 75% of the UAA (MAPA, 1995). This decline has been most pronounced in dry cereal areas, where the arable area has fallen from 18.6 million ha in 1972 to 16.4 million ha in 1993 (Barceló *et al.*, 1995).

Although reliable livestock statistics before 1970, and even during the 1980s, are lacking, the most widely accepted trends reflect a fall in livestock numbers until the late 1970s, and a widespread increase of stock densities afterwards. While this increase has been associated with intensification in certain parts of Spain, it has also been linked to changes in livestock species with a generalised shift from sheep and goats to cattle. Changing breeds with a move towards more productive but higher input-dependent species, and changing management practices aimed at reducing manual labour, have, however, led both to overgrazing in easily accessible areas and to abandonment and invasion by scrub on less accessible sites (Beaufoy *et al.*, 1994; Donázar *et al.*, 1997). Since Spain joined the EEC in 1986, these trends have continued, although a proportion of the apparent increases in the number of animals may also be due to both better book-keeping and the obligation for farmers to now declare all their stock in order to get subsidies. Spanish livestock production lies now in second place in the EU with regard to pigs, sheep, goats and poultry meat, and in third place with regard to beef cattle and egg production (MAPA, 1995).

The farm intensification process has often been accompanied by an increase in input use – in particular stock feed, fertilisers, herbicides and pesticides – with resulting problems of soil and water pollution. Although problems are less pronounced in Spain than in most other EU countries, fertiliser and biocide dosages (especially in irrigated and greenhouse systems), along with manure generation by intensive livestock systems (especially along the north-west coast of Spain), have in some regions reached levels as high as those in central and northern European countries. While average surpluses of nitrates and phosphates in Spain (19 kg N/ha and 28 kg P_2O_5/ha) still remain below the EU average, almost one-fifth of all Spanish farms have exceeded the 170 kg N/ha threshold established through Regulation 676/91/EEC (Brouwer *et al.*, 1995). As a result, a total of 361 MECU were spent on phytosanitary products in 1993 alone (MAPA, 1995). Further, and according to 1992 data, more than half of sampled water points (in 10 out of 88 aquifers) contained NO_3 levels above 50mg/l (ITGME, 1993).

Environmental consequences

Changes in farming practice identified above are the causes of a series of environmental problems. Intensification of production in agriculturally favourable areas, the abandonment of production in less favourable areas, and the homogenisation of crop varieties and livestock breeds have all contributed to accelerating environmental degradation. It is now widely acknowledged that modern agricultural practices have led to a major reduction in biodiversity and to an impoverishment of landscapes, largely because of increased uniformity in land uses and practices associated with the intensification process (Baldock, 1990; Tucker and Heath, 1994; Pain and Pienkowski, 1997; Tucker and Evans, 1997). In Spain, in particular, there appears to be a strong relationship between extensive arable farming methods and the diversity and richness of bird and butterfly species that depend on these systems for survival[32]. The diversity of uses in different fields in extensive arable systems has created a lattice of complementary habitats that harbour a wide variety of plant species, and that are also fundamental for the maintenance of bird diversity (Peco and Suárez, 1993; De Juana *et al.*, 1993; Suárez *et al.*, 1997a; Díaz *et al.*, 1997).

---

[32] There is, for example, a clear correlation between extensive arable farming systems and high butterfly numbers (Valladares, 1993).

Intensification has also contributed to the loss of landscape and cultural diversity. The co-existence of different landscape elements and land uses in traditional Spanish farm landscapes (and in other parts of the Mediterranean basin; see also Chs. 5 and 11) created an interface between nature and social organisation that allowed numerous interactions in both directions. These 'cultural landscapes', characterised by extensive agricultural systems that have existed for centuries, are particularly important in ecological and historical terms, but are now in serious danger of survival (Lucas, 1992; Meeus, 1993). As a result, remnant cultural landcapes have become the subject of research by the *International Union for the Conservation of Nature*, aiming at establishing a 'red list of threatened cultural landscapes' in which Spain will feature prominently (Morey, 1992). Further, the farm intensification process has also contributed to the draining and ploughing of many wetlands in coastal and inland locations, and over 60% of the total wetland area in Spain has disappeared over the last 50 years (Montes and Bernués, 1994). The loss of these distinctive ecosystems has also led to a serious impoverishment of landscape diversity and the disappearance of a fundamental type of habitat to many species.

The abandonment of farms in the most marginal and unproductive areas and changes in grazing patterns are also generating other significant environmental problems, especially through increased fire hazards, the loss of fertile soils, and increased erosion risks (Pérez Trejo, 1992). Particularly serious problems have resulted from the abandonment of terracing, but others include the loss of landscape and biodiversity associated with homogenisation caused by both scrub encroachment and the planting of fast-growing tree species on abandoned land. The maintenance of a threshold density of rural population is thereby seen as a key component of agri-environmental programmes (and hence of the structural and functional systems they maintain), but the abandonment of traditional farming practices has also often led to rural population decline with resulting environmental degradation. Finally, the loss of genetic heritage associated with the use of only few crop strains and livestock breeds could become a problem in the near future. The abandonment of local breeds by livestock farmers who seek higher productivity may lead not only to the extinction of over 50 breeds already under threat, but also to the demise of the traditional extensive and semi-intensive farming systems that sustain them (García Dory et al., 1985).

Implementation of agri-environmental policies before 1992

Political background

The introduction of agri-environmental schemes has been a new departure for Spain, in contrast to many other EU countries who have had considerable experience with established mechanisms for countryside protection (Baldock and Lowe, 1996). The lack of prior agri-environmental tradition can be largely explained with reference to the situation of Spanish agriculture at the time of entry into the EEC in 1986. At that time, the primary aim of agricultural policy was mainly to overcome the traditional structural deficits that limited Spain's agricultural productivity (a productivity that was much lower than that of most of its future EEC partners), and in doing so it aimed at increasing the competitiveness of Spanish farming. In the mid 1980s, therefore, problems arising from surplus production, as well as the possible negative environmental effects of agriculture, were scarcely recognised among the Spanish farming sector. An agri-environmental debate was virtually non-existent at the time, with public environmental concerns largely focused upon urban problems, nuclear energy, and industrial environmental impacts. It was only in scientific circles that the relationship between farming and environmental conservation were discussed (De Juana *et al.*, 1988; Lasanta, 1988; Ruiz, 1988).

During the early 1990s, the debate began to spread to the emerging environmental lobby, but national policy-makers continued to focus on localised environmental impacts of isolated agricultural projects (e.g. irrigation schemes). From 1992 onwards, however, and largely as a result of the initiative of certain regional governments (backed by nature conservation groups and farmers' associations), the first proposals were made for the declaration of ESAs under EEC Regulation 797/85 (Naveso, 1992, 1993; Urdameneta and Naveso, 1993). Unfortunately, the lack of political impetus at the time prevented these proposals from being implemented, and the potential of this early Community agri-environmental legislation was, therefore, never fully used in Spain.

Implementation of EU regulations

The approval of Regulation 797/85 coincided with Spain's admission to the EEC. However, as the following section demonstrates, its implementation in Spain was essentially oriented around the twin issues of income support and productivity improvement.

The translation of the objectives of Regulation 797/85 into Spanish law demonstrates the lack of priority given to environmental objectives at the time. With regard to aid for the improvement of efficiency in farming structures, for example, the Regulation was interpreted as "a means of improving farm incomes as well as the living, working and production conditions of the farming population" (Real Decreto, 808/87). Extensification and set-aside aid were interpreted as means "to complement the actions undertaken by the EC bodies for the different market organisations, aiming to attenuate part of the effects that such actions may have on farmers' income" (Real Decreto, 1435/88). The application of Regulation 797/85 was, therefore, almost exclusively aimed at structural improvements of farms on the basis of efficiency, mechanisation and intensification – highlighting the continuing Spanish emphasis on establishing policies aimed at overcoming structural problems (see above). This meant that both before and after EEC accession, policy mechanisms failed to consider the conceptual and technological changes that would be needed to guarantee the parallel adoption of EEC environmental standards. While the process of designing specific schemes to be applied under Regulation 797/85 was characterised by a notable absence of involvement by environmental NGOs and state environment agencies, farmers' organisations were strong supporters of the schemes, precisely because they interpreted the schemes as direct subsidies which would help them remain competitive against their new Community partners.

As a result, agri-environmental schemes under Regulation 797/85 (and its amendment Regulation 2328/91) have only been applied to a limited degree in Spain. First, the proposed *ESA scheme* was not implemented by the central government, despite strong backing from regional governments and producer organisations. Second, the *Extensification Scheme* was not applied, largely because its implementation made little sense in a country that already had large areas characterised by extensive agricultural systems in which farmers were more concerned with productivity increases than decreases (Palacios, 1998). Third, implementation of the *Set-aside Scheme* clashed with problems of rural depopulation in areas where population densities were already low, and also contradicted agricultural reform laws imposing a minimum threshold of land utilisation (for job creation purposes) that had been passed in Andalusia and Extremadura. Set-aside was also opposed (unofficially) by many state agronomists who were reluctant to adopt a scheme designed to reduce European surpluses in a country which had not contributed to this surplus, where productivity was much lower than the Community average, and where the creation of an additional 4 million ha of fallow land would cause problems in distinguishing traditional fallow rotation from set-aside fallow land. As a result of these constraints, set-aside was implemented on only 70% of the elegible area defined by the EC, and the subsidy level was set at only 40 to 60% of the level originally stipulated by the EC. Consequently, the take-up rate for set-aside was poor, with only 1,646 farms with 91,367 ha participating in the scheme between 1988 and 1992 (MAPA, 1990-94).

The situation was slightly different with regard to implementation of the LFA policy in Spain. This policy was the only one that had precedents within Spanish agricultural policy (e.g. the *Mountain Agriculture Act* passed in 1982). When Spain joined the EEC, pre-existing national policy was extended to include not only mountain areas, but also areas threatened by depopulation and other zones with specific agricultural disadvantages. As a result, LFAs now cover 41 million ha (equivalent to 81% of the national land area and including almost three quarters of the national UAA)[33]. Consequently, the LFA scheme was the most important EEC regulation implemented before 1992 in Spain (along with structural aid), both in terms of the number of subsidy recipients and with regard to budgetary expenditure (the latter despite the fact that subsidy levels were set lower than those stipulated by the LFA Regulation). Indeed, during the period between 1986 and 1992, almost 1.4 million farmers received payments through the LFA scheme with a yearly average of 328 ECU/farm (MAPA, 1990-94)[34].

Implementation of Regulation 2078 in Spain

Implementation of Regulation 2078 in Spain has to be understood in the context of the 'reluctant' socio-political framework outlined in the previous section. At the time when Regulation 2078 was introduced, Spain had only little experience with implementation of AEP, and the persistent productivist ethos that had marred implementation of agri-environmental schemes under Regulation 797/85 has continued to strongly influence the implementation of Regulation 2078.

The Spanish agri-environmental programme under Regulation 2078 comprises two parts: one developed by the Central Government, and the other developed by the regions (MAPA, 1994). As mentioned above,

---

[33] LFAs also include land not classified as UAA.

[34] Other EU policies implemented in Spain with environmental effects associated with farming include forestry aid under Regulation 797/85, Directive 79/409 (Birds Directive), Directive 91/676 (Nitrate Directive), Regulation 2080/92 (Afforestation on Farmland), Directive 92/43 (Habitats Directive) and EC regional policies such as Objective 1, 5b and LEADER. Their impact on farming systems is highly uneven, and a detailed discussion of the environmental implications of their implementation lies beyond the scope of this chapter.

agricultural and environmental responsibilities have been handed over to the 17 regional governments, which means that all agri-environmental schemes must be implemented regionally (see also Ch. 7 on Germany for a similar situation). 'Horizontal' schemes (cereal extensification, organic farming, rearing of local breeds and agri-environmental training) and those concerning protected areas (national parks, wetlands protected under the RAMSAR agreement, *Special Protection Areas* for birds) are implemented by MAPA and apply for the whole nation. Each region has to implement these schemes, using broadly similar policy instruments across Spain[35]. In contrast to this 'double legislation' (i.e. national and regional), agri-environmental schemes that are to be applied in specific zones chosen by individual regions ('zonal' schemes) are formulated and implemented by the regions themselves, without input from the national government. This two-part strategy is also evident in the joint funding arrangements, with EU contributions (75% in Objective 1 areas and 50% in Objective 2 and 5b areas) varying in both cases: environmental schemes proposed by the central government are co-financed on a 50-50 basis by MAPA and the regional governments, while the regions are fully responsible for co-financing the agri-environmental schemes they propose for specific areas. Similarly, the processing of applications, payments to farmers, and scheme monitoring are the responsibility of the Agriculture and/or Environment Departments of the regional governments. MAPA only acts as an intermediary between the regions and the EU in processing and monitoring payments and in justifying expenditure levels. As will be discussed in detail below, this regional agri-environmental implementation structure has severe repercussions with regard to the commitment of individual regions to the implementation of Regulation 2078, resulting in highly differentiated budgets and scheme implementation across Spain.

Any analysis of the implementation of Regulation 2078 in Spain also needs to consider, first, policy-makers' expectations and, second, the reality of scheme implementation on the ground. Although the former reveal the motivations behind the inclusion of environmental measures in Spanish agricultural policies, problems associated with the lateness of AEP implementation, together with funding problems, have caused considerable delays in the translation of policy-maker's expectations into reality. These conflicts are evident in the implementation of both horizontal and zonal schemes. Thus, although the central government passed the horizontal schemes in January 1995 and the measures for protected areas in April and June 1995 (with a target budget of 1,300 MECU and a target area of 5.3

---

[35] This situation is similar to that in Germany (see Ch. 7) where the GAK provides a national framework for basic AEP implementation.

million ha), regional implementation of these schemes could only begin after June 1995 and still has to be completed in some regions. Further, implementation of agri-environmental schemes developed by the regions themselves (zonal schemes) was even further delayed, with the majority of schemes implemented as late as 1996 or 1997 and with some still to be completed.

The only schemes that have escaped such delays are those for the reduction of water use near the *Tablas de Daimiel National Park* and the *Lagunas de Ruidera Natural Park* (Castilla-La Mancha), the *scheme aiming to protect the dry-cereal habitats of steppe birds* (Castilla-León), and the agri-environmental plan for the *Covadonga Mountain National Park* (Asturias). There may be two reasons why these schemes were implemented relatively early. First, plans for all three schemes had already been prepared in 1992 for application in accordance with Articles 21-24 of Regulation 2328/91. The subsequent implementation of Regulation 2078 allowed Spanish policy-makers to adapt these already formulated schemes to the new regulation. As a result, two of the three schemes were implemented in 1993 – even before the inclusion of Regulation 2078 into Spanish law. Second, all three schemes were also examples of a bottom-up approach in scheme implementation – sparked by pressure from local environmental NGOs, farmers' unions and scientists – which may have contributed to considerably speeding up the process of implementation compared to the more sluggish top-down process outlined above.

In light of the above observations, the following sections analyse, first, the Spanish agri-environmental programme as initially designed and envisaged by policy-makers, and, second, the reality of implementation and initial acceptance on the ground. The analysis is based on projected budget figures for the national programme (including already allocated funds). It should be noted that, although the approved budget by the Commission has been based on the period between 1993 and 1997, all available official figures on budget allocation for Spanish regions and aid schemes refer to the period between 1994 and 2000. This may be partly due to the substantial delays in programme implementation mentioned above, but also to the fact that Spanish policy-makers may be convinced that Regulation 2078 will still be in existence in the year 2000. As outlined above, implementation of agri-environmental schemes in Spain is still in its infancy, since some schemes initially envisaged have not yet been implemented, while others have been abandoned altogether (and it is also likely that some new schemes will be proposed for the next five-year period). The results of the second part of the analysis (implementation and acceptance) are, therefore, only preliminary.

Policy-makers' expectations and the design of the Spanish agri-environmental programme

Table 8.1 shows that the original design of the Spanish agri-environmental programme included all measures offered by Regulation 2078, both for national schemes and for most schemes designed by individual regions (the latter often aiming to offer seven or more out of the ten possible measures). However, budgetary allocations have been highly uneven between individual schemes and regions – a characteristic of Spanish implementation that deserves more detailed analysis. In the following discussion, therefore, the Spanish agri-environmental programme will be analysed from two perspectives. First, environmental objectives are considered and, second, regional disparities in budgetary allocations for agri-environmental schemes are assessed in detail.

Table 8.2 suggests that in terms of budget allocation the main environmental objectives of the Spanish agri-environmental programme are landscape preservation and extensification. With over 600 MECU, schemes aimed at landscape protection take up nearly half of the overall budget, and this figure increases further if the maintenance of abandoned land (7% of the budget) is also included within the wider notion of 'landscape conservation'. The second most important set of schemes (in budgetary terms) are those aimed at the extensification of production. This group includes extensification (30% of the budget), 20-year set-aside for cropland (7%) and livestock reduction (2%). In contrast, the remaining agri-environmental schemes account for less than 9% of the total budget. In particular, there is a remarkable lack of emphasis on the reduction of chemical inputs and on the promotion of organic farming (1.1% and 2.2% respectively), especially when compared with other European countries (see other chapters in this book). Low levels of investment in this area are due partly to the low-intensity nature of the majority of Spanish farming systems (see above) and to a widespread belief that Spanish agriculture does not have pollution problems – despite isolated problems caused by nitrates (Vera and Romero, 1994; Brouwer *et al.*, 1995; Palacios, 1998) and pesticides (Muñoz, 1991).

It should, however, be noted that the analysis presented here may be influenced by the specific categories used to define individual schemes under Regulation 2078 in Tables 8.1 and 8.2 – particularly with regard to the apparently low committment to reductions of chemical inputs. Almost all landscape conservation schemes in Spain include some measures encouraging both the reduction of chemical inputs and the reduction of stocking density, but these do not appear in any of the above figures. For

Table 8.1 Estimated budgets for schemes under Regulation 2078 by region 1994-2000 (in MECU)

Cluster of 2078 Measures	Conversion to, or continuation of, organic farming	Extensification of arable land and/or permanent crops		Extensification of grassland	Local breeds	Protection of environment, natural resources, countryside and landscape			Public access and leisure activities	Education and training	Total
Single measures	Organic farming	Fertiliser/Pesticide reductions	Maintenance or introduction of extensive production	Livestock reduction	Rearing of local breeds	Environment and landscape protection	Upkeep of abandoned farmland or wood land	20-year set-aside[b]	Public access and leisure activities	Education and training	
	Reg. 2078 Art 2 (1.a)	Reg. 2078 Art 2 (1.a)	Reg. 2078 Art 2 (1.b)	Reg. 2078 Art 2 (1.c)	Reg. 2078 Art 2 (1.d)	Reg. 2078 Art 2 (1.d)	Reg. 2078 Art 2 (1.e)	Reg. 2078 Art 2 (1.f)	Reg. 2078 Art 2 (1.g)	Reg. 2078 Art 2 (2)	
Andalusia	6.1		49.9	3.9	2.8	83.7		27.7	0.8	4.6	179.4
Aragón	1.9		63	5.1	1.1	16.2	13	5.4	*	2.3	108
Asturias	0.3				1.7	28.9	8.3			0.2	39.3
Baleares	0.9		0.6		0.1					0.2	1.8
Canarias	1.1				1.9	30.3	1.1	1.8	0.3	1.5	37.9
Cantabria					0.8	2	1.9			0.1	4.9
Castilla-L. Mancha	2.6		84.1	2.2	1	149.5	4.6	1.8	*	1.9	247.8

Castilla y León	2.5		80.5		2.8	166	47.2	4.1		3.1	306.2
Catalonia	4.3	8.4	6.9	6.2	0.6	53.2		14.1	0.1	1.3	95.1
Extremadura	2.1		44.1	6.7	1.4	25.3	8.6	1.8	0.5	1.1	91.7
Galicia	0.7	3.3			0.7	16.6		2.4		2.3	26
Madrid	0.5		10.4		0.1	5.4		12.4	0.2	0.1	29.1
Murcia	0.7	2.9	21.8		0.2	0.6	1.4	1.2		1	29.8
Navarra	0.4		7.1		0.1	1.9	2	0.6		0.1	12.2
Basque Country[a]											
La Rioja	0.9		1.8	0.2	0.4	0.3		2.4	0.2	0.6	6.7
Valencia	2.6		16.7		0.4	25.3	1.8	9.3	0.3	0.8	57.2
TOTAL	**27.6**	**14.6**	**386.9**	**24.3**	**15.8**	**605.3**	**90.1**	**85**	**2.4**	**21.2**	**1,273.1**

(*) Measures implemented after budget estimation and therefore not included in breakdown estimations.
(a) Measures planned in the Basque Country for which budget breakdown is not available.
(b) Estimated budget for a five-year period.

Source: MAPA, 1994

Table 8.2 Estimated budget (in MECU) for different schemes in the Spanish agri-environmental programme for the 1994-2000 period

Types of schemes	MECU
Landscape protection	605.2
Extensification	386.8
Upkeep of abandoned land	90.1
20-year set-aside	85
Organic farming	27.2
Livestock reductions	24.3
Education and training	21.2
Rearing of local breeds	15.8
Fertiliser/pesticide reductions	14.5
Public access/recreation	2.4

Source: MAPA, 1994

example, the zonal scheme for landscape maintenance in the Canary Islands allocates a third of its budget to the maintenance of traditional forms of agriculture, a third to the fight against erosion and a third to crop extensification. Further, all measures within that scheme aim at prohibiting the use of herbicides, restricting livestock densities, and reducing the use of chemical fertilisers (with the aim of replacing them with 'green' fertilisers). Another example where the specific environmental categories are blurred are the (financially) important landscape protection schemes which seek to protect fauna and flora in extensive croplands. Here, 29% of the budget has been allocated to crop extensification, 27% to soil conservation, 22% to the promotion of crops used for cover by steppe birds, 16% to the reduction of chemical inputs, 7% to the encouragement of environmemtally-friendly farming techniques and 0.4% to the maintenance of traditional crop varieties. In all cases, agri-environmental payments are linked to restrictions in the use of chemical inputs, neither of which receive specific compensation payments. Finally, the reduction of chemical inputs also features highly in demonstration projects, taking up 78% of the 'education and training' budget (but again not distinguishable in the figures presented in Table 8.2).

These three examples suggest that, although the majority of agri-environmental schemes are predominantly aimed at landscape protection and production extensification, measures aimed at reducing the use of external inputs and stocking densities are more important than Table 8.2

would initially suggest (i.e. they are implicit rather than explicit parts of the schemes). Nonetheless, the area targeted by extensification and landscape protection schemes makes up almost 90% of the total programme target area (Oñate *et al.*, 1998) – a logical agri-environmental approach in a country with a large land area covered by extensive farming systems that contain the most valuable agri-ecosystems and that are at greatest risk of disappearance. In these least favoured areas of the country, serious conservation problems would result from farm abandonment, in particular through increased fire hazards and the possible extinction of wildlife species that rely on traditionally farmed agricultural landscapes (Suárez *et al.*, 1997b).

Yet, overall expenditure only gives a partial insight into the Spanish agri-environmental programme. An analysis of agri-environmental expenditure by regions, therefore, complements the above discussion and provides the basis for understanding socio-economic factors that may have influenced the design of Spanish AEP. As for Germany (see Ch. 7), a regional analysis is particularly important in Spain as the regions' political and financial autonomy in agricultural matters has played an important role in their commitment towards AEP implementation. In Figure 8.1, agri-environmental budgets are shown as expenditure/ha/UAA in each autonomous region for the seven-year period between 1994 and 2000. As the figure shows, the regional distribution of agri-environmental budgets is very diverse. While average agri-environmental allocations amount to 48.7 ECU/ha for that time period, the Balearic Islands will only spend 6.7 ECU/ha while in the Canary Islands 246.2 ECU/ha will be available.

Several trends are apparent from Figure 8.1. Inland regions have budgets that are closer to the average (40-60 ECU/ha), while peripheral regions show much greater variations. A possible explanation for this is that in inland Spain subsidies for extensive systems predominate, and that the overall emphasis in these regions is on horizontal schemes aiming at extensification of arable systems. In contrast, the marginal regions have a greater diversity of farming systems, all of which have their location-specific environmental problems. Consequently, in these areas, greater inter-regional variations in the types of schemes implemented are to be expected. Examples of this can be seen in budget variations between the four northern regions on the Cantabrian coast (north-west Spain): despite their relative similarity with regard to agricultural systems based on cattle breeding, subsidies range from around 30 ECU/ha/UAA in Galicia and Cantabria to 130 ECU/ha/UAA in Asturias.

Such inter-regional variations raise the question of the extent to which the pattern of implementation of agri-environmental schemes reflects socio-economic factors, rather than being the result of specific

Figure 8.1 Regional distribution (ECU/ha of UAA) of the planned Spanish agri-environmental budget for the period 1994-2000

Source: MAPA, 1994

environmental 'needs' of the agricultural systems in question. Two alternative socio-economic hypotheses might thereby be formulated. First, agri-environmental budgets may be related to the economic wealth of a region, suggesting that the more prosperous regions would be in a better position to implement agri-environmental schemes. In such areas there may also be greater overall interest in preserving traditional agricultural systems due to pressures exerted by relatively wealthy urban populations. Second, agri-environmental payments should have more weight in regions where the farming sector is of greater relative importance (in percent of UAA; share of employment in the primary sector; or contribution of agriculture to regional

GDP). In these areas, higher agri-environmental payments may be linked to an increased awareness of the public and policy-makers to farming matters.

However, detailed analysis shows that budget allocations among the regions do not in fact correlate with the factors such as 'relative weight of agricultural sector in region', 'percentage of UAA in region', 'regional agricultural employment' or 'regional wealth' (CEDOC, 1987; Domingo, 1994; CREM, 1995; MAPA, 1995; INE, 1996a, 1996b). The relative importance of the agricultural sector or the relative wealth of a region do not, therefore, explain the differences in agri-environmental budget allocations in Spanish regions highlighted in Figure 8.1, while locality-specific factors appear to be the main explanation for budget discrepancies. Thus, regions with higher agri-environmental budgets are usually those where schemes pay relatively high subsidies per ha UAA. These schemes are generally aimed at the conservation of landscapes and agricultural practices within geographically targeted areas with high natural and/or cultural values which are usually threatened by intensification or abandonment. In these areas there is a tendency, therefore, to invest large amounts of money for the maintenance of traditional farming systems. In the Canary Islands, for example, conservation measures for the countryside include prescriptions which require large amounts of costly labour inputs (e.g. repairs to stone walls, manual weed clearance, etc.). If farmers were not paid large sums in these areas, the likely disappearance of traditional crops and farming practices would lead to serious erosion problems (Hernández, 1996). This, in turn, would lead to the destruction of landscapes with high touristic value. The case of mountain communal pastures threatened by abandonment in Asturias, and the case of the green belt around Madrid where farmers face pressures from land speculators in the proximity of the capital, are similar examples that require relatively high payments/ha/UAA to encourage the maintenance of traditional framing practices. Further, in Catalonia and the Valencia Region a large part of the agri-environmental budget is targeted at the preservation of traditional farming practices within RAMSAR wetlands (e.g. Ebro river delta, Albufera wetland in Valencia) threatened by intensification (Fasola and Ruíz, 1997).

In contrast to these highly targeted schemes, regions with an intermediate agri-environmental budget usually have a higher percentage of extensive cereal systems and hence a large proportion of land that could potentially be covered by agri-environmental schemes (e.g. Castilla-La Mancha, Castilla-León, Extremadura, Aragón or Murcia). This inevitably reduces payments per ha UAA (i.e. a broader and shallower approach).

The only Spanish region where none of the above explanations seem to apply are the Balearic Islands. Although this region has the highest per capita income in Spain, it comes last with regard to agri-environmental payments/ha/UAA, and no zonal schemes are currently envisaged there. The UAA covers 54% of the Balearic Autonomous Region (close to the national average of 49%), but the sector is of minimal importance in the region's economy (only 1.5% of the GDP and 2.4% of the workforce). Although more research would need to be conducted to understand the current patterns of weak AEP implementation in this region, possible explanations could be that the economy of the islands is almost entirely geared towards the coast (tourism) and that there is currently little threat of intensification or land abandonment in most of the islands' agricultural areas – although it is striking that the Canary Islands, as the most similar counterpart to the Balearic Islands, has the highest payments/ha/UAA.

The reality of scheme implementation on the ground

The discussion so far has addressed the distribution of agri-environmental budgets in Spain. This section briefly investigates the reality of scheme implementation on the ground with the aim of highlighting the large discrepancies that exist between AEP formulation and the number and types of schemes that have actually been implemented to date in Spanish regions.

As of December 1997, a total of 77 schemes had been fully or partially implemented, representing 37.5% of the 205 schemes initially proposed[36]. The proportion of approved horizontal and protected area schemes of national and international importance is slightly above average with 63 implemented schemes out of 166 originally proposed (38%), and slightly below average in the case of zonal schemes with only 14 out of 39 schemes implemented so far (36%). Among the zonal schemes, there is no correlation between scheme type (i.e. livestock reduction, landscape protection, etc.) and successful implementation. As would be expected from the discussion above, the percentage of implemented schemes varies greatly between regions, although the inter-regional variation neither follows a clear geographic pattern, nor is it related to the wealth of the regions or the regional importance of the agricultural sector.

These implementation patterns show that, in many cases, regional governments have taken a long time to implement schemes. Partly, this has been due to the timing of final scheme approval by the national government (January-June 1995), which has meant that only a small proportion of the schemes were implemented by the regions before 1995. Indeed, Table 8.3 shows that only two schemes were implemented in 1993, five in 1994, while

---

[36] This figure can only be an approximation because of implementation of new schemes that were not planned initially, and because other originally planned schemes have been abandoned altogether.

the bulk have only been implemented very recently (36 in 1995, 26 in 1996, and 8 in 1997). Undoubtedly, the pace of scheme implementation has also been affected by the highly variable administrative structure and expertise among different regional governments, available budgets (also in terms of scheme administration and monitoring), and agri-environmental interests of specific regional actors involved in the policy-making process. Overall, only first tentative steps have been made in the process of implementation of the relatively ambitious Spanish agri-environmental programme.

Table 8.3 Agri-environmental schemes implemented by the autonomous regions between 1993 and 1997

Year	Horizontal schemes (national) (n)	Protected areas schemes (national) (n)	Region-specific schemes (regional) (n)	Number of implemented schemes (n)
1993	0	1	1	2
1994	3	1	1	5
1995	21	6	9	36
1996	19	5	2	26
1997	5	2	1	8

Source: authors

Participation   rates   and   early   scheme   successes: some   preliminary indications[37]

It is evident from the above that the Spanish agri-environmental programme is still small and, as yet, in its early stages of development. Nonetheless, implemenation has increased steadily since the first schemes were established, partly as a result of gradual parliamentary approval for the planned schemes, and partly due to their increasing acceptance by the farmers themselves. However, implementation delays have had a severe impact with regard to payments to farmers. By the end of 1995, for example, farmers had only received payments for the following schemes: *reduction in irrigation water use* near the Daimiel National Park in Castilla-La Mancha

---

[37] It should be noted that the dificulties of co-ordination between the national agricultural ministry and the regional administrations limits the accuracy of the data presented in this section. The figures are, therefore, only preliminary.

(for 1993-1995), *wildlife protection on extensive cereal croplands* in Castilla-León (for 1994 and 1995), and *landscape conservation on common extensive grasslands and native livestock breeding* in Asturias (only for 1995). By the end of 1997 the situation had improved, with about 90 schemes providing regular payments to farmers.

Table 8.4 shows implementation results of the Spanish agri-environmental programme in terms of participants, total area and livestock units entered, and expenditure. Despite the currently limited scope of the Spanish agri-environmental programme (see above), the figures show that land area and livestock units entered into agri-environmental schemes have doubled each year, and that the number of management agreements has increased steadily. Similarly, the number of both farmers and officials receiving training and participating in educational courses (not shown in the Table) has increased significantly from about 400 in 1995 to 3,500 in 1997. Parallel to this, total agri-environmental expenditure has increased over the years to a total of 187 MECU (by December 1997). In light of these figures, the trends over the past five years suggest an optimistic outlook for the future of the Spanish agri-environmental programme.

Table 8.4 Implementation results of the Spanish agri-environmental programme

Year	Participants	Area entered	Livestock units entered	Expenditure
	(N°)	(ha)	(LU)	(MECU)
1993	1,335	420	0	12.2
1994	2,305	836	0	17.5
1995	7,533	1,450	3,476	29.6
1996	28,408	5,588	11,330	56.5
1997	33,323	8,668	33,245	75.9

Source: authors

Although both the percentage of farms included in agri-environmental schemes (2.1%) and the area covered (3.3%) do not yet comprise a significant proportion of the Spanish agricultural sector, some schemes already have considerable impacts in the specific areas where they are being applied. For example, the 175,000 ha of land already entered into the *scheme aimed at reducing the use of irrigation water* near Daimiel National Park represent almost 100% of the original area targeted by the scheme. Further, the *scheme for the conservation of communal pastures in Asturias* has also been successful, with nearly 100,000 ha already entered, representing two thirds of the eligible area. Meanwhile, the *scheme for the protection of cereal steppes in Castilla-León* has met with less enthusiasm, with only 16% of the initially expected 1.2 million ha included by December 1997.

In Spain as a whole, schemes falling into the categories of *landscape conservation* and *fire prevention in extensive grasslands* have had the highest uptake rates, both in terms of contract numbers and area entered into the schemes. As a result, farmers participating in these schemes have also received the largest agri-environmental payments. This category is followed by schemes aimed at wildlife protection in extensive croplands. The third category in terms of acceptance comprises horizontal schemes for extensification of cereal production. Altogether, these three categories comprise nearly half of all participants, area entered and payments. Future research, in particular through scheme monitoring programmes, will be necessary to investigate in more detail the effectiveness of these first Spanish agri-environmental schemes in terms of both socio-economic and environmental impacts.

Conclusions

Compared to many other EU countries, Spain has been relatively slow to implement its agri-environmental programme in response to Regulation 2078. Scheme implementation has suffered continuous delays, leading to less than 40% of initially envisaged schemes to be implemented by the end of 1997. Undoubtedly, the traditional productivist orientation of agricultural decision-makers is a key explanation for this delay (Wilson *et al.*, 1999), but widespread government budget restrictions, together with severe financial competition with forestry schemes associated with Regulation 2080/92 (often with objectives that clash with agri-environmental schemes), have also played a role. The slow pace of implementation has also been influenced by the fact that policy-makers lacked previous experience with such schemes – a situation exacerbated by the on-going confrontation of policy-makers with agricultural interest groups who have continued to emphasise the importance of further restructuring and modernising Spanish farming.

The chapter has also highlighted how environmental and historical factors have led to the present combination of traditional environmentally valuable extensive agricultural systems in many areas of Spain, resulting in a rural landscape that is one of the richest in the EU with regard to abundance and diversity of wildlife. Yet, agricultural practices that have contributed to the creation and maintenance of valuable habitats have also been paralleled by intensification and land abandonment which, in turn, have led to severe environmental degradation in some areas. This has meant that agri-environmental schemes have often clashed with opposing interests of the farming lobby who have regarded these schemes as a constraint to modernisation, rather than as an opportunity to guarantee the continuation of farming in certain areas, to protect the environment, and to act as a substitute for traditional production subsidies.

As a result of the existence of many threatened and valuable wildlife habitats in the Spanish countryside, the Spanish agri-environmental programme has been focused mainly on the protection of extensive agricultural systems, while paying less attention to agricultural pollution problems. This reflects the spatial and conservation importance of 'cultural landscapes' in Spain, as well as highlighting the importance of the key policy aim of reducing (or even reversing) rural depopulation. However, this policy approach also reflects the reduced importance of pollution problems in extensive agricultural systems, as well as the pressure exerted by the agricultural lobby for the modernisation and intensification of agricultural production in the more intensively farmed regions of the country – the latter resulting in the fact that fewer agri-environmental schemes have so far been implemented in Spain's intensive agricultural areas.

Two further contradictions in the environmental targeting approach of the Spanish agri-environmental programme can be identified: first, the lack of priority given both to agricultural systems capable of yielding the greatest conservation value and to those threatened by erosion problems and, second, the importance placed on schemes located within areas of special natural value (i.e. national or natural parks, wetlands included in the RAMSAR agreement, and *Special Protection Areas* for birds). Thus, there is remarkably little emphasis on schemes targeting Mediterranean mountain areas and *dehesas* (open savannah-like woodlands which cover over two million ha), although these ecosystems contain a large proportion of extensive livestock breeding areas in Spain. This is particularly revealing as the mountainous and hilly areas with extensive grazing and marginal croplands are very common in many parts of Spain and suffer from serious problems of land abandonment and depopulation, often leading to severe soil erosion. Spanish *dehesas* have not received the attention they should get in proportion to their area and natural values, and the same is the case for the 2.2 million ha of olive groves who have been largely left out by the Spanish agri-environmental programme. Indeed, schemes implemented in these types of landscape account for only 5% of the total agri-environmental budget.

Meanwhile, about 40% of the budget has been allocated to areas that already had some type of environmental protection. In part this is due to the fact that protected areas in Spain cover large areas (2.9 million ha in 1994; Fernández, 1996), and the chance of inclusion of some of these areas into the Spanish agri-environmental programme has, therefore, been high, but it may also simply reflect the high conservation value of extensive agricultural systems often located within these protected areas. Thus, the recognition that conservation of these protected areas inevitably involves the continuation of traditional farming practices has certainly contributed to the emphasis given to schemes targeting areas that are already protected in some form, but it does not, however, fully explain the large gap that exists between these types of ecosystems and the neglected landscapes mentioned above. It could be argued, therefore, that areas with established protection status are over-represented in the Spanish agri-environmental programme, while other equally vulnerable systems are under-represented.

In addition to these targeting contradictions with regard to specific types of agricultural systems, the Spanish agri-environmental programme also displays considerable inter-regional variations. This has been largely due to the relative autonomy of the regional governments in agricultural and environmental policy decision-making matters. Although there are no statistically significant correlations, it appears that less money per ha UAA is spent in regions where farming plays a larger role in the regional economy, as in these regions budget allocations depend more heavily on the implementation of deep and narrow (i.e. small-scale but high-cost) schemes (e.g. avoidance of intensification in rice plantations leading to irreversible damage to RAMSAR wetlands). However, the relative wealth of regions seems to have no influence on regional budget allocations, even though regions are forced to pay part of AEP costs themselves. This lack of clear socio-economic trends in the design of the Spanish agri-environmental programme is not easy to explain, but it may be linked to the absence of overall political guidelines during the drafting stage. The current Spanish agri-environmental programme may, therefore, be more a collection of individual schemes generated by the presence of specific agricultural and/or environmental problems than a single coherent political instrument.

The outlook for the Spanish agri-environmental programme is, nevertheless, relatively good. Despite the fact that Spain's agri-environmental programme is still in its infancy, there are some promising signs as some schemes have already been successfully implemented and more schemes are likely to come on stream in the near future. Most schemes implemented to date have been well accepted, with the exception of schemes that have offered excessively low payments or that contain management prescriptions that are perceived to be too severe (the latter is particularly the case with the *20-year set-aside scheme*). The pace of scheme approval and implementation has quickened in recent years, and a catalytic effect of the first schemes can be expected. Thus, once the first schemes give positive results and have proven to Spanish farmers that it can be an advantage to be a scheme participant, the implementation and acceptance of the rest is likely to improve. On this basis, the renewal and/or extension of schemes included in the first five-year period of Regulation 2078 will play a key role, and there is a clear wish among increasing numbers of agricultural decision-makers in Spain for agri-environmental schemes to continue beyond the initial phase.

9 Austria: towards an environmentally sound agriculture

Michael Groier and Elisabeth Loibl

Changes in agricultural practices and resulting environmental effects

Agriculture in Austria is largely determined by its alpine topography. As a result, a large part of the UAA is permanent grassland, with alpine pastures covering another 8% of Austria's total land area[38]. Some 35% of all farmers are categorised as mountain farmers, occupying comparatively small farm units with an average size of about 29 ha. A significant proportion (66%) are part-time farmers (Dax and Wiesinger, 1998). As a result, mountain farmers in Austria have faced unfavourable working conditions, yet at the same time have enjoyed the positive economic effects of pluriactivity (direct marketing, tourism, etc.) derived from the high environmental quality of alpine landscapes which themselves have been the result of centuries of low-intensity and environmentally friendly farming (Groier, 1993; Hovorka, 1998).

Similar to other industrialised countries, agricultural structural change after the Second World War accompanied major shifts in Austrian agriculture (particularly in the lowlands), including increasingly capital-intensive ways of farming, rationalisation, intensification (increasing energy input through massive increases in mechanisation and chemical inputs), specialisation (move towards pure livestock or arable farms; impoverishment of crop rotation; industrial mass production independent of area), increasing dependence on fertiliser distributors and agri-multinationals, and an increasing rift between extensive mountainous and less-favoured regions and intensively cultivated lowlands (Krammer and Scheer, 1978). Although application rates for fertilisers and pesticides in Austria remain among the lowest in Europe, agricultural pollution (especially N-contamination of groundwater) has been increasingly concentrated in intensively farmed regions, particularly in areas with maize-

---

[38] Overall, Austria has 263,500 farms on 3.4 million ha UAA (in 1995).

growing and intensive pig and poultry rearing[39]. This intensification has led to environmental degradation including the impoverishment of the cultural landscape through consolidation of holdings, a reduction of wildlife habitats, a decline in ecosystem quality and biodiversity, and nitrate and pesticide pollution of ground water (Hofreither and Rauchenberger, 1995; Wagner, 1997). Further, it has often also led to decreasing standards of animal welfare on holdings with factory-farmed livestock and poultry.

Partly as a result of the increasing divergence between lowland and upland farming, environmental problems in the mountainous regions of Austria have been very different from those in the lowlands. Mountain farming has largely remained an extensive form of cultivation, which means that positive environmental effects usually predominate, although negative effects have also become apparent in some upland regions. In contrast to the lowlands, these problems are usually not the result of intensification but are linked to the winding-down of farming operations often leading to reduced grazing of alpine pastures[40]. Such problems have been exacerbated by a general shift in cultivation from higher altitudes to lower lying areas and the conversion of extensive grassland to forest, all resulting in the loss of the traditional character of the cultural landscape in mountain areas (Groier 1993).

Implementation of agri-environmental policy before 1995

Before 1995 (when Austria joined the EU), AEP operated exclusively under a national policy-making framework. Since its beginnings in the early 1980s, Austrian policy has been characterised by a horizontal approach focusing on the 'ecologisation' of the entire agricultural area, and differs, therefore, from the more targeted approaches in countries such as the UK or Denmark (see Chs. 3 and 6). Thus, a different set of agri-environmental measures have been developed, aimed essentially at dealing with environmental problems throughout the country. Since their onset however, these measures have been developed with possible EU membership in sight. As a result, they have often corresponded closely to equivalent EU regulations and directives.

---

[39] These areas include the south-eastern plains, the Lower Austrian plain and hill country, the Alpenvorland, and the Carinthian basin.

[40] In some cases, however, farmers have also begun to overstock the fragile mountain meadow ecosystems, often leading to severe environmental degradation and erosion.

The changing framework of policy implementation

Austria's agri-environmental philosophy has to be understood within the framework of agricultural and environmental policy developments after the Second World War. The agro-political context of the 1950s and 1960s with its emphasis on agricultural and production subsidies, for example, closely mirrored that of other European countries (albeit outside the framework of the CAP). Nature protection was discredited through its ideological association with fascism, and the paradigms of 'rebuilding' and 'progress' overshadowed any concerns for specific AEP. However, the 1970s and 1980s already saw a rapidly growing environmental movement (see below) and a new understanding of nature protection based on scientific knowledge, highlighted through the implementation of soil protection schemes developed by individual provinces. Although much emphasis was still placed on market regulation, Austria initiated a special programme for mountain farmers in 1972, which already highlighted the importance of maintaining viable farming communities in upland areas. This was supplemented in 1974 by an amendment to the *Agriculture Act* which already included some elements of 'landscape conservation'.

The 1980s, meanwhile, saw a re-orientation of agricultural policy, with the introduction of so-called 'ecological and social agricultural policy'. Increasing problems with the financing of surpluses, the alarming decline in farm numbers, combined with continuing intensification in intensively used areas, led to the introduction of the quota regulations with agri-environmental components (for selected agricultural commodities), the promotion of production alternatives, and the first considerations of outright financial support through agri-environmental measures. This marked an overall shift in attitudes towards environmental problems in the Austrian countryside, further fuelled at the time by reports from the media and environmental consulting agencies suggesting that modern agriculture had a damaging effect on the environment. It came as no surprise, therefore, that Austria placed specific emphasis on direct payment agri-environmental support mechanisms during the late 1980s and early 1990s, thereby pre-dating the introduction of post-accession Regulation 2078. Within this new orientation, the support of organic farming was declared a priority issue in terms of environmentally friendly farming and the orientation of direct payments (Hess and Vogl, 1997; Groier, 1998a).

Policy milestones in this respect included the *Animal Husbandry Act* 1976/80 (introduction of maximum stocking rates), policies related to organic farming (1983), taxes encouraging reduction of inputs or production (e.g. fertiliser tax 1986, maize seed tax 1987) and general support for extensive production in animal husbandry. In particular, the late 1980s saw a plethora of new policies supporting environmentally friendly forms of farming, including the *Agriculture Act* 1988 (maintenance of natural resources, landscape conservation), specific support for ecological farming (support for green fallow in arable areas from 1988), support for energy biomass production (from 1988), financial support for organic farming associations (from 1989), cultivation restrictions for farmers concerning water protection (*Water Act* 1959/90) and regulations on nitrate pollution in drinking water (1989)[41].

The period between 1990 and 1995 (before EU membership) was characterised by further changes in environmental thinking, which included a reunification of 'nature' and 'environmental' protection philosophies (which had become separated conceptually during the 1980s), a growing emphasis on comprehensive and integrated environmental protection concepts, and increasing incorporation of agricultural aspects into environmental strategies aimed at long-term solutions. As a result, the early 1990s saw the consolidation of an environmentally oriented direct payment system which eventually became the basis for the large horizontal agri-environmental programme ÖPUL (implemented 1995) discussed below. In the build-up to EU membership, Austrian AEP also saw an increasing convergence with EU agri-environmental programmes, best highlighted through the *Agriculture Act* 1992/95, which included specifications for adaptation to the CAP and the introduction of 'extensification' based on EU guidelines. Important steps during that period include, in particular, financial support for organic farming (conversion only in 1991; from 1992 permanent support through area-based payments), an innovative 'eco-points' system (implemented in Lower Austria; see also Ch. 7 on the German MEKA programme), support for crop-rotation, green fallow, and environmentally friendly fertiliser storage (all from 1991) and support for 'ecological schemes' (including regional and landscape schemes). The *Agriculture Act* 1992/95, therefore, highlighted the increasing emphasis placed on environmentally friendly farming by giving more regard to the ecological compatibility of agricultural practices, and by providing a framework for subsidies based more on environmentally friendly production methods and product quality[42].

---

[41] These policy developments were accompanied by wider changes in environmental policies, including the establishment of the first national park (Hohe Tauern 1981) and Austrian accession to the RAMSAR Convention (1983).

[42] Additional environmental legislation included a tightening of the *Water Act* 1959/90 (including new threshold levels for N-applications and livestock densities), accession of Austria to the *Alpine Convention* (1991) and legal mechanisms controlling genetic engineering of agricultural products (1994).

The agri-environmental debate

The agri-environmental debate in Austria cannot be separated from discussions about socio-economic issues in agriculture. From the beginning, issues about agriculture and the environment have been closely linked with the problem of socio-economic disparities between mountain and lowland farmers. During the 1960s and 1970s, the former were not only at a competitive disadvantage due to orographic and climatic conditions, but agricultural policy was also oriented to the more favoured areas (and usually larger farms) which received the bulk of subsidies. Although policies were put in place that helped address this problem (see above), this unequal situation has persisted to the present day (Hovorka, 1996).

In the late 1970s, mountain farmers publicly raised the question why extensive farming in the Austrian Alps had not seen more financial support guaranteeing the long-term survival of their farms and families – criticisms that were also supported by intellectuals from urban areas at the time. It was argued that this lack of support was surprising, as extensive mountain agriculture was seen to be more environmentally friendly than lowland farming, and was also seen to produce important landscape 'values' crucial for the Austrian tourism industry (see also Ch. 4). Conversely, mountain farmers criticised that surplus producing agricultural holdings were subsidised and continued to consume large amounts of public revenue, despite the fact that they were causing increasing environmental degradation. This debate eventually resulted in the introduction of policies specifically addressing the needs of mountain farmers in the 1970s (special supplement for mountain farmers), with the specific aim to maintain small farm holdings that faced difficult farming conditions in upland areas (Krammer and Scheer, 1978; Groier, 1993).

Yet, debates at the time were still characterised by disagreements regarding the overall impact that Austrian agriculture had on the environment. Krammer and Scheer (1978) in particular, explored in detail why environmental damages caused by agriculture were not the subject of more widespread public debate. They argued that, first, intensification levels of Austrian agriculture on the whole had been low compared to other European countries, and that it was easy, therefore, to shift the blame of countryside degradation onto other European countries while acting as if everything 'at home' was in order. Second, farmers' political interest groups at the time had successfully presented agriculture as making an exclusively positive contribution to the maintenance of a functioning and 'clean' environment. Third, debates were also influenced by the fact that environmental damage caused by agriculture was not immediately visible and traceable. It was argued that impacts on landscape and food quality occurred with considerable time-lags, which meant that these impacts were not immediately apparent at the time. Finally, they argued that the general lack of information with regard to scientific facts concerning agriculture and environment, and the lack of information of the wider public about the potential threats of agriculture to human health, had hindered the early development of a widespread debate and the resulting implementation of AEPs.

Krammer and Scheer's study had a major impact on policy thinking, and launched the environmental question firmly onto the agricultural agenda. Protagonists who had previously been slandered as 'greenies' were now taken more seriously. Thus, in the course of the 1980s, the relationship between the agriculture lobby and environmentalists changed from confrontation to collaboration, which enabled environmentalists' views to be increasingly accommodated in the AEP framework. At the beginning of the 1990s, for example, an environmental NGO carried out an extensive media campaign informing a large part of the population in detail about environmental problems caused by agriculture. The overall result of this new collaboration between environmental actors was a policy package that addressed both environmental and socio-economic issues.

Yet, it would be wrong to argue that the debate surrounding environmental impacts of agriculture has completely disappeared in the late 1990s, and even today discussions about the severity of environmental pollution caused by agriculture continue unabated. It is mainly the agriculture lobby and farmers with large holdings who reject connection between their farming methods and health-threatening levels of nitrate in groundwater. The Austrian public has also been relatively lethargic when it comes to agricultural pollution issues, and people have only tended to become active when their health was directly threatened by agricultural practices (e.g. food poisoning scandals; BSE crisis) (BMLF, 1997). This is part of the reason why it will still take some time before legal guidelines will completely regulate environmental pollution caused by agriculture.

The establishment of the Austrian agri-environmental programme ÖPUL

Programme development

Regulation 2078 gave Austria new opportunities for the establishment of agri-environmental schemes, and allowed a substantial expansion of its existing agri-environmental programme (Groier, 1998a). There had been substantial pre-accession negotiations regarding the compatibility of Austrian AEP with EU regulations, and the fact that most of the Austrian policies were compatible with the CAP (and required little change) played some part in persuading voters during the public referendum in June 1994 to vote for EU membership. During these membership negotiations, Austria had already presented the first version of its agri-environmental programme, ÖPUL I (*Austrian programme for the promotion of extensive farming methods compatible with the requirements of environmental protection and the maintenance of the countryside*). According to the official Austrian interpretation, this programme had already been 'approved in advance' by the EU Commission before the close of negotiations (Groier, 1995). Environmental issues were addressed in the statement of intent by the EU in the treaty of accession, and the 36th statement on agri-environmental schemes in the document on membership conditions stated that the EU would take the necessary measures "to enable the new Member States to carry out the speedy implementation of the agri-environmental scheme to the benefit of their farmers in keeping with Regulation (EEC) No. 2078/92, and to secure the co-funding of this programme within the limits of existing domestic funding" (Hovorka, 1996, 4). Co-funding of the Austrian agri-environmental programme was expected to be about 175 MECU per year.

ÖPUL I (and its successor ÖPUL '98) went through a series of policy-related and legal development stages which included a variety of policy actors from state-related agencies and non-state organisations (BMLF, 1996a). The 'discussion phase' (from mid 1992), for example, involved the establishment of working groups that discussed possibilities for the adaptation of existing agri-environmental measures to Regulation 2078. These early negotiations involved the Chamber of Agriculture, the Ministry of Agriculture and Forestry (BMLF), the Ministry of Environment, the National Environment Agency, and WWF Austria. The drafting of the first programme took place in summer 1993 and included an overview of all previous agri-environmental subsidies available to farmers through the BMLF. By January 1994, the programme was submitted to the EU, and further amendments were added later that year on the basis of suggestions form the BMLF, various Austrian regions, the Chamber of Agriculture, and the Austrian Farmers' Union. By May 1994, publication of the first version of ÖPUL I could be presented (Hovorka, 1996).

Based on the large funding basis provided by both the EU and the Austrian government, ÖPUL I was intended to extend previous measures, as well as introducing entirely new measures for environmentally friendly farming. New measures (in operation from autumn 1994) included, for example, payments encouraging abandonment of yield-enhancing substances on arable and grassland areas, incentives for the stabilisation of crop rotations, and inducements for extensive cereal farming. Already existing payments under previous agri-environmental schemes (e.g. *organic farming subsidy*; *crop rotation subsidy*; *alpine pasturing premium*; see above) were adjusted and extended within ÖPUL I to fit in with Regulation 2078 specifications. Further, previous state subsidies for farming and agri-environmental schemes funded by the regions (e.g. alpine pasturing payments), were also integrated into ÖPUL I. Overall, 25 different measures have been offered under ÖPUL I available at both the national and regional level (i.e. some measures are only region-specific) (Wagner, 1996).

The drafting of ÖPUL I was an incremental process. Throughout 1994, parts of the original draft of ÖPUL I were changed as a result of both internal discussions and negotiations with the EU Commission. In autumn 1994 ÖPUL was close to its final version, and an explanatory leaflet concerning ÖPUL I could be sent to farmers. After some final revisions in early 1995, ÖPUL I was submitted to the Commission in its final form in February 1995, and was approved by the EU in June 1995 (Hovorka, 1996; BMLF, 1996a).

As will be outlined in detail below, ÖPUL I was so successful with farmers that the budget had already been exhausted by the end of 1995. As a result, any new applications were stopped in January 1996 (except for organic farming), and payments in two of the most costly measures (basic premium and crop rotation stabilisation; see Table 9.1 below) were reduced. A modified version of ÖPUL I (ÖPUL '98) was subsequently submitted to the EU in summer 1997 and approved by the Commission in October 1997. Due to the recency of ÖPUL '98, the following discussion will focus mainly on implementation and effectiveness of ÖPUL I.

Aims and objectives of ÖPUL I

ÖPUL I and its successor programme ÖPUL '98 (hereafter ÖPUL) is a nation-wide (horizontal) programme co-funded by the Commission under Regulation 2078. Currently, it is the largest and most ambitious agri-environmental programme in the EU, both in terms of participants and funding (see also Ch. 12). The 25 individual measures offered under ÖPUL target different land uses and production systems and operate at different scales, ranging from individual wildlife habitats to whole-farm measures. ÖPUL is based on the philosophy that policy should not only help reduce environmental damage, but should also prevent future damage according to the precautionary principle. This forms the basis for the six components of the programme: maintenance of extensive forms of cultivation; extensification of production on arable land; extensification of grassland farming; encouragement of environmentally friendly farming practices and conservation of biodiversity; creation and conservation of landscape elements; and improving farmers' education (Table 9.1).

The aims of ÖPUL closely mirror the objectives stated in Article 1 of Regulation 2078 and include the promotion of agricultural methods that help minimise environmentally damaging effects of agriculture, while at the same time contributing to a better market balance through reduced production (Groier, 1995). The programme also aims at increasing the use of environmentally friendly extensive methods in crop production and animal husbandry, and at promoting cultivation methods compatible with environmental conservation and the maintenance of landscape elements, natural resources, and soil and genetic diversity. Further, incentives are given for long-term set-aside of agricultural areas for conservation reasons, and for the promotion of environmental education of farmers. Finally, ÖPUL aims at ensuring appropriate incomes for farmers.

ÖPUL has the most complex set of agri-environmental measures in the EU (25 overall). Some measures target all agricultural land in Austria, while others specifically target grassland and arable areas (Figure 9.1). The programme is structured into two parts, including 'Part A' measures that are offered throughout Austria, and 'Part B' measures only offered in certain regions. Part A measures offer the same terms and payments throughout the country and include all measures listed under (1.), (2.), and (3.1) in Table 9.1 above (excluding measure 1.4). Part B measures address specific regional problems and include all other measures listed in Table 9.1. Each region (and each farmer) can, therefore, select the 'menu' of measures relevant to their agricultural and environmental problems and adapt them to their specific requirements. Further, regions can also define specific measures in the form of regional projects (measure 4.5 in Table 9.1).

First assessment of the impacts of ÖPUL I

ÖPUL I takes up over a third (37%) of the entire Austrian budget for direct payments in agriculture (the remaining 63% are for compensatory payments as well as compensatory allowances under Objective 5a). The great variety of measures, together with relatively high payments available under different measures, have been responsible for the very high uptake rates in the programme. In 1997, the area covered by ÖPUL I already amounted to 2.6 million ha, equivalent to 76% of Austria's UAA (excluding alpine pastures), and on average participant farms have entered 3.3 measures (out of 25) (BMLF, 1996c). In the same year, the total number of

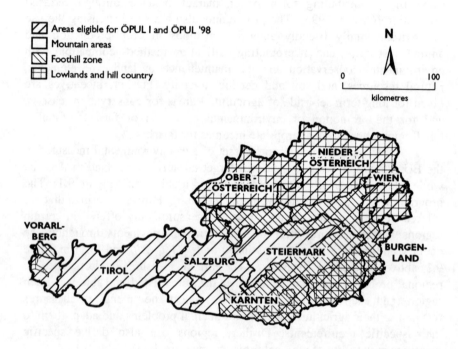

Figure 9.1   Areas eligible for ÖPUL and the main landscape types in Austria

Source: Authors

Table 9.1 Measures under ÖPUL I

1. Extensive forms of cultivation (whole farm)	2. Extensive arable land use (specific areas on the farm)	3. Extensive grassland use (specific areas on the farm)	4. Environmentally friendly farming practices and conservation of biodiversity	5. Creation and conservation of landscape elements	6. Educational measures
1.1 Basic subsidy	2.1. Extensive cereal production (foodstuff sector)	3.1 Non-application of easily soluble commercial fertilisers and extensive use of chemical crop protection in grassland	4.1 Erosion prevention in fruit growing	5.1 Landscape elements and biotope development areas with 20-year set-aside	Not yet implemented
1.2 Organic farming	2.2 Non-application of specific yield-enhancing agents		4.2 Erosion prevention in viticulture		
1.3 Non-application of specific yield-enhancing agents	2.2.1 Growth regulators	3.2 Mowing restrictions		5.2 Provision of areas for ecological objectives (5-year set-aside)	
1.3.1 Grassland and arable land	2.2.2 Easily soluble commercial fertilisers and growth regulators		4.3 Erosion prevention in arable farming		
1.3.2 Fruit, vine and ornamental plant growing	2.2.3 Easily soluble commercial fertilisers and synthetic chemical crop-protection agents		4.4 Keeping and rearing endangered breeds	5.3 Provision of areas for ecological objectives on selected cyclical set-aside	
1.3.2.1 Integrated controlled fruit growing	2.2.4 Fungicides		4.5 Regional projects		
1.3.2.2 Integrated controlled viticulture	2.2.5 Synthetic chemical crop-protection agents		4.6 Mowing of slopes and mountain meadows		
1.3.2.3 Integrated production of ornamental plants	2.2.6 Integrated production in vegetable cultivation		4.7 Alpine pasturing and herding supplement		
1.4. Extensive grassland cultivation in traditional areas			4.8 Upkeep of ecologically valuable areas		
1.5 Reduction of livestock density			4.9 Growing of rare agricultural crops		
1.6 Crop rotation stabilisation			4.10 Upkeep of abandoned agricultural and woodland areas		

Source: BMLF, 1996

participants amounted to 162,000, equivalent to 85% of all eligible Austrian agricultural and forestry holdings (farm numbers based on latest farm census in 1997). In total, 522 MECU were paid out for ÖPUL I in 1997 alone, with average payments per farm at 3,200 ECU. Table 9.2 highlights that the total cost of the programme increased substantially between 1995 and 1996 (particularly because of the expansion of measure 1.6 *crop rotation stabilisation*), while the number of initial participants decreased in the same period (from 68% to 64%). This decrease was based on both continuing consolidation of farms and changing statistical baseline data. Based on an amendment to the *Agricultural Act* 1992/96, payments for the two measures *basic subsidy* (measure 1.1) and *crop rotation stabilisation* (measure 1.6) were reduced, resulting in the fact that the agri-environmental budget for ÖPUL has decreased for 1997[43].

Table 9.2 Participation in ÖPUL I and budget for 1995/96

Year	UAA under contract (million ha)	Participants	Budget (MECU)
1995	2.6[a]	179,478	549
1996	2.6[a]	168,804	613
1997	2.6[a]	162,000	522

(a) Estimated total subsidised area is based on data from BMLF (1996d); this figure includes estimations about the extent of alpine pastures based on the assumption that 1 LU = 1 ha alpine pasture; the actual area is probably much larger.

Source: BMLF, 1996a, 1996b, 1996c, 1996d

Preliminary research on the effectiveness of the Austrian agri-environmental programme suggests that the main reason for high uptake has been that the programme is offered on a nation-wide basis (horizontal programme) (BMLF, 1996b, 1996c). Further, some of the most expensive measures only have modest environmental restrictions (e.g. measure 1.1 *basic subsidy*), making it possible for farms with very varied and also relatively intensive forms of production to take part. There is no doubt that farmers' experience with agri-environmental schemes (especially *organic farming*) before the implementation of ÖPUL was also an important factor in persuading farmers to participate (Groier 1995, 1998b).

---

[43] No figures for 1997 are available yet. The budget is likely to be similar to that of 1995.

Yet, and as Table 9.3 highlights, participation in individual measures has varied greatly. Thus, farmers in grassland-dominated or mountainous areas have tended to be most interested in measures that contain more stringent environmental prescriptions applying to the whole farm such as *organic farming* (measure 1.2); and measure 1.3 on *non-application of special yield-enhancing agents on the whole farm*. Farmers in regions with intensive cultivation of arable land, meanwhile, have been more interested in measures applying to individual areas on the farm (e.g. the cluster of measures mentioned under '2' in Tables 9.1 and 9.3). Further, certain types of farms seem to have benefited more from ÖPUL than others. On the one hand, medium-sized farms with permanent grassland in mountainous regions have received relatively high payments by entering well paid and environmentally oriented measures specifically designed for this type of farming (e.g. measure 4.6 *mowing of slopes and mountain meadows* and measure 4.7 *alpine pasturing and herding supplement*), and the same is true for larger farms in favourable arable areas that have received higher than average payments. On the other hand, farms with intensive pig and poultry rearing have received comparatively low payments, mainly because they have relatively small farm areas and because they only enter measures with low payments and modest environmental restrictions (BMLF, 1996c).

Discussion and future perspectives

Before joining the EU in 1995, Austria already had a well developed bundle of agri-environmental measures which, on the one hand, together with existing subsidies and new measures, were further developed into the Austrian environmental programme ÖPUL I and provided Austria with a vital head start when it came to implementation of Regulation 2078 in 1995. Based on its previous experience with horizontal schemes, the new agri-environmental programme ÖPUL I was established in 1995 – the largest agri-environmental programme in the EU both in terms of uptake and budget. Drafting of the programme coincided with Austria's EU membership negotiations and, therefore, took place under great time pressure (similar to the situation in Sweden; see Ch. 4). This explains partly why some elements of ÖPUL I did not work perfectly in the first year, resulting in the fact that some amendments had to be made subsequently (e.g. changes to measure guidelines and payment levels; halt to new

Table 9.3 Uptake of different measures under ÖPUL I (in 1996)

Measure classification	Measure	Contracted area (ha UAA)	Partici-pants (N°)	Total cost MECU	%
1.1	Basic subsidy	2,314,451	161,806	90.8	17.4
1.2	Organic farming (including monitoring)	247,260	18,485	63.1	12.1
1.3.1	Non-application of specific yield-enhancing agents (grassland, arable land; total farm)	300,632	33,700	40.6	7.8
1.3.2.1	Integrated controlled fruit growing	8,248	2,633	4.3	0.8
1.3.2.2	Integrated controlled viticulture	37,187	13,203	21,4	4.1
1.3.2.3	Integrated production of ornamental plants	377	45	0.1	0.02
1.4	Extensive grassland cultivation in traditional areas	114,208	10,609	20.4	3.9
1.6	Crop rotation stabilisation	1,163,223	68,333	95.0	18.3
2.1	Extensive cereal cultivation	242,338	28,108	43.6	8.4
2.2	Non-application of yield-enhancing agents arable (individual areas)	319,695	82,017	21.0	4.0
3.1	Non-application of external inputs: grassland (individual areas)	236,593	45,868	29.7	5.7
3.2	Adherence to mowing restrictions	5,042	2,630	0.7	0.1
4.1	Erosion prevention in fruit growing	7,811	2,419	0.7	0.1
4.2	Erosion prevention in viticulture	4,647	3,030	0.5	0.1
4.3	Erosion prevention in arable farming	437	148	0.01	0.0
	Keeping rare endangered breeds				
4.4	Regional projects	-	-	1.6	0.3
4.5	Mowing mountain meadows	-	1,014	6.5	1.2
4.6	Alpine pasturing	236,770	61,828	44.6	8.6
4.7	Upkeep of ecologically valuable	267,590[a]	8,525	20.1	3.9
4.8	areas	34,314	43,602	11.3	2.2
	Growing of rare agricultural crops				
4.9	Upkeep of abandoned woodland	4	30	0.0	0.0
4.10	areas	667	329	0.2	0.04
	Landscape elements (20-year set-				
5.1	aside)	343	730	0.4	0.08
	Ecological objectives (5-year set-				
5.2	aside)	549	1,570	0.8	0.2
	Ecological objectives (5-year				
5.3	cyclical set- aside)	4511	1,783	0.3	0.06
	Total	2,600,000	162,000	520.4	100

(a) This figure includes estimations about the extent of alpine pastures based on the assumption that 1 LU = 1 ha alpine pasture; the actual area is probably much larger.

Source: BMLF, 1997

applications after 1996[44]). Even today, ÖPUL is subject to further changes and refinement through the new ÖPUL '98 and the planned programme ÖPUL 2000.

In general terms, ÖPUL I aimed at promoting environmentally friendly agriculture at the national scale, as well as helping to maintain small-scale family farming. Although initial discussions about implementation of ÖPUL I were influenced by how Germany had implemented its agri-environmental schemes (i.e. on a regional basis with separate agri-environmental programmes for each individual region; see Ch. 7), a more practical model was selected for ÖPUL based on one national horizontal programme that also comprised region-specific measures.In contrast to many other EU-countries, organic farming in Austria has become established as a guiding principle of AEP (more than 10% of programme budget) – a pattern that started well before EU membership and implementation of Regulation 2078 (Groier, 1998a). Currently, nearly 8% of Austrian farms (9% of total UAA) are organic farms (according to Regulation 2092/91), and the share of organic products is increasing rapidly because of increasing promotion by two of the largest supermarket chains. It is evident that in future great effort will be made to maintain and further develop this specific type of farming practice, especially because organic farming is one of the key strategies for the realisation of both sustainable agriculture and integrated regional development (Cernusca *et al.*, 1997).

Although ÖPUL I was a great success right from the start (especially with regard to uptake by farmers), some pre-existing and very stringent environmental measures were cancelled in 1994 (e.g. fertiliser tax; maximum stocking rates per farm) in order not to impede competitiveness of Austrian agriculture after EU integration. Thus, in contrast to long-established EU Member States, Austria had to take into account the agro-political implications of CAP adoption including, for example, large reductions in producer prices with potentially severe repercussions for Austrian farmers. As a result, a key precondition for the successful EU membership referendum in Austria was the incorporation of a relatively clear income-support orientation in ÖPUL I. When analysing the geneses of the ÖPUL I and ÖPUL '98 programmes, it is evident that environmental experts were only involved in the general preparatory phases, not in the concrete drawing up of the programme within the implementation process.

Partly as a result of the income orientation of the programme, ÖPUL saw a very high uptake by farmers. This raised the costs of the programme well beyond initial expectations in 1996, and consequently the EU co-

---

[44] With the exceptions of organic farming and some environmentally-oriented measures.

funding rate was raised retrospectively from initially 31% to nearly 50% (for 1995-1997). The share of future EU co-funding will depend largely on the first programme evaluations of ÖPUL I and the effectiveness of its successor programmes ÖPUL '98 and ÖPUL 2000. ÖPUL has been subject to a permanent evaluation process since its inception. This was one of the rationales for the launching of a new modified version of the programme (ÖPUL '98), which also took into account some of the criticisms made by the EU Commission in 1997.

A second conceptually improved evaluation report will be submitted in 1999 and will form the basis for the design of ÖPUL 2000. This new version of ÖPUL is likely to include modifications related to the improvement of regional ecological effectiveness of certain measures (regional water and nature protection programmes), the further promotion of organic farming, and the implementation of improved nature protection measures.

Although ÖPUL I more or less fulfilled its initial objective of maintaining extensive and environmentally friendly farming methods, the extensification of intensive farming systems (as well as the creation of habitat networks in intensively farmed areas) will have to be developed further. This indicates that continuous efforts will have to be made to further optimise what is already an ambitious programme in order to realise a sustainable, environmentally sound agriculture throughout the entire country.

10 Switzerland: agri-environmental policy outside the European Union

Hansjörg Schmid and Bernard Lehmann

Swiss agriculture: a special case?

Switzerland is not a member of the EU, and Swiss AEP operates outside the policy framework of the CAP. Regulation 2078, therefore, has no direct influence on the Swiss agri-environmental programme. This special situation makes Switzerland and interesting case study to analyse in the context of this book. Switzerland has implemented an ambitious agri-environmental programme, and the aim of this chapter is to analyse in what ways this programme may be different or similar to policies developed in EU countries outlined in this book – in other words, is Swiss AEP comparable with EU policies?

Most of Swiss agriculture is concentrated in the central lowlands (covering about 30% of the country) which have relatively favourable terrain and soils suitable for intensive arable farming (see Figure 10.1 below). Half of the country is mountainous, with extensive livestock-oriented farming in the more suitable valley and foothill regions and seasonal extensive livestock grazing on alpine pastures (Table 10.1). Of the one million ha agricultural land almost three quarters are grassland, emphasising the important role of livestock and dairy production in Swiss agriculture. Dairy products make up about a third of the gross agricultural product[45], beef and veal 17%, while crops and vegetables only generate about 18% of the gross product. The wide range of different farming activities and intensities has created different types of environmental problems, ranging from severe nitrate pollution problems in the lowlands to farm abandonment and resulting loss of cultural landscape values in mountain areas (see also Ch. 9 on Austria). As will be discussed in detail

---

[45] The gross agricultural product is the cash value of agricultural products when they leave the farm.

below, these different problems have posed severe challenges for Swiss AEP-makers.

Table 10.1 Land use in Switzerland

Land use	% of land area
Forests	30
Lakes, glaciers, unproductive areas	25
Agricultural area	25
Alpine pastures	14
Built-up areas	6

Source: Schweizerischer Bauernverband, 1996

Swiss agriculture is characterised by small farms with an average of 17 ha for full-time farms (compared to >60 ha in the UK, for example). Average farm sizes are even smaller in upland areas, where 40% of all Swiss holdings are located (out of a total of 80,000 farms). Further, more than 30% of Swiss farmers are part-timers, and the number of full-time farmers has decreased by 40% since 1970. Especially in mountain areas, Swiss farmers have to complement their often meagre farm incomes with off-farm jobs, usually as forest workers, on construction sites, and in tourism or tourism-related activities (e.g. farm accommodation, skiing instructors in winter, mountain guides in summer).

As in other European countries, the share of people working in Swiss agriculture has dwindled to about 4% of the workforce over the last few decades, with the most severe changes occurring in remote and agriculturally marginal upland areas not touched by tourism. Land abandonment has often resulted in poor maintenance of fragile upland ecosystems created by centuries of farming (e.g. species-rich nutrient-poor alpine pastures) and a decline in the maintenance of privately owned forests that are important for avalanche protection (epitomised, for example, during the severe avalanche problems in February 1999). In the lowlands, meanwhile, rapid post-war urban growth and the expansion of road infrastructure have encroached upon good agricultural land, particularly in urban fringe areas where most of the land suitable for permanent cropping is located (covering only 25,000 ha overall). The latter has not only been an environmental problem through the loss of countryside amenity values and wildlife habitats, but has also been an agricultural problem in a country that only has a food self-sufficiency rate of about 60%[46]. The whittling away of agricultural land through urban development has, therefore, led to increasing intensification on the remaining agricultural land in the lowlands, often leading to further environmental degradation.

Changes in agriculture and environmental effects

The experience of food shortages during the First and Second World War accentuated the need for an efficient agriculture that would ensure national self-sufficiency. The basis for Swiss agricultural policy was established through the *Agriculture Act 1951* which provided a framework of support and assistance to Swiss farmers. Apart from aiming to guarantee adequate food supplies, the Act also aimed at preserving agricultural structures and maintaining viable farming communities (especially in upland areas). Consequently, most subsidies were 'productivist' in nature, in addition to providing direct income support through capital grants and special contributions to farmers in mountain zones. Subsidies were also provided for agricultural research and education, and price and sales guarantees were put in place for several products together with protectionist import restrictions.

Although self-sufficiency levels were increased substantially on the basis of these subsidies, the downside was an intensification of agricultural production and a dramatic increase in the use of external inputs. The use of chemical fertilisers, for example, increased from 13 kg/N/ha in 1960 to 72 kg/N/ha in 1990, although in recent years this figure has been reduced to 62 kg/N/ha (Schweizerischer Bauernverband, 1996). The resulting nitrate pollution problems in the lowlands were the most severe environmental problem resulting from these post-war policies, in particular through the pollution of drinking water (Gruber, 1992). There were fewer concerns with regard to environmental degradation through overgrazing (average of only 19.4 LU/farm), as the number of cattle did not increase substantially after the Second World War (the number of cows even decreased from 900,000 in 1956 to 760,000 in 1996). This was partly due to the introduction of milk quotas in 1977 (which effectively stopped any major changes in the number of dairy cows after that date) and to technological progress which resulted in much higher average milk production per cow. The only severe environmental problems related to livestock came from intensive pig-

---

[46] Due to the orientation of Swiss farming towards livestock production, the degree of self-sufficiency for animal products is relatively high with 84%, but only 40% of consumed plant products originate in Switzerland itself.

breeding installations where numbers had increased from 1.2 million in 1956 to 1.6 million in 1996, with associated problems of liquid manure storage and disposal.

Swiss AEP has mirrored the differing severity of environmental problems caused by agriculture. As will be discussed in detail below, great emphasis has been placed on water protection regulations in order to reduce nitrate levels in drinking water. In addition, Swiss policy has concentrated more than any other European country on the promotion of 'integrated farming' – a type of farming which entails location-specific timing and concentrations of external input applications, thereby leading to substantial reductions in nitrate use without greatly influencing yields. A recent study by the *Swiss Federal Institute for Technology* analysing the 'nitrate problem', for example, shows that there is still further potential for the reduction of nitrate pollution, and that on most Swiss farms the quantity and timing of N-fertiliser applications are still not optimal. If all farms, and especially the 'worst' culprits, improved the efficiency of fertiliser applications, it would be possible to reduce nitrate use by about 16,000 t/N/year, which corresponds to about 13% of estimated nitrate pollution in Swiss agriculture (Häfliger *et al.*, 1995).

Policy responses to environmental degradation

The first criticisms of productivist agricultural policies in Switzerland emerged in the 1970s – much earlier than in most EU Member States. By the early 1970s, for example, the limitations of the price guarantee system were recognised, and the *Department of National Economic Affairs* set up a think-tank to study the viability and credibility of the direct payment system. Yet, although the group submitted a number of alternative compensation payment systems, their proposals were not followed up because of resistance by conservative agricultural circles (who were largely lobbying for powerful farmers in the lowlands) who wanted to see a continuation of quantity-based production subsidies. Established policy circles – in particular the *Swiss Farmers' Union* – also continued to advocate the Swiss approach of interventionist and protectionist agricultural policies which were seen as the only solutions to solve the emerging agricultural problems (Müller, 1998). Farmers preferred to be 'rewarded' by the consumers through pricing policy rather than being increasingly dependent on the state (Schweizerisches Bauernsekretariat, 1990). In the 1970s, this productivist discourse continued to be fuelled by the fact that most people still remembered the crucial role that Swiss agriculture had played during the

Second World War, when it had been able to feed most of the population despite of adverse economic and political circumstances. It was argued, therefore, that, as long as border protections could be maintained, there was little reason why farmers, together with their political representatives and farmers' unions, should change their outlook (Hofer, 1998).

This conservative and production-oriented outlook effectively stalled any further debate surrounding a re-orientation of Swiss agricultural policies during the 1970s and early 1980s. It took until the end of the 1980s for the general mood among policy makers – fuelled increasingly by an outspoken conservation movement that demanded better food quality and countryside management – to change in such a way that new types of agricultural policies could be introduced. A policy change also became necessary because of increasing pressure resulting from GATT negotiations which necessitated European-wide revisions of agricultural instruments (Wilson *et al.*, 1996; Curry and Stucki, 1997). The idea of direct payments to agriculture became politically more acceptable (as opposed to the earlier idea that agriculture could be regulated through pricing policies alone). The result was the constitution of a panel of experts in 1987 consisting of various organisations and institutions including agricultural interests, consumer groups, food marketing and processing businesses, and representatives from trade and research interests. By 1989, this expert group had drafted a new agricultural policy which had direct payments as its key element, aiming at both income support for farmers and financial rewards for environmentally friendly farming practices (Bundesamt für Landwirtschaft, 1990).

Calls for changes in policy directions were also based on the fact that in the late 1980s the protectionist high-price approach became unworkable. With farmgate and supermarket prices for food being considerably higher in Switzerland than in the EU (e.g. milk price in EU only 45% of Swiss price; wheat 40%; beef 56%), Swiss consumers began to increasingly purchase foodstuffs abroad (especially non-perishable goods), resulting in the loss of market shares for Swiss farmers. This meant that production costs of Swiss agriculture had to be reduced, and new marketing opportunities had to be established (e.g. marketing of local organic products; see below). On the basis of this rapidly worsening crisis, the Swiss Farmers' Union reluctantly agreed in 1990 to accept the introduction of direct payments which would reduce pressures on product prices, while at the same time providing incentives for environmentally friendly farming (especially through integrated production practices). The farm lobby, nonetheless, referred to the date of introduction of direct payments as 'black Monday' (Hofer, 1998) – indicating the continuing reluctance of farming circles to acknowledge that a new policy trajectory was necessary in order to maintain the viability of Swiss farming.

The new policy was introduced in January 1993 in the form of two new articles (Articles 31a and 31b). Article 31a introduced mechanisms for the lowering of prices of major agricultural products and the introduction of direct payments to compensate farmers for ensuing income losses. Article 31b provided the framework for implementation of agri-environmental schemes (Schweizerischer Bundesrat, 1992)[47]. Articles 31a and 31b were the results of political negotiations between a variety of actors, including the Green Party and parties from the Left and farmers' unions, leading to a relatively comprehensive policy package that addressed problems at the national, regional and local levels. Although Article 31a payments have provided the largest proportion of compensatory payments to farmers, the long-term aim is to achieve a balance between 31a and 31b payments – emphasising the increasing importance attached to subsidies that are linked to environmentally friendly farming prescriptions (cross-compliance).

Swiss agri-environmental policy

In contrast to most EU countries discussed in this book, the Swiss approach to AEP has been characterised partly by regulatory mechanisms. Although the voluntary principle plays an important role with regard to certain agri-environmental schemes in Switzerland (see below), many environmentally harmful farming practices are regulated by law rather than through voluntary participation in agri-environmental schemes. The following will, therefore, discuss regulatory and voluntary mechanisms separately.

Legally-binding agri-environmental mechanisms (regulatory)

Five environmental laws regulate key elements of environmental management in the Swiss countryside at the federal level (Rieder and Anwander Phan-Huy, 1994). These are binding to all land-users, and the breaching of any of these regulations may entail financial penalties or other types of legal punishments. The federal *Water Protection Act 1991*, for example, contains several legally binding prescriptions concerning water pollution on farms (e.g. prescriptions about on-farm liquid manure storage and applications). This Act also imposes a certain maximum limit of

---

[47] These policy developments were further strengthened in 1996 through a new article in the Swiss constitution which further boosted the philosophy of farm incomes to be supported by direct payments aimed at rewarding farmers for environmentally-friendly farming practices.

LU/ha/UAA (levels depend on production zones), and has consequently required reductions of stocking rates on many farms since 1991. The *Environmental Protection Act* 1983, meanwhile, operates on the basis of the PPP and enforces strict regulations regarding chemical inputs on farms (e.g. maximum permissible levels; no fertiliser use near wetlands or woodlands) and on-farm soil and air pollution (e.g. emission standards for farm machinery). This shows that contrary to most EU countries that aim at regulating stocking rates or chemical input applications through voluntary agri-environmental schemes (e.g. UK, France, Germany), in Switzerland livestock densities and fertiliser/pesticide applications are largely controlled through regulatory mechanisms. Arguably, this leaves farmers with less freedom to manage their own land, but proponents of the regulatory framework have argued that this approach leads to better environmental protection on farms.

Other federal laws that regulate farmers' environmental management practices include the *Town and Country Planning Act* 1979 (regulations about farm consolidation; prevention of urban sprawl into the countryside), the *Animal Protection and Health Act* 1978 (animal welfare and hygiene; regulations about farm buildings for livestock), and the *Nature and Landscape Protection Act* 1966 (regulations regarding specific landscape features and areas of high ecological value often involving a management agreement with the landholder).

Production subsidies with environmental prescriptions and agri-environmental schemes (voluntary)

Since 1993, new agricultural policies have influenced farming practices through the introduction of production subsidies with environmental prescriptions (cross-compliance) (Article 31a), and by offering voluntary agri-environmental schemes (Article 31b). Overall, the Swiss direct payment system consists of five elements, including supplementary direct income payments (Article 31a), direct payments to compensate natural disadvantages (some of which have environmental implications; see below), agri-environmental schemes (Article 31b), direct payments linked to food production and quality (some of which have environmental implications), and hardship payments.

As Table 10.2 highlights, 4,857 MECU were spent between 1993 and 1996 on direct payments to farmers, of which about 27% had direct environmental implications (including agri-environmental schemes, direct payments for cultivation of steep meadows/alpine pastures, and subsidies for green fallow and renewable resources). However, to obtain supplementary income payments under Article 31a (40% of total payments), farmers also have to comply with a variety of criteria of which some include environmental prescriptions on the basis of the principle of cross-compliance. Thus, since 1996, apart from specific socio-economic criteria[48], farmers have to either participate in *ecological compensation schemes* or produce renewable resources on at least 5% of their farm area (from 1998 7% for farms in lowland areas). Taking cross-compliance under Article 31a into account, therefore, means that about two thirds of all direct payments to Swiss farmers have some implications for environmentally friendly farming practices, with a budget/ha/UAA by far exceeding that of other European countries. Thus, while about 1,500 ECU/ha/UAA have been available in Switzerland for agri-environmental measures between 1993 and 1996 (without any co-funding from the EU!), Austria – with the highest agri-environmental expenditure in the EU – has 'only' spent about 450 ECU/ha/UAA between 1993 and 1997 (including co-funding from the Community) (see Ch. 9), while the German agri-environmental budget of 75 ECU/ha/UAA (1993-1997) fades into virtual insignificance in comparison, despite being one of the highest agri-environmental spenders in the EU (see Ch. 7). In monetary terms, therefore, Switzerland emerges as the most committed European country with regard to implementation of policies with agri-environmental components. Average payments per holding have amounted to 18,000 ECU in Switzerland for the period between 1993 and 1996 (about 33% of all payments have gone to mountain farmers), while in Austria 'only' 6,000 ECU have been available on average (1993-1997). Discrepancies also exist with regard to payments for specific schemes. Organic farming payments in Austria are about 500 ECU/ha, while in Switzerland about 700 ECU/ha are available to farmers. The greatest differences exist with regard to support of alpine pastures and mountain meadows, where Swiss payments are almost double those in Austria.

As Table 10.2 highlights, one of the key elements of the new Swiss agricultural policy are agri-environmental schemes implemented under Article 31b. Although AEP only comprises 17% of the total budget for direct payments, this is nonetheless one of the highest AEP budgets in relation to direct subsidies or compensatory payments in the whole of Europe. As these schemes are aimed at directly addressing environmental problems in the Swiss countryside, and are not primarily directed at income aid (which is provided through the other direct payments indicated in Table 10.2), the issue of distinguishing between environmental schemes and

---

[48] Farms have to be above 3 ha; they are not allowed to employ more than 7 farm workers; the farmer has to be below 65 years of age; and the total agricultural income per year is not to exceed ECU 95,000.

Table 10.2 Direct payments to farmers in Switzerland 1993-1996

Type of direct payment	Payments 1993-1996 (MECU)	% of total payments
Supplementary direct income payments (Article 31 a)	1,953	40
Direct payments to compensate natural disadvantages	1,096	23
• Direct payments to livestock farms in mountain areas	*673*	
• Direct payments for cultivation of steep meadows/alpine pastures	*423*	
Agri-environmental schemes	820	17
• Schemes according to Article 31b	*677*	
• Extensive production of cereals	*143*	
Direct payments linked to food production and quality	745	15
• Subsidies for cows not in milk	*270*	
• Subsidies preventing silage feeding in dairy production	*156*	
• Subsidies encouraging milk use for cheese production	*117*	
• Subsidies for cultivation of fodder grains	*143*	
• Subsidies for green fallow and renewable resources (non-food crops)	*59*	
Hardship payments	243	5
Total	**4,857**	**100**

1 SFR = 0.63 ECU

Source: Bundesamt für Landwirtschaft, 1997

'hidden' income-support schemes is less problematic in Switzerland than in other countries discussed in this book.

Overall, five voluntary agri-environmental schemes have been implemented in Switzerland, all offering direct payments to farmers for specific environmentally friendly farming practices. All schemes are horizontal and available to any farm in the country[49], and farmers can participate in several schemes at the same time (with the exception of *integrated production* and *organic farming*) (Figure 10.1). The schemes *integrated production, ecological compensation* and *organic farming* are aimed at environmental protection, while the *free range farming scheme* and the scheme for *animal-friendly indoor farming installations* target the well-being of farm animals. On-farm targeting differs between the schemes: farmers participating in the schemes *integrated production* and *organic farming* must enter all their land, while those entering the *ecological compensation scheme* only have to farm 5-7% of their farm in environmentally friendly ways to be eligible for payments. In the following, a brief outline of these schemes is provided with regard to specific management prescriptions and payment levels.

Ecological Compensation   All measures comprised in this scheme apply for a minimum of six years. There are three categories of payments. The first category comprises payments for the continuation of extensive management of hay meadows, hedge management/restoration, and woodland management; the second category provides subsidies for environmentally friendly farming on both flower-rich fallow land and extensively managed meadows in arable areas; the third category gives financial aid for sustainable management of fruit orchards. All measures prohibit the use of chemical fertilisers and herbicides/pesticides, and on most land the application of organic manure is also forbidden. Farmers entering the *Ecological Compensation Scheme* have to agree to delay the cutting of hay on meadows before a fixed date which reflects the main seeding period of endangered plants (i.e. lowlands and foothill zone 15th June; lower mountain zones 1st July; high alpine meadows 15th July). Participants entering arable land into the scheme have to stop any arable production on that land, and on grassland farms the extent of pasture has to be maintained at 1994 levels (baseline year). Payment rates for the *Ecological Compensation Scheme* reflect the principle that participation in agri-environmental schemes should

---

[49] Farms have to be above 3 ha; they are not allowed to employ more than 7 farm workers; and the farm can not be managed by a national or regional authority. There is no age limit as is the case with Article 31a.

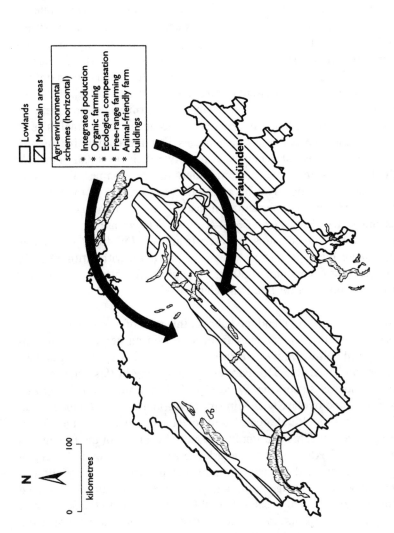

Figure 10.1 Agri-environmental schemes in Switzerland under Article 31b

Source: Authors

not negatively affect farmers' incomes. Payments are, therefore, intended to compensate farmers for the cost increases and/or revenue losses associated with abandoning conventional farm management practices on all, or part, of their farm. This has meant that in some cases payments have been set at very high levels, particularly when compared to payments in agri-environmental schemes in EU Members States. Participants in the measures for *management of flower-rich fallow land* and *extensive management of hay meadows*, for example, currently receive about 1,900 ECU/ha (same rate for all farmers) – a sum that would be considered excessive in most EU Member States (see other chapters in this book). These very high payments reflect, first, that Switzerland is one of the wealthiest countries in Europe (second only to Luxembourg in terms of per capita GDP) and can, therefore, afford the 'luxury' of high agri-environmental payments, second, that great emphasis is placed on encouraging farmers to farm in environmentally friendly ways and, third, that payments take into account the small size of most Swiss farms (see above), which means that the cumulative income through agri-environmental schemes is usually relatively small (i.e. only small eligible areas involved). As in other agri-environmental schemes discussed in this book, the payments also reflect the severity of management changes required through particular measures, and payments for other measures under the *Ecological Compensation Scheme* are usually lower than the above-mentioned sums, ranging from 300-750 ECU for private woodland management (in this case payments decrease with altitude) or 10 ECU/fruit tree/year (maximum of 300 trees eligible) for sustainable orchard management (Bundesamt für Landwirtschaft, 1997).

Integrated Production As mentioned above, this type of agri-environmental scheme sets Switzerland most apart from its European neighbours and, as will be discussed below, *Integrated Production* also takes up the largest part of the budget under Article 31b. Farmers participating in this scheme must follow the standards set by the *Professional Organisation for Integrated Farming* (accredited by the Swiss Ministry of Agriculture), and must farm at least 5% of their agricultural area (7% in lowlands) under the principles of integrated production. This can imply substantial changes in the timing and application rates of external inputs in order to achieve the required nitrogen balance on the farm, and the use of herbicides/pesticides is only allowed when the expected damage through pests (as a result of reduced applications) is expected to exceed 'tolerable' levels. Due to the severity of required changes payments are set at relatively high levels, ranging from 750 ECU/ha for integrated production of special crops (vineyards, fruit production, vegetables, etc.), to 500 ECU/ha for other crops (cereals, potatoes, root crops, etc.), to 'only' 270 ECU for integrated grassland management. In order to prevent excessive payouts to large farms only the first 50 ha are eligible for full funding, and only 50% are paid for any further land.

Organic Farming Similar to organic farms in EU countries who have to adhere to strict guidelines (e.g. Regulation 2092/91), Swiss farmers wishing to participate in the *Organic Farming Scheme* must follow the standards set by the *Swiss Organic Farming Association*. Farmers accepted into the scheme are allowed to sell their products with the organic label (the so-called 'Knospe' label) at slightly higher rates than 'conventional' products. Organic farmers have to fulfil all the requirements for integrated production mentioned above, and in addition the use of synthetic pesticides/herbicides and most synthetic fertilisers is forbidden. Due to both the severity of changes needed to convert farms to organic production and because integrated production methods are the baseline requirements for acceptance into the scheme, payment levels are again set very high. Farmers receive 1100 ECU/ha for organic production of special crops (vineyards, fruit production, vegetables, etc.), 880 ECU/ha for other crops (cereals, potatoes, root crops, etc.), and 330 ECU/ha for grassland. As for integrated production, the first 50 ha of a farm are eligible for full funding, while only 50% are paid for any further land entered.

Free Range Farming Scheme Contrary to the three above-mentioned schemes that directly target environmental concerns, this scheme is aimed at increasing the well-being of farm animals. Payments ranging from 75 ECU/LU for cattle and 150 ECU/LU for poultry are available to farmers willing to adopt free range farming practices. Participants also have to adhere to strict guidelines about adequate conditions within cowsheds and poultry rearing installations.

Scheme for animal-friendly indoor farming installations Similar to the above scheme, this scheme is aimed at improving animal welfare in indoor farming installations. Introduced in 1996, the scheme aims at providing an alternative for farmers who are not able to provide outdoor farming facilities for their livestock. Participants have to make provisions for animals to be able to move around in their buildings, and payments range from 40-75 ECU/LU/year depending on the type of animal.

Farmers' acceptance of agri-environmental schemes

As highlighted in the previous section, Swiss agri-environmental schemes under Article 31b are horizontal, target many farmers, and have budgets per ha/UAA that often exceed those of agri-environmental schemes in EU countries. As a result of these relatively favourable conditions, farmer participation in schemes has been very high. Table 10.3 shows that both land entered into the various schemes and total payments to farmers have increased steadily between 1994 and 1996, with total payments in 1996 being four times higher than in 1994. The *scheme promoting integrated farming*, in particular, stands out as one of the largest agri-environmental schemes in Europe, with 646,000 ha enrolled into the scheme equivalent to 60% of the entire Swiss agricultural area (excluding alpine pastures), and with payments to farmers amounting to 263 MECU in 1996 alone (70% of all agri-environmental payments) – more than three times the available budget in the relatively large MEKA programme in Germany in the same year (see Ch. 7). *Organic farming* is the second largest agri-environmental scheme in Switzerland with 54,000 ha entered (5% of Swiss agricultural area; in comparison 7% of the Austrian agricultural area is farmed organically). As farmers are not permitted to enter both schemes (see above), this means that 700,000 ha (65% of total agricultural area; 60% of farms) are cultivated according to environmentally friendly farming principles (in 1996). Further, measures falling under the umbrella of the *ecological compensation scheme* (sustainable management of fruit orchards; extensive management of hay meadows; extensively managed meadows in arable areas) altogether have covered an area of about 75,000 ha in 1996 (7% of agricultural area), and the *measure encouraging sustainable management of fruit orchards* has also been well received by farmers, with 2.4 million fruit trees entered into the scheme by 1996.

Despite this promising start and the generally favourable response by farmers towards schemes under Article 31b, the aim of Swiss policy-makers is to further increase the number of participants in schemes. Thus, instead of the current 7% of land entered under the *ecological compensation scheme* it is hoped that at least 10% will be entered in the near future. Further, although the *free range farming scheme* has shown remarkable increases (almost double the number of LU entered in 1996 compared to 1995), only about 20% of all livestock in Switzerland are currently in the scheme and the aim is to substantially increase that figure in the 21st century. The most ambitious goals have been set for a further increase in participation in both the *integrated farming* and *organic farming* schemes.

Table 10.3 Land entered and payments to farmers in Swiss agri-environmental schemes 1994-1996

Schemes and measures[1]	1994		1995		1996	
	MECU	1000 ha	MECU	1000 ha	MECU	1000 ha
Integrated production	43.9	298	98.5	364	262.8	646
Organic farming	3.6	21	8.9	28	24.8	54
Sustainable management of fruit orchards	13.2	2.1 million trees	20.9	2.2 million trees	22.6	2.4 million trees
Free range farming scheme	4.4	118,000 LU	5.5	146,000 LU	20	255,000 LU
Extensive management of hay meadows; hedge and woodland conservation	9.2	22	12	23	16.4	31
Extensively managed meadows in arable areas	3.6	2	5.1	2.8	8	4.8
Animal friendly indoor farming installations	0	0	0	0	3.8	94,000 LU
Total	77.9		150.9		358.4	

(1) The measure for environmentally friendly farming on flower-rich fallow land is not listed as payments and land entered are negligible

Source: Bundesamt für Landwirtschaft, 1997

Although these schemes have already been very successful (see above), the ultimate aim is to achieve participation of all Swiss farmers in either of these schemes by the year 2002 (Schweizerischer Bundesrat, 1996).

Early indications are that Swiss agri-environmental schemes have been relatively successful in preventing further environmental degradation in the worst affected intensively farmed areas (where participation has been relatively good), and that they have helped to maintain farming activities in marginal upland areas (e.g. Hanser, 1991; Sironi and Peter, 1993). A recent investigation by a Swiss/UK team of researchers in the region of

Graubünden (eastern Switzerland; see Figure 10.1), for example, revealed that farmer participation in individual measures encouraging the continuation of environmentally friendly farming practices on steep mountain meadows and alpine pastures was almost 100% (Wilson *et al.*, 1996). Farmers in the region commented very favourably about the important additionality effects that agri-environmental schemes were having for their overall farm incomes, and a substantial proportion of farmers interviewed argued that participation in schemes had made them recognise how environmentally valuable their farmland was – especially with regard to aesthetic and scenic values and as a resource attracting crucial tourist income. Officials implementing the schemes in Graubünden were generally satisfied with the way the schemes were running, but complaints were voiced – as elsewhere in Europe – that the budgets for the monitoring of scheme compliance were too limited to ensure that farmers were always complying with scheme prescriptions. The problem of scheme monitoring may be a particular concern in relatively inaccessible mountain areas.

Is the Swiss agri-environmental programme comparable with EU policies?

The above analysis of the Swiss agri-environmental programme has highlighted that the Swiss approach to countryside protection has been very similar to that of its EU neighbours. Although Swiss AEP has been developed outside the framework of the EU and the CAP accompanying measures, Article 31b – which provided the framework for Swiss AEP – shares many similarities with Regulation 2078. However, it was also highlighted that there are some differences between the EU and Swiss approaches, particularly with regard to the Swiss emphasis on regulatory countryside protection mechanisms. In the context of this book, which mainly analyses implementation of Regulation 2078 in EU countries, it is, therefore, crucial to ask the question how comparable Swiss AEP is with EU policies? This question is particularly important in view of possible Swiss EU membership in the near future (despite narrow rejection of Swiss membership in recent public referenda).

Swiss AEP has not operated in isolation from the rest of Europe and has not been developed in a policy vacuum. As both Wilson *et al.* (1996) and Curry and Stucki (1997) have highlighted, during the formulation of its agri-environmental programme Switzerland has not only built on its own experiences with countryside protection mechanisms (dating back to the 1970s), but it has also taken into account agri-environmental programmes in neighbouring EU Member States, particularly the Austrian ÖPUL programme (see Ch. 9) and the German MEKA and KULAP schemes (see Ch. 7). Popp (1990) argued, for example, that the Bavarian KULAP programme provided important insights for the development of Article 31b in Switzerland, and discussions about EU-compatibility of the MEKA scheme in Baden-Württemberg in 1993 were also intensively followed by Swiss policy-makers. However, other countries have also learnt from the Swiss experience during formulation of their agri-environmental programmes, and the ÖPUL programme in Austria, in particular, was formulated after extensive discussions with Swiss policy-makers about their experiences with countryside protection schemes in mountainous areas (e.g. restrictions on the feeding of silage to livestock apply in both the Swiss agri-environmental programme and ÖPUL)[50]. Thus, there has already been a tendency for mutual and reciprocal influence in AEP formulation between Switzerland and EU Member States.

The similarities between the Swiss agri-environmental programme and other EU AEPs would suggest that implications of Swiss EU membership would not be too dramatic. Indeed, there are already signs of convergence between AEPs in countries currently outside the EU (e.g. Poland, Czech Republic, Hungary and Slovenia) with Regulation 2078 (Petersen, 1999), and the same is true for Switzerland. This can be largely explained by the fact that agricultural policies in all European countries have been influenced to a great extent by the liberalisation of world trade through the GATT agreements which, arguably, have shaped the trajectories of AEPs much more than, for example, the wish to protect the European countryside (Potter, 1998). Convergence of AEP between EU and non-EU Member States may, thus, be less a result of European transnational efforts at harmonisation of AEP, than a response to increasingly similar socio-economic, structural and environmental problems. It could be argued, therefore, that Swiss AEP shows more similarities with some neighbouring EU countries such as Austria or Germany than would be true for countries within the EU such as, for example, Greece (see Ch. 5) and Sweden (see Ch. 4).

There are, nonetheless, some important differences between Swiss and EU agri-environmental approaches. The Swiss emphasis on regulatory mechanisms to solve pollution problems caused by agriculture, for example, goes against the voluntary principle inherent in EU AEP. Although the same may be true for EU countries that have favoured an approach based on the

---

[50] The Swiss emphasis on animal welfare is another interesting case in point. Switzerland has, so far, been the only European country to implement substantial schemes tackling animal welfare issues, and EU policy-makers are currently contemplating incorporation of new policy mechanisms similar to those already implemented in Swizterland into *Agenda 2000* that would help address animal welfare problems across the EU.

PPP (e.g. Sweden, Denmark, and to some extent Germany), the fact that agricultural pollution issues are not explicitly addressed in the current Swiss agri-environmental programme would cause problems if the Swiss programme had to be adapted to Regulation 2078. Of similar importance would be the issue of very high agri-environmental payments. As was stated above, average agri-environmental payments per ha/UAA in Switzerland by far exceed even the most generous payments in EU Member States such as Austria or Germany. However, cutting the high agri-environmental payments to Swiss farmers could result in severe hardship – especially in the environmentally and socio-economically vulnerable mountain zones. It is no coincidence, therefore, that the most vociferous opponents of Swiss EU membership have traditionally been the Swiss farmers who fear that they would have to pay the highest price for EU accession compared to other economic sectors in Switzerland. Yet, there is no reason why the Swiss system could not operate as successfully as the Austrian ÖPUL programme (which has much lower payments for its farmers).

Changes to Swiss AEP have been substantial in the 1990s, and policies are still subject to continuous restructuring. Although Articles 31a and 31b have provided a relatively comprehensive framework for countryside management, the aim is to introduce a new agricultural policy by 1999 which will require minimum ecological standards which farmers will have to fulfil in order to obtain direct payments (currently farmers still receive payments to compensate for the loss of income due to changes in the pricing system) (Schweizerischer Bundesrat, 1996). Swiss discussions about the de-coupling of agricultural subsidies from agri-environmental payments, therefore, mirror current discussions surrounding *Agenda 2000* in the EU (e.g. Buckwell *et al.*, 1998; Potter, 1998). It is very likely, therefore, that Swiss AEP will become even more similar to EU policies in the next few years.

11 Portugal: agri-environmental policy and the maintenance of biodiversity-rich extensive farming systems

Peter Eden and Miguel Vieira

Portuguese agriculture: constraints and opportunities

Agriculture in Portugal has been influenced by a diverse landscape with large geological, climatic and topographic variations over a relatively small territory. Northern parts of the country are influenced by Atlantic climatic conditions with 400 to 3,000 mm of rain, while the south is characterised by a Mediterranean climate with considerably lower average rainfall (350-600 mm). Farm structures differ considerably across the country, with the north characterised by small family farms with average sizes of less than 5 ha, usually practising polyculture with a small irrigated area and with some tree crops and livestock. Farms in the south are considerably larger with an average size of over 20 ha and with many farms of over 500 ha. Traditional crops in the south include cereals, olives, vines and livestock which graze the *montados* (holm and cork oak woodlands with natural grazing). Southern agricultural landscapes in Portugal contain many of the most important and best preserved Mediterranean wildlife habitats on the Iberian peninsula (Beaufoy *et al.*, 1994).

Portugal's agriculture has remained relatively extensive, resulting in low levels of self-sufficiency. Thus, earlier in the 20th century the government attempted to make the country self-sufficient in cereals and promoted a campaign to intensify production through high grain prices (Black, 1992). This led to the clearance of large areas of *montado* and the ploughing up of shallow soils to expand the cropping area and, consequently, caused great problems of soil erosion. Yet, as in Spain (see Ch. 8), Portugal does not have the same type of environmental problems that northern European countries have with regard to pollution from excessive use of external inputs. As will be discussed in detail in the next section,

Portuguese environmental problems are rather caused through the mismanagement of valuable habitats, largely as a result of socio-economic changes that have taken place over the recent past. Nonetheless, Portugal still contains many important and biodiversity-rich wildlife habitats which have been shaped by centuries of extensive (and arguable environmentally sustainable) farming practices. Indeed, that many traditional farming systems have survived to the present day has allowed the conservation of some of the most important European habitats and species, although many of these habitats are now being threatened by rapid changes in agricultural practices (Beaufoy *et al.*, 1994).

Yet, Portuguese agriculture has not only undergone changes from an environmental perspective. When Portugal joined the EEC in 1986, rural Portugal was already going through a crisis as a result of more than 40 years of political and economic isolation (Williams, 1992; Syrett, 1995). Since the 1960s, in particular, the rural economy suffered increasingly from misguided political decisions, and consequently the drift from the land accelerated with rural people moving to coastal industrialised areas or emigrating to other European countries (IEADR, 1993). Rural areas had been particularly badly affected by socio-political events related to the left-wing agrarian reform following the 1974 political revolution. Most commentators agree that this agrarian reform failed completely and destroyed the agrarian structure of the larger farm businesses found in the centre and south of the country (Black, 1992). Accession to the EEC was, therefore, initially seen by farmers as a positive move that would help counteract previous decades of rural decline. Indeed, EEC membership provided an opportunity to gain access to European funding and to new markets and technology, but adaptation to the new conditions proved extremely difficult for Portuguese farmers due to strong competition from other European producers which caused the collapse of many internal markets and accentuated the drift from rural to urban areas. Smaller farms located in the north, in particular, became uneconomic and unable to support the families who worked them, although in some areas small local industries have helped maintain some of these smallholdings as part-time farms by giving alternative employment. In the south, increased industrial and tourist employment opportunities developed in coastal areas around Lisbon, Setúbal and the Algarve led many rural people to move to the cities. It is only recently that areas in the interior of southern Portugal have designated industrial zones in an attempt to attract new business and maintain rural communities.

European funding has had a differential impact in Portuguese rural areas. Larger farms, particularly in the south, invested heavily in modernisation of buildings and equipment, making use of European funding, but also borrowing from banks which were happy to lend due to the rising prices of farmland. Yet, the CAP reform towards extensification in 1992 changed the whole logic of these investments, causing immense problems to farmers who had just started to modernise their 'backward' holdings. The result has been that debts are often no longer covered by the falling value of farms (negative equity), thus creating a difficult financial situation for many rural communities (only few farms have overcome these financial problems so far). The result of these developments has been a continuous drop in the active population involved in agriculture from 26% in 1981, to 17% in 1991, to only 12% in 1996. Agriculture now has much less importance in areas close to industrial centres and tourist areas such as the Algarve and much of the coastline.

Changing agricultural practices and environmental impacts[51]

The entry of Portugal into the EEC in 1986 caused fundamental changes to Portuguese agriculture, in particular through the intensification of crops and rotations and the introduction of new cultures often less suited than traditional crops to Portugal's environmental conditions. The main driving force for these changes were the CAP subsidies for selected products and the concurrent drop in Portuguese market prices after the opening of the borders to foreign competition. As a result, cereal production was strongly intensified with the introduction of new machinery and crop varieties, resulting in higher use of fertilisers, herbicides and fungicides.

A few examples may illustrate the rapid changes that have taken place and the increasing environmental impact that modern agriculture is now having in Portugal. Irrigation of areas with cereals using central pivot irrigators, for example, has become more common due to continued high subsidies given to irrigated crops. This has meant that traditional rotations of 3-5 years have often been replaced by continuous cereal growing. It has also led to increased water use (a scarce commodity in many parts of Portugal) and associated pollution of both subterranean and surface waters. In particular, environmentally demanding crops such as sunflowers (for oil production) have been highly subsidised and, consequently, the area of sunflower crops has increased dramatically in southern parts of Portugal, replacing less environmentally damaging crops such as chick-peas and melons in traditional rotation. Similarly, there has been a substantial

---

[51] Official information about the impacts of different agricultural practices on the environment is still scarce in Portugal, and only in a few years time will 'official' results of environmental research projects become available.

expansion in the production of maize, particularly in southern regions with intensive irrigation and fertilisation, and fruit and vegetable production also increased considerably in the Algarve and along the west coast.

The main environmental impacts of this intensification and change in agricultural land use have been associated with the draining and ploughing of wetlands with associated wildlife losses (especially rare birds). General loss of habitats has also had severe effects on threatened species requiring vast and undisturbed areas for feeding and reproduction such as the lynx, certain raptors (especially the imperial eagle, the golden eagle, Bonelli's eagle and vultures), the great bustard and other steppe birds, as well as many wintering species from northern Europe. These impacts have been exacerbated by the introduction of new intensive technologies such as greenhouses and drip irrigation, making use of more plastic materials and agro-chemicals. Further, imported exotic breeds have increasingly been used for crossing local livestock breeds to increase meat production and profits, leading to the depletion of the genetic pool of local breeds of horses, cattle, sheep, goats and pigs.

Yet, at the same time as Portuguese agriculture has intensified during the 1990s, there has also been a trend towards extensification and abandonment of traditional cultures and farming systems in marginal farming areas (Black, 1992). Some of this extensification has been linked to policies related to the 1992 CAP reform, but trends towards extensification and abandonment had been apparent since World War Two. Especially on poor soils there has been pronounced extensification or abandonment of cereal farming, with reversion to natural pastures and extensive livestock grazing. Large areas with poor soils in isolated regions are now completely abandoned, with concurrent environmental problems linked to scrub encroachment and soil erosion on unmaintained agricultural terraces. Traditional fruit orchards and olive groves, usually associated with small farms particularly suffering from market competition, have also often been abandoned. In the case of olive groves, the abandonment is largely due to the lack of human resources in depopulated rural districts and the difficulty of mechanising olive picking operations. The abandonment of olive groves has had particularly negative impacts on the number of migratory birds that use the groves for wintering.

The important wildlife habitats of the extensively used *montados* have particularly suffered from recent changes. As a traditional 'silvi-agri-pastoral farming system' (Black, 1992; IEADR, 1993), covering about 25% of the Portuguese UAA, the *montados* rely on a complex and continuous extensive management system of both forest and grazing land. However, such 'dual' management does not fit into the CAP regulations which clearly divide land management into either agriculture or forestry (Regulations

2078 and 2080/92 respectively). The general trend of land abandonment in the *montados* could, therefore, not be halted by agri-environmental schemes that were unsuitable to farmers in these areas (see below), resulting in many areas in the abandonment of the traditional *montados* management regime, the removal of trees, and overgrazing. From an environmental perspective this has led to a lack of tree regeneration, the ageing of the *montados* woodlands, scrub invasion and associated loss of biodiversity.

The discussion so far has highlighted that in Portugal, as in other Mediterranean countries (see Chs. 5 and 8), the survival of biodiversity-rich wildlife habitats has relied on century-old extensive farming systems. However, many areas of high environmental importance are losing their value because of rural depopulation and the abandonment of traditional farming practices that have helped maintain high biodiversity. Portuguese policy-makers, therefore, had to recognise that the key to enhancing environmental management in the Portuguese countryside is to find a strategy which would help conserve the human management activities needed to maintain the environmental values of the different traditional farming systems. Traditional Portuguese farming systems need not only to be subsidised but also to be updated to provide sufficient income for the local population. This requires outside support, practical research, and the development of commercial structures (including marketing strategies). At the same time, the professional ability of farmers to manage their land sustainably has to be improved through training courses and improved extension services. To some extent, the Portuguese agri-environmental programme in response to Regulation 2078 has attempted to address these concerns.

The Portuguese agri-environmental programme

The politics of agri-environmental policy in Portugal

As other chapters in this book have highlighted, policy change usually takes place as a result of the recognition of problems by a variety of environmental actors and interest groups. In Portugal, the debate over the relations between agriculture and the environment started late and only gained momentum in the 1990s with the advent of the CAP reform. Before accession to the EEC in 1986, political parties, farming organisations and most of the farmers were indifferent to the need of integrating the environment into agricultural policies. Low public interest in the environment can also be explained by the fact that environmental NGOs were virtually non-existent before 1986, depriving the political debate from a critical and environmentally conscious voice. This means that without the external pressure resulting from the CAP reform, changes in Portugal would have been slower and much more gradual. Accession to the CAP, therefore, forced Portuguese policy-makers to quickly adapt to a new policy situation and to question the productivist ideology that has dominated agricultural decision-making. To some extent, this has increased communication between different actors, highlighted for example in the fact that the proposed zonal agri-environmental schemes (see below) will each have a management committee composed of representatives from the Ministry of Agriculture, the Ministry of the Environment, the Regional Planning Unit, local farmers' associations and local county councils. This committee may also consult with other bodies such as local agricultural universities or relevant NGOs involved in the region. Yet, the Portuguese administration lacks trained human resources to deal with the new challenges emanating from Regulation 2078, and policy-making is further complicated by the fact that Portugal had no experience with agri-environmental schemes before 1992 (see also Chs. 5 and 8). Regulation 797/85, for example, was only partially implemented, and there was no reference to *Article 19* in the final policy response. Similarly, Regulation 2328/91 (the amendment to Regulation 797/85) was implemented as a policy aimed at improving the efficiency of agricultural structures, without specific reference to Articles 3 and 21-24 aimed at encouraging environmentally friendly farming.

Agricultural policy-making in Portugal has also been affected by highly uneven political power among its farmers. While small family farmers in the north are poorly organised with regard to political lobbying and farmers' unions, southern farmers are usually better organised and have more political influence (partly linked to their greater wealth). This fundamental difference between north and south has resulted in a different participation of farmers in the public debate about both the adaptation of Regulation 2078 to the Portuguese context and its implementation on the ground. Thus, northern farmers did not have any substantial participation in the drafting process of the national agri-environmental programme in response to Regulation 2078. Southern farmers' organisations, meanwhile, took a very conservative position towards the CAP reform and lobbied strongly for Regulation 2078 to be regarded as an income support policy with only minimal environmental obligations. The Portuguese administration was strongly influenced by the powerful southern farmers' lobby, and, as a result, the Portuguese agri-environmental programme has been implemented differentially between the north and the south. In the north, policies under Regulation 2078 are more socially oriented (at least in theory) in order to address the problems of land abandonment (i.e. more measures for rural communities), while in the south income support for individual farmers has been the prime objective (see also Figure 11.1 below). The environmental component of the policies has been relatively minimal throughout, although (and as will be discussed in detail below) some positive policy elements have been introduced that are genuinely aimed at improving environmental management of the Portuguese countryside. Indeed, the application of Regulation 2078 in 1994 was the first opportunity for Portuguese farmers to benefit from environmentally based supports, including organic farming and the establishment of ESAs (see Table 11.1 below).

Despite the fact that some communication has taken place in the last few years between a variety of policy actors, agricultural policy-making in Portugal is still characterised by a highly centralised agricultural administration. Overall responsibility for the design and administration of agricultural policies and the Portuguese agri-environmental programme under Regulation 2078 continues to rest in the hands of the central office of the Ministry of Agriculture in Lisbon (Ministério da Agricultura, 1991, 1994). Information about the different schemes and measures is divulged to the farmers in a top-down manner, and farmers' applications are dealt with at the local level through county extension offices of the Ministry of Agriculture with the help of local farming associations and co-operatives. Although the processing of applications is done by regional Ministry of Agriculture departments, and decisions on acceptability are also taken at a regional level, regional and local offices perform mostly bureaucratic tasks and do not have any significant autonomy. Indeed, over the last 20 years, duties of local administrators have changed, leading to more paper work and leaving the farming community with little technical and organisational support. This is particularly exemplified by the fact that the *Institute for Funding and Support for the Development of Agriculture and Fisheries* is responsible for the financial management of the Portuguese agri-environmental programme – and not the regional or local extension services – and this institute is also in charge of monitoring compliance with the different measures (as in many other EU countries, organic farming and integrated production are monitored by independent bodies). This hierarchical administrative structure which has increasingly concentrated decision-making powers at the centre has, therefore, important implications for the implementation of AEP in that it allows little flexibility or adaptation of specific policies to regional or local circumstances.

Arguably most important, however, is that most agricultural policy-makers in Portugal are still caught in the productivist ethos. Only very recently has the environment begun to be seen as an important factor for Portuguese society. Although in 1988 the Environment Ministry was created

Table 11.1 Planned and existing agri-environmental schemes in Portugal

Scheme	Objectives	Proposed targeting	Expected eligible area (ha)/eligible stock (LU)
1. Reduction of Agricultural Pollution			
1.1 Reduced use of agri-chemicals	Controlled use of agri-chemicals on farms	Horizontal	40,700
1.2 Integrated crop protection	Improved application and timing of agri-chemicals	Horizontal	5,300
1.3 Integrated crop production	Reduction of use of agri-chemicals and improved timing of applications	Horizontal	1,000
1.4 Organic farming	Introduction or continuation of organic farming practices	Horizontal	8,200
2. Extensification and/or maintenance of traditional agricultural systems			
2.1 Traditional polycultural systems	Halt abandonment of traditional farming systems	Zonal (northern and central Portugal)	69,000
2.2 Dryland cereal farming systems	Maintain cereal rotation on small farms	Zonal (areas with marginal soils)	53,800
2.3 Water meadows ('*lameiros*')	Preserve flora and traditional irrigation systems (local breeds)	Zonal (northern and central Portugal)	26,900
2.4 Extensive grazing systems	Avoid abandonment or intensification of these systems	Zonal (extensive grazing systems)	191,500
2.5 Traditional olive groves	Maintain traditional olive grove management	Zonal	53,700
2.6 Fig groves of '*Terras Novas*'	Stop abandonment of traditional fig groves	Zonal	3,000
2.7 Terraced vineyards	Maintain traditional vineyard landscapes	Zonal (Douro Valley)	10,200
2.8 Fruit orchards with local varieties	Preservation of local/regional fruit varieties	Horizontal	1,500
2.9 Traditional dry orchards	Preserve typical landscape	Zonal (Barrocal region in Algarve)	12,500

2.10 Traditional dry almond groves	Preserve traditional landscape	Zonal (hilly interior in northern Portugal)	6,600
2.11 Holm oak landscapes ('*montados*')	Preserve ecosystem for environmental reasons	Zonal (interior southern Portugal)	125,000
2.12 Arable conversion to extensive pastures	Conversion to extensive pastoral systems	Zonal (areas with poor soils)	44,000
2.13 Local breeds	Conserve genetic diversity	Horizontal	50,000 LU
2.14 Extensification of livestock production	Reduction of stocking densities of dairy herds	Zonal	2,000 LU
3. Conservation of natural resources and rural landscapes			
3.1 Maintenance of abandoned forest areas	Reduce fire risk and erosion	Zonal	41,900 (with 3.2)
3.2 Maintenance of small forest areas on farms	Fire control	Zonal (pine, oak and chestnut forests in northern Portugal)	41,900 (with 3.1)
3.3 Preservation of native trees and shrubs	Preservation of ecological value	Horizontal	21,000
3.4 Maintenance of farmland	Reduce fire risk	Zonal (interior forest areas)	5,300
3.5 Environmentally Sensitive Areas	Maintain traditional farming systems	Zonal (only Castro Verde zonal scheme implemented so far)	64,000
4. Training Courses and Demonstration Projects			
4.1 Training courses	Training for extension services and farmers	Horizontal	1,140 training courses
4.2 Demonstration projects	Establishment of demonstration units	Horizontal	50 demonstration projects

Source: IEADR, 1994; Ministério da Agricultura, 1994, 1995; EC, 1997a

with a section dedicated to nature conservation, the environment is poorly integrated into the wider policy framework. Worst of all, the environmental administration is severely under-staffed and under-funded, often leading to a breakdown in communication between the Environment Ministry and other policy actors.

Agri-environmental schemes

As with implementation of Regulation 2078 in many other EU countries (see other chapters in this book), it is important to distinguish between ambitions and facts of the Portuguese agri-environmental programme. Table 11.1 outlines implemented and proposed schemes under Regulation 2078 in Portugal. It is important to note that only part of these schemes have so far been implemented, and that the targeted eligible area has not yet been achieved in most schemes due to budgetary restrictions. For example, although seven ESAs have been planned (scheme 3.5 in the Table), only one scheme (Castro Verde) has so far been implemented (see below). Similarly, although the scheme *maintenance of traditional polycultural farming systems* (2.1) targets a relatively large area (69,000 ha) with small farms in the north and centre of Portugal (in urgent need of funding of rural communities to prevent land abandonment), there are currently no mechanisms under Regulation 2078 able to generate new economic activities in depressed rural areas at the required level. This scheme, therefore, is currently a hypothetical scheme rather than reality, and plans for its implementation will in fact be discontinued after 1998 (see below). Further, although Portugal has proposed a relatively ambitious programme of training courses and demonstration projects (4.1 and 4.2), these initiatives have so far suffered from low success rates, largely because of a lack of interest from local and regional bodies. Yet, as Table 11.1 highlights, Portugal has made a concerted effort to suggest a relatively ambitious and expensive agri-environmental programme, and with regard to real agri-environmental expenditure per ha/UAA (1993-1997) Portugal emerges as a 'medium' expenditure country with about 50 ECU/ha/UAA (including EU contribution) (IEADR, 1995; EC, 1997a). This places Portugal well above Greece and Spain in terms of financial commitment to agri-environmental schemes (see Chs. 5 and 8), and even puts it above relatively 'large' implementers such as France (see Ch. 2). It remains to be seen, however, whether planned implementation will be followed through with tangible policies and opportunities for farmers 'on the ground'.

As Table 11.1 highlights, the Portuguese agri-environmental programme has four main objectives: the reduction of agricultural pollution, extensification and/or maintenance of traditional agricultural systems, the conservation of natural resources and rural landscapes, and the establishment of training courses and demonstration projects (IEADR, 1994; Ministério da Agricultura, 1994). By far the largest areas targeted by schemes[52] fall under *extensification and/or maintenance of traditional agricultural systems* which aim at addressing many of the problems of Portuguese agriculture outlined below (Figure 11.1). The schemes *extensive grazing systems* (2.4 in the Table) and *montados* (2.11), in particular, have expected eligible areas well above 100,000 ha and will include substantial numbers of farmers once they are fully implemented. Schemes for the *maintenance of traditional polycultural and dryland cereal farming systems* (2.1 and 2.2) are also relatively important, as well as the *scheme for the maintenance of traditional olive groves* (2.5). Table 11.1 emphasises that relatively small areas are targeted for the reduction of agricultural pollution, with the exception of the *scheme for reduced use of agri-chemicals* (1.1) which will have an eligible area of over 40,000 ha, thus reflecting the relatively low priority given to agricultural pollution problems outlined above. An interesting aspect of the Portuguese agri-environmental programme are the schemes related to the maintenance of traditional forest ecosystems on farms (3.1-3.3), which in most other EU countries are part of Regulation 2080/92 rather than 2078[53]. Schemes aimed at the *reduction of fire risk and erosion* are similar to some of the planned schemes in the Spanish agri-environmental programme (see Ch. 8), but the *scheme for the preservation of native trees and shrubs* (3.3) and the large scheme for the *maintenance of the montados* (2.11) emphasise the importance of remnant semi-natural forest and shrub associations on Portuguese farms and the need for specific policies to address the special management needs of these ecosystems.

The Portuguese agri-environmental programme is still in its infancy, and, as in Spain and Greece, only the first initial steps towards implementation have been undertaken. The programme was only ratified in 1994, and many schemes have not yet been implemented on a large scale (IEADR, 1994; Ministério da Agricultura, 1994). It is, therefore, too early to comment on the relative success of the various schemes, and only little information is available about farmers' reactions to existing and proposed schemes. One of the exceptions where some information on scheme effectiveness is available is the *organic farming scheme* (1.4). Information

---

[52] At the time of printing, no accurate information was available about the planned budgets for individual schemes.

[53] Exceptions are some of the ESAs in the UK which target oak woodlands (see Ch. 6) and Swiss (Ch. 10) and Austrian (Ch. 9) agri-environmental programmes.

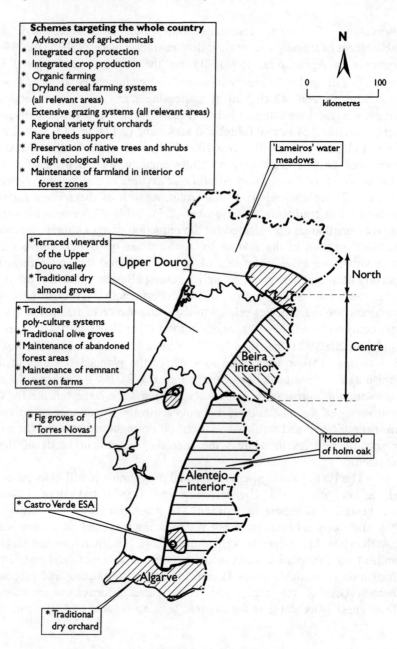

Schemes targeting the whole country
* Advisory use of agri-chemicals
* Integrated crop protection
* Integrated crop production
* Organic farming
* Dryland cereal farming systems
  (all relevant areas)
* Extensive grazing systems (all relevant areas)
* Regional variety fruit orchards
* Rare breeds support
* Preservation of native trees and shrubs
  of high ecological value
* Maintenance of farmland in interior of
    forest zones

N

0   100
kilometres

'Lameiros' water
meadows

*Terraced vineyards
 of the Upper
 Douro valley
*Traditional dry
 almond groves

Upper Douro

North

* Traditonal
poly-culture systems
* Traditional olive groves
* Maintenance of abandoned
forest areas
* Maintenance of remnant
forest on farms

Centre

Beira
interior

* Fig groves of
'Torres Novas'

'Montado'
of holm oak

Alentejo
interior

* Castro Verde ESA

Algarve

* Traditional
dry orchard

**Figure 11.1   Agri-environmental schemes in Portugal under
                Regulation 2078**

Source: Authors

is available because Portugal had already partly implemented Regulation 2092/91 (organic farming) before putting into place its new agri-environmental programme in 1994. Farmers' initial response to schemes under Regulation 2092/91 was relatively poor, largely due to a lack of interest and financial support. The first true financial mechanism for organic farming was established under Regulation 3828/85 in 1992, although farmers could only apply for reimbursement of investment costs. The implementation of the *organic scheme* under Regulation 2078 introduced compensation payments for conversion to and maintenance of organic farming, increasing substantially both the interest of farmers and the area under organic farming (8,200 ha target area). The rising interest of farmers in converting to organic farming stems largely from the fact that payments are now seen to be 'adequate' (IEADR, 1995). Further, technical support that can be obtained from an already existing organic farming association has helped to attract more applicants to this scheme. Another scheme that appears to have been relatively successful is the *scheme for the maintenance of local breeds* (2.13). Early indications are that this scheme is proving to be extremely important and effective and has contributed to enhancing the interest of farmers in increasing both the number of rare animals and the number of different rare breeds under threat from crossing with exotic breeds.

Possibly the best documented scheme so far has been the *Castro Verde zonal scheme* (see Figure 11.1), the only ESA established so far in Portugal (Associação de Agricultores do Campo Branco, 1995). This ESA is located within the Castro Verde CORINE Biotope Area (central Portugal), and aims at the maintenance and improvement of steppe bird habitats (great bustard, little bustard, sandgrouse, stone curlew, etc.), the sustained improvement of farm incomes through further extensification of farming systems, and the encouragement of environmentally friendly farming methods for soil and water protection (Ministério da Agricultura, 1995). This scheme, therefore, has a relatively strong environmental component compared to many of the other schemes mentioned in Table 11.1. Castro Verde is an undulating and dry region with very poor soils where the extensive production of cereals, together with extensive sheep grazing, are the two main farming activities. Facing the reduction of cereal prices that followed the CAP reform, Castro Verde farmers soon realised that in an area where average cereal production does not exceed 1.2 tons/ha, support mechanisms proposed under the *ESA scheme* could be an important contribution to their incomes. The response to the scheme has, therefore, been relatively positive, and farmers are beginning to realise the ecological importance of the threatened bird species that use the habitats created by their traditional and extensive farming methods. The *Castro Verde scheme* has been particularly successful due to good communication between the various actors involved in implementing this *ESA scheme*, including the Ministry of Agriculture, extension services, local farmers' associations and the farmers themselves (Ministério da Agricultura, 1995). It is currently hoped that the Castro Verde ESA provides a positive example of successful AEP implementation from which the other six planned Portuguese ESAs will greatly benefit.

Despite these success stories, however, Portuguese policy-makers are aware of the current shortfalls in their agri-environmental programme. In order to correct some of the limitations of the current programme, and to further increase the impact of schemes in rural areas of high natural value, the Commission has recently approved a Portuguese proposal to modify its agri-environmental programme for the period 1998 to 1999. Principal alterations include, for example, increased payments in order to enrol more farmers into existing schemes (also for farmers *converting* to organic farming), the abolishment of maximum ceilings (area and LU eligible for schemes per farm), and the enlargement of zonal schemes to include more farms and wildlife habitats. The schemes for arable conversion to extensive pastures (2.12 in Table 11.1) and extensification of livestock production (2.14), meanwhile, will be discontinued because of poor take-up rates and the impracticability of implementing these schemes within the framework of Regulation 2078.

Conclusions

Portugal shares many of the problems about AEP implementation with its Mediterranean counterparts. As in Spain and Greece, Portugal has been a relative latecomer with regard to implementing AEP, and has lacked the experience with agri-environmental schemes that has given a vital head start to most of the northern EU Member States. In particular, there has been a lack of trained people both in terms of administration and within the farming community to understand and deal with the difficulties posed by new agri-environmental schemes, which in turn has resulted in considerable administrative difficulties. Similarly, most Portuguese policy-makers are still caught in the productivist ethos, largely because of the immense structural deficiencies of its agricultural sector with poor yield performances and many uneconomic small family farms. Farmers and farmers' organisations have also been slow to accept the notion of AEPs, and their lack of familiarity with the concept of being paid for environmental conservation has led to suspicion and an initially low level of participation.

However, in contrast to Spain (see Ch. 8) and Greece (Ch. 5), ambitions of the Portuguese agri-environmental programme have come closer to reality – best expressed in the relatively high agri-environmental expenditure per ha/UAA. There is, however, no doubt that had it not been for the CAP reform in 1992, the introduction of AEP in Portugal would have been a much slower process. It has also been highlighted that AEP in Portugal serves mainly as an income support mechanism, a fact related closely to the strong lobbying power of the larger and politically more powerful southern farmers' lobby. This means that the environmental component of most of Portugal's agri-environmental schemes has been relatively weak – exacerbated by the fact that the Ministry of Agriculture in Lisbon has always had a very narrow species conservation policy, ignoring that most of the existent important habitats have been created (and are dependant on) traditional farming systems. The result has been that Portuguese policy-makers were slow at recognising the opportunities provided by Regulation 2078, and accounts for the considerable delay in putting into place the first agri-environmental schemes after 1994 (a process which is still ongoing). Yet, it has to be acknowledged that the Portuguese agri-environmental programme also had to tackle substantially different socio-economic and environmental problems compared to most northern EU Member States. In most cases, the main goal in Portugal is the maintenance of extensive farming systems which support important species and habitats, while in northern Europe the objective is usually the reduction of 'inputs' (see other chapters in this book). Unfortunately, as this chapter has outlined, most schemes designed under the Portuguese programme are far from making full use of the potential for promoting sustainable environmental and socio-economic development in rural areas (at least for the time being).

Nevertheless, four years after implementation of the Portuguese agri-environmental programme some positive results are already apparent. First, implementation of AEP has opened up the debate between various actors in the policy-making process, in particular between the Ministry of Agriculture and other state actors (e.g. the Ministry of Environment), but also between state and non-state actors involved in the implementation process. Second, agri-environmental schemes have also undoubtedly made the farming community and the general public more aware of the interrelationships between farming and the environment (e.g. in the relatively successful *Castro Verde ESA*), and a very gradual shift in attitudes is perceptible among some parts of the farming community who have begun to realise the important environmental potential of their land.

12 Regulation 2078: patterns of implementation

Henry Buller

> *"Were we to represent Europe by a colour, that*
> *colour would undoubtedly be green."*
> (EC, 1992b, 7)

Introduction

The agri-environmental policy of the EU, as contained within Regulations 2078 and 746/96, seeks to promote and encourage agricultural production methods compatible with the protection of the environment and the maintenance of the countryside while, at the same time, contributing to the provision of an appropriate income for farmers. Within the context of a wider European territory, such a broad policy goal confronts a significant variety of different national (and indeed sub-national) profiles, not only with respect to agricultural production methods and practices and the trajectories of their recent evolution, but also with regard to broader environmental and rural traditions. Indeed, as the Commission itself acknowledges, while the CAP has achieved a certain degree of harmonisation of national agricultural development strategies, it is still in their rural and agrarian characteristics that European nations continue to display their most fundamental differences (EC, 1992b; Buller, 1998a). Thus, it is against a highly variable backdrop that an EU-led concern for reconciling agricultural production, environmental protection and rural sustainability has emerged. Herein lies a fundamental tension. On the one hand, the EU strives to obtain broadly comparable environmental standards within the wider European space. Yet, on the other hand, it needs to maintain that rural-agricultural-environmental diversity and multifunctionality that is so characteristic of that European rural space. Understanding that tension is critical for any study of the implementation of EU AEP.

The implementation of AEP also reflects the interaction of different policy-making arenas. While we might present AEP implementation in terms of a process of Europeanisation, where pre-existing domestic policies and policy instruments are adapted and transformed to fit in with the exigencies of EU rules, we need also to take into account the importance of domestic agendas not only in defining the trajectories of implementation but also in defining the orientation of EU policy. Whatever weight we ultimately give to these top-down and bottom-up inputs, one thing is certain; the invention and establishment of AEPs and actions is fundamentally bound up with the process of European integration, both in the sense that it has largely been as a result of the territorial and environmental impacts of CAP-led processes of agricultural change that the agri-environmental agenda has emerged and, second, in the sense that the EU's own mission to harmonise European environmental quality standards has provided the legislative foundation for that agenda's subsequent development.

In this chapter, we adopt an overtly comparative stance that builds upon the individual national case studies presented in Chapters 2 to 11. Our starting point is our belief that the patterns and styles of implementation of EU AEP are fundamentally conditioned by the culture and traditions of individual Member States (Buller, 1997a), a proposition that has similarly underlain other studies of 'Europeanisation' processes (for example, Buller *et al.*, 1992; Lowe and Ward, 1998). These cultures and traditions have largely been exposed in the preceding chapters of this book. Here, we seek to identify and explain the spatial, policy and institutional patterns that emerge when we consider the translation of an EU regulation into on-the-ground schemes and measures. Additionally, we seek to identify what broad farming systems and environment/landscape types are affected by agri-environmental schemes. Before considering the implementation and impact of Regulation 2078 in detail, however, we need to review the agri-environmental background of the Member States under discussion and, in doing so, compare and contrast the varied development of distinct national agri-environmental agendas.

The emergence of national agri-environmental policy agendas

"Sufficient numbers of farmers must be kept on the land.
There is no other way to preserve the natural
environment, traditional landscapes and a model of
agriculture based on the family farm as favoured by
the society generally."
(EC, 1991a, 9-10)

The preceding chapters in this book have clearly demonstrated two things. First, the pace of agricultural modernisation and indeed the starting points of that process, have been highly variable between the EU Member States. Clear contrasts exist between the UK, the archetype of early liberal and export-oriented agricultural modernisation where the average farm size significantly exceeds the EU average and where European style 'peasant' family-farming traditions have long since all but vanished, and Spain, Greece and Portugal, where agricultural modernisation and intensification have been much more recent phenomena and have, crucially, coincided with membership of the EU and adhesion to the CAP. While we are reluctant to adopt too readily a classic 'north/south' explanation for such differences, partly because other 'northern' states such as Sweden also underwent agricultural modernisation and intensification relatively recently, there is clearly, as the European Commission itself acknowledges (EC, 1997a), a major difference between 'southern' and 'northern' holdings.

The second observation to emerge from the preceding national profiles is that, despite the considerable variability in the pace and timing of agricultural modernisation, the process of agricultural change has followed broadly similar trajectories within all ten countries under investigation in this book. For each, the authors record ubiquitous processes of production intensification leading to higher yields per unit area. In all, this modernisation has been achieved through the increasing application of chemical and other entrants, through changes to the organisation of agricultural land holdings, through plant and animal modification and through increased mechanisation. At a European as well as at a national scale, the result has been an increasing specialisation and concentration of agricultural production, leading to the development and reinforcement of broad regional production models.

While there is no doubt that agricultural modernisation has greatly increased the relative domestic and international economic strength and performance of European farming, this has largely been achieved through massive restructuring, labour shedding and increasing financial involvement of the public sector. Further, agricultural intensification and the resulting regional specialisation has also had two important consequences for rural space. First, as countless authors and commentators have demonstrated (from Carson, 1962, to Conway and Pretty, 1991), many modern industrial agricultural techniques have a considerable negative effect upon the natural environment and upon landscape in which they are found (and indeed beyond, as in the case of the pollution of drinking water aquifers). Second, the process of agricultural concentration in certain key producer regions has strongly affected those more marginal and less-favoured regions that, for a variety of physical, structural and social reasons, have not developed similar intensive practices. Such areas are faced rather with de-intensification, extensification or withdrawal of an increasingly unprofitable extensive and/or peasant agriculture, processes which, in their turn engender rural community decline, out-migration land abandonment and the subsequent ecological problems of soil erosion, afforestation, forest fires and landscape dereliction (Buller, 1992; Lowe, 1992). Thus the polarisation of European agricultural production has also led to a polarisation of European agri-environmental concerns; on the one hand, those linked to processes of intensification and high input use and, on the other hand, those linked to de-intensification and farm withdrawal.

This duality is attractive in that it, first, emphasises the divergent and, to a certain extent, opposing trends resulting from agricultural modernisation and, second, broadly coincides with more traditional divisions such as those between upland and lowland, between extensive husbandry and arable farming, between 'northern' and 'southern' models. Yet, it also masks the wider variety and more complex geography of agri-environmental concerns that are found across Europe (Baldock and Lowe, 1996). Indeed, Member States have come to AEP from a variety of different starting points. While Regulation 2078 to some extent imposes a common agenda upon which they have focused subsequent policy actions – based essentially upon landscape management, natural resource and nature protection, and the improvement of access (Article 1) – Member States have all brought to these actions, and indeed to the definition of the European agenda, their own distinctive agricultural, rural and environmental concerns, enclosed, for the most part, within distinctive social, political and administrative frameworks.

Thus, at a broad European level, we can trace the origins of current AEP (including both Regulations 797/85 and 2078) back to specific national preoccupations. If we consider the full range of agri-environmental measures currently in operation, we might identify four, largely national and sub-national, policy traditions and concerns that have strongly influenced the elaboration and adoption of existing rules.

Nature and landscape protection

In a number of EU states, considerable attention has traditionally been given to the relationship between, on the one hand, farming practices, agricultural structures and rural well-being and, on the other hand, countryside management, landscape and nature protection. Such states where a 'naturalist' tradition infuses the notion and conceptualisation of rurality (Hoggart *et al.*, 1995) have come to AEP with a strong set of policy antecedents both in nature and landscape protection and in agricultural land management. Clearly, the UK has been, to some extent, a policy 'leader' in this field (Hart and Wilson, 1998). Not only does the UK have a long history of contractual environmental management of agricultural land, but it also possesses a strong and active set of institutions and interest groups that have, since the beginning of the 20th century, promoted countryside management. A rural development agenda that has linked agricultural well-being to landscape and nature protection has underpinned UK policy since the 1942 Scott Report and indeed before (Whitby and Lowe, 1994). Coupled with a voluntary approach to landscape maintenance, enshrined in the 1949 and 1968 *Agriculture Acts*, this has emerged as the dominant agri-environmental preoccupation in Britain and has heavily influenced the ways in which subsequent AEP has been adopted and implemented. Further, it also accounts for the key role played by the UK in securing EU approval for Member States to offer premiums to farmers for environmentally friendly practices under *Article 19* of Regulation 797/85, a policy ideally suited, at the time, to prior British experience and central to British concerns (Whitby, 1994; Potter, 1998; Buller, 1998b).

Germany too is marked by a strong naturalist tradition, linked, as in Britain, to an early and powerful urbanisation. Late 19th century moves to create protected rural areas went hand in hand with critiques of (and alternatives to) modern urban life (such as those of Ernst Rurdorff and Rudolf Steiner), and with the reinforcement of German romanticism in which the forest played a crucial part. As in Sweden and Austria, these traditions have found expression in the key notion of, often regionalised, cultural landscapes in whose construction, and indeed maintenance, agricultural activities play a central part. Yet, despite similar aesthetic and naturalist preoccupations, the immediate roots of German AEP are largely different from those of the UK. In the absence of an all pervading, almost emblematic national sense of 'countryside', so characteristic of the British experience, German concerns have been more closely linked to the original CAP agenda of maintaining farm incomes (Höll and von Meyer, 1996) onto which have been grafted more recent anxieties over the effects of farm pollution (see Ch. 7). As Wilson *et al.*, 1999 have argued, these differences in part explain the relative tardiness of Germany's response to Regulation 797/85, though by 1990 Germany had overtaken the UK in terms of the amount of agricultural land contracted under *Article 19* schemes (EC, 1991b).

In other states such as France, concern for nature and landscape protection, though undoubtedly present, has been highly focused within specific zones and has not permeated the policy domain as a whole (see Ch. 2). Elsewhere (for example in Denmark as well as Spain), landscape concerns have also been linked to specific issues and territories rather than being part of an all-embracing protectionist rural culture.

Economic support of marginal agricultural activities and compensation for natural handicaps

A second concern is more prevalent in those nations or regions where a large agricultural population persists, operating in relatively remote rural areas. In much of central southern France, parts of Spain and Portugal and much of Greece (and northern Sweden, albeit in a different agricultural and environmental context), the dominant rural environmental agenda is that of combating the environmental and socio-economic effects of land abandonment and/or farming withdrawal by maintaining and supporting agricultural activities where these are threatened by the economic marginalisation of production activities and by the socio-economic decline of rural communities. Here, the critical environmental issue is that of land abandonment and the loss of cultivated or grazed land to natural recolonisation or afforestation (Beaufoy *et al.*, 1994).

Although a distinct policy domain, LFA schemes and the support of agricultural activities (and thereby rural communities) in areas where natural handicaps would otherwise lead to farm abandonment has been a significant pre-cursor to AEP in France and Spain. Different from the support of marginal farming areas in that it targets particular landscape-farming systems (such as extensive grazing on alpages) rather than economically marginal territories, LFA policy can be found in virtually all the states under study here. In Sweden, for example, it has been an important element in maintaining meadows within an otherwise densely forested landscape. In Britain, the links between LFA policy, upland grazing systems and ESA designations are also clear-cut. Similarly, in France a large proportion of the original ESAs designated in the late 1980s and early 1990s are to be found in the mountain zones of the south east, and the same is true for agri-environmental schemes in upland areas in Germany. Indeed, in this latter country by far the highest proportions of farmers participating in agri-environmental schemes are found in the upland regions of the south (see below).

In terms of AEP, concerns for maintaining agricultural activities and, as a result, rural community viability in marginal and handicapped regions, have married well with the emerging European interest in 'High Nature Value' farming and 'High Natural Value' areas (Baldock *et al.*, 1996). The particular emphasis placed today upon the protection of such areas, many of which coincide with LFAs and extensive grass-based husbandry systems, has given this particular set of concerns a renewed relevance in the implementation of contemporary AEP, as we shall demonstrate below.

The regulation of farm-based pollution

If landscape and nature protection and agricultural withdrawal constitute two central issues upon which European AEP has been built, a third issue (though it emerged later) has been equally important in defining the subsequent European agenda: the need to address farm-based pollution, whether resulting from entrants or from animal wastes, was, as we have seen in the introduction to this book, a key factor in the development of the 1992 agri-environmental Regulation. While concern for the polluting effects of certain agricultural techniques has developed its own regulatory agenda, emerging from the introduction of normative EU rules governing water contamination by nitrates and pesticides and from growing recognition of increasing levels of contamination, a number states or regions where concern for the environmental consequences of intensive forms of farming was gaining in strength, sought to place the reduction of agricultural pollution high on the 1992 European AEP agenda.

In this respect, Germany and Denmark stand out. As the relevant chapters in this book point out, both countries had developed their own detailed programmes for addressing the issue of farm-based pollution before Regulation 2078 and both sought, specifically through the agri-environmental Regulation, to continue this particular emphasis. While, to a certain degree, they (and in particular Germany) succeeded in shifting the European agenda and in diversifying agri-environmental concerns away from the predominantly countryside management thrust of Regulation 797/85, the reduction of agricultural pollution, as we shall demonstrate below, has not emerged as the principle focus of those aid schemes that have subsequently been implemented by the majority of Member States.

Agricultural modernisation and structural reform

Although it might initially appear contradictory to claim that agricultural modernisation has been an important goal of AEP, it is clear from the Spanish and, though to a lesser extent, Greek experience, that agri-environment schemes have formed part of broad programme of EU-led actions designed to aid agricultural reform and support the competitiveness of farmers through income support within an enlarged European agricultural community. In nations or regions characterised by very low population and livestock densities, the northern European concern for extensification and surplus reductions makes little sense. Instead, the maintenance of rural populations and low intensity agriculture through measures acting essentially as income support has a far greater pertinence and relevance in protecting and maintaining a distinct 'southern' model of farm structure that is increasingly under threat (EC, 1997a).

In addition to these four dominant agri-environmental concerns, a number of more localised issues are also discernible, reflecting the responses of different natural environmental systems to change. The dryer European states record concern over the risk of forest fires on land taken out of agricultural production. In Sweden, emphasis is given to natural grasslands in maintaining breaks in an otherwise closed forest landscape or in maintaining a stable cover in sensitive areas. Heavily urbanised northern European states place a greater value upon the recreational value of rural land and perceive certain agricultural trends as a threat to future access and enjoyment of the countryside.

As we have shown in the introductory chapter of this book, Regulation 2078 brought to these essentially national agendas a series of additional EU imperatives; the need to integrate environmental and agricultural policy, the need to reduce EU agricultural overproduction (and the costs thereby incurred), and the need to support farm incomes. Nevertheless, the key link between AEP and the CAP, of which it forms part, lies in the fact that, for the most part, the environmental, social, economic and territorial issues that the former seeks to address have been largely consequent upon the differential and uneven effects of the latter (Brouwer and Lowe, 1998). As the different chapters of this book have repeatedly shown, Regulation 2078, like LFA policy and preceding AEPs, is essentially responding to CAP-driven changes in the rural environment and economy.

The adoption of Regulation 2078

Council Regulation 2078 was adopted on the 30th June 1992. Member States were required to submit, by the 30th July 1993, draft regulatory frameworks for the implementation of five-year (1993-1997) agri-environmental aid schemes in accordance with Article 3 of the Regulation. These five-year frameworks were to include the specific schemes identified in Article 2 of the Regulation as well as any other 'existing or proposed laws, regulations or administrative provisions by which they intend to apply this Regulation' (Article 7.1).

The cost of Regulation 2078

In practice, the initial establishment of Regulation 2078 has deviated substantially from the originally intended procedure. Three differences might be identified. First, the twelve Member States in 1992 did not all meet the 30th July deadline for the submission of draft general frameworks. Certain States, notably the UK, Germany, France and the Netherlands, having a pre-established AEP (founded largely upon Regulations 797/85 and 2328/91) were able to respond quicker than others to the timetable laid down in Brussels. Others, such as Portugal, had to negotiate with the Commission for the inclusion of specific regional schemes. Second, the EU itself expanded from 12 to 15 states in 1995 thereby introducing not only a new set of demands for co-financing from Austria, Sweden and Finland, but also a new set of agri-environmental concerns. Third and finally, the number of proposed schemes and, as a result, the anticipated cost of the national five-year programmes and their component zonal elements, has greatly exceeded the initial provisions of Regulation 2078 (Table 12.1), both as a result of the high number of programmes proposed by Member States and by the membership of Austria, Sweden and Finland. As Priebe (1997) has admitted, the initial assumption of the Commission, that there would be one 'scheme' per country soon proved to be unrealistic in the face of an increasingly regionalised response to the Regulation.

Table 12.1 EAGGF Guarantee contribution to the financing of agri-environmental programmes under Regulation 2078

Year	Source	EAGGF Budget estimate MECU
1991 (EU-12)	Commission estimate	2256
1993 (EU-12)	Initial programme forecasts	5830
1995 (EU-15)	Budget of approved programmes	3915
1997 (EU-15)	Expenditure (estimate)	3787

Source: EC, 1997c, 1997f

In 1993 and 1994, the *Star Committee* of the European Commission, charged with overseeing implementation and approving aid schemes, sought to negotiate and introduce national budgetary allocations by Member State. The EAGGF budget for the first five-year period of Regulation 2078 (1993-1997), based upon estimations from the 15 Member States, initially stood at 4,397 MECU in 1996 (EC, 1997c). However a number of Member States have subsequently reduced the expansion of their own agri-environmental programmes for 1996 and 1997 or, as in the case of France, froze the allocation of new money, either because of internal financial constraints or because they had already exhausted their allocated budgets. Others, such as Austria, have picked up shortfalls occasioned by their late start.

The distribution of agri-environmental expenditure (including both national and European funds) varies considerably across the Union (Table 12.2). In part this is due to the different levels of European co-funding (75% in Objective 1 areas, 50% elsewhere) and to the different starting dates of the five-year agri-environmental programmes. While Germany, Spain, France, the UK and the Netherlands began funding schemes in the first year (1993) of the policy, other states including Ireland, Belgium, Italy and Greece, as well as the three new Member States, Austria, Finland and Sweden, did not begin spending money on agri-environmental schemes until 1995 or 1996. This has meant that while some countries are currently (1997-1998) redesigning the agri-environmental programmes to take account of implementation issues and changes in priorities for the next round of five-year engagements, (for example, France, Denmark and the UK; see Chs. 2, 3 and 6) others are still in the relatively early stages of implementation.

The allocation of EAGGF funds as the co-funding element of the total budgets is clearly concentrated in the larger Member States. Germany accounts for 24% of the total currently allocated EAGGF agri-environmental expenditure for the 1993-1997 period, with France and Italy accounting for 13.4% and 11.4% respectively. However, the size of the national territory and the national UAA is not the sole explanatory factor. Other smaller nations also record significant budgetary allocations reflecting their commitment to placing high proportions of their agricultural land surface under agri-environmental programmes. Thus, Austria and Finland also account for significant proportions of the entire EAGGF agri-environmental expenditure for the 1993-1997 period, while Spain records a far lower proportion (3.3%). Such variations in expenditure reflect different national agendas and priorities. It is notable, for example, that Austria and Finland allocate a far higher proportion of their total EAGGF Guarantee Section budgets (which include most forms of agricultural support) to AEP (around 22% and 20% respectively) than all other Member States (EC, 1997a). The UK, on the other hand, not only accounts for a low proportion of the EAGGF agri-environmental expenditure for the 1993-1997 period (2.5%), but this in itself represents only a very small proportion (1%) of the total EAGGF Guarantee expenditure in Britain (EC, 1997c) – reinforcing Hart and Wilson's characterisation of the UK as an agri-environmental 'policy receiver' in the 1990s (see Ch. 6).

Table 12.2 Total co-financeable expenditure under Regulation 2078 and EAGGF contribution by Member State for the five-year period 1993-1997

State	Total co-financeable expenditure (1993-1997)	EAGGF contribution	Assumed Member State contribution	Proportion of total EU 15 EAGGF agri-environmental budget
	(MECU)	(MECU)	(MECU)	(%)
Austria	1,553	806	746	21.30
Belgium	6	3	3	0.08
Denmark	38	19	19	0.50
Finland	798	399	399	10.54
France	1,018	509	509	13.44
Germany	1,294	918	376	24.24
Greece	15	11	4	0.29
Italy	714	432	282	11.43
Ireland	217	163	54	4.30
Luxembourg	9	4	4	0.11
Netherlands	49	25	24	0.66
Portugal	197	148	49	3.92
Spain	167	125	42	3.30
Sweden	252	126	126	3.33
UK	192	98	94	2.59
TOTAL	**6,244**	**3,787**	**2,458**	**100**

Source: EC, 1997c, and author's calculations and estimations based upon EC, 1997c

Thus far, we have considered EAGGF agri-environment expenditure for the five-year period of 1993 to 1997. This, however, is a problematic data set largely because it fails to account for the different start-up dates of national programmes. If we focus on agri-environmental expenditure for the year 1997 (both because this yields the most up-to-date information and because this is the first year in which all 15 Member States actually spent money on agri-environmental schemes) and relate that to the total declared UAA per country, we reveal considerable variations in the levels of expenditure (Table 12.3). Overall, the Member States can be grouped together into three sets: those displaying a high 2078 EAGGF budget allocation/UAA ratio (Austria, Sweden, Finland, Ireland and Luxembourg);

those displaying a medium ratio (Italy, Germany and Portugal); and those displaying a low ratio (Belgium, Denmark, France, the Netherlands, Greece, Spain and the UK).

Table 12.3 EAGGF expenditure on Regulation 2078 by Member State against total UAA by Member State for the year 1997

State	EAGGF Expenditure (MECU)	Total national UAA (1000 ha)	Expenditure ratio (ECU/ha)
Austria	265	3,487	76.0
Belgium	2	1,350	1.4
Denmark	9	2,756	3.3
Finland	143	2,699	52.9
France	144	30,335	4.7
Germany	304	17,136	17.7
Greece	10	3,930	2.5
Italy	336	17,215	19.5
Ireland	100	4,444	22.5
Luxembourg	4	126	31.7
Netherlands	12	1,986	6.0
Portugal	58	3,882	14.9
Spain	54	26,930	2.0
Sweden	83	3,342	24.8
UK	36	17,775	2.0
Total	**1,557**	**137,393**	**11.3**

Source: Eurostat, 1996; EC, 1997a

In the first group, we find three mountainous states where the UAA covers only a relatively small proportion of the total land area. Austria, Finland and Sweden are also the latest European states to join the EU, entering in 1995 well after the 1992 reforms of the CAP. These three states alone account for over 35% of the total EAGGF expenditure to date on Regulation 2078, despite their late accession. Significantly, the UK – which, like Denmark, has a strong tradition of national agri-environmental concerns – numbers among those states with the lowest ECU/ha rate. This, in part, reflects the spatial strategies adopted by Member States. Those nations with low budget/UAA rations have, in general, adopted geographically targeted schemes within sensitive areas, while those with higher ratios have frequently sought wide horizontal national schemes. This distinction is something we shall return to below.

The organisation of programmes

Article 3 of Regulation 2078 identifies the specific form of the required national multi-annual agri-environmental programmes. Three forms are identified, though the first is clearly regarded by the Regulation as the standard form :

1. *Zonal programmes*: 'Each zonal programme shall cover an area which is homogeneous in terms of the environment and the countryside and shall include, in principle, all of the aids provided for in Article 2' (Article 3.2.).
2. *Local zonal programmes:* 'Where there is sufficient justification, programmes may be restricted to aids which are in line with specific characteristics of an area' (Article 3.2).
3. *General regulatory frameworks:* 'By way of derogation ... Member States may establish a general regulatory framework providing for the horizontal application throughout their territory of one or more of the aids referred to in Article 2' (Article 3.4).

By 1997, some 150 agri-environmental programmes had been approved by the Commission (EC, 1997a), the vast majority being zonal programmes as defined by Article 3 of Regulation 2078. To date, all Member States have submitted such programmes. For the most part, these have been organised and presented at the regional level: the German *Länder* (NUTS 1), the Spanish and the French regions (NUTS 2). Thus, for example, Baden-Württemberg, Picardie and Castilla-y-León all have their own, distinct agri-environmental programmes. In other states (Denmark, Belgium, Ireland, the Netherlands, Austria, Finland and Sweden) a national approach has been adopted, central government submitting a programme for the entire nation. The UK and Portugal are distinguished by a semi-regionalised approach, the former having established distinct programmes for England, Wales, Scotland and Northern Ireland, the latter by adopting a general national programme for all regions except for the Açores and Madeira which have distinct regional programmes. In the bulk of Member States, these programmes have been modified since their original approval by the Commission.

Zonal programmes combine general aid schemes, available to all qualifying farmers within the administrative territory concerned (such as, most commonly, extensification schemes, the preservation of rare breeds, grassland maintenance schemes or aid for organic farming) with more spatially specific aid schemes which are offered only to those farmers operating within designated zones (more common for landscape and nature protection aid schemes, the provision of access schemes and those linked to the management of abandoned farm and woodland). France, for example, has implemented 24 regional programmes, which include the full range of aid schemes applied either to the entire regional territory (such as organic farming aids), or to localised sub-areas within the regions (the 217 local operations with independently negotiated premium levels and conditions; see Ch. 2).

In addition to their zonal programmes, two of the Member States studied in this book (in addition to Ireland and Finland) have adopted general regulatory frameworks for the horizontal application throughout the national territory of one or more of the aid schemes (though these may include within them sub-measures targeted at particular farm systems, such as elements of the Austrian ÖPUL programme):

- Germany: the national framework for the improvement of agricultural structures and for coastal protection (*Gemeinschaftsaufgabe zur Verbesserung der Agrarstruktur und des Küstenschutzes* - GAK)
- Austria: the national environment programme (ÖPUL)

These provide a general policy framework for a series of agri-environmental aid schemes. However, while the Austrian ÖPUL programme has been developed (and negotiated) as an all-embracing legal and policy framework for the implementation of all adopted aid schemes under Regulation 2078, the German GAK covers only part of the aid schemes available through the Regulation (extensification schemes, the maintenance of extensive grassland systems and organic farming). The French *Prime à l'Herbe* (grassland premium) is the only truly national aid scheme offered in France in that it applies to the entire national territory. Other aid schemes are operationalised within a regional framework (though they, of course, might also be available through the entire territory in that all regions might offer them, as is the case for organic farming).

Finally, all Member States also offer local aid schemes which are usually regionally or sub-regionally operationalised and are, therefore, contained within the broader regional programmes (for example, the French local operations or individual ESA schemes in the UK). These concern only specifically designated territories. They tend, however, to be focused upon two distinct concerns. First, the vast bulk of landscape and nature protection schemes under Article 2.1d take the form of local zonal programmes, with regional and sub-regional and local government being the principal designatory authorities. Second, a significant number of aid schemes seeking to reduce pollution arising out of agricultural activities (either through the reduction of entrants or long-term set-aside; Articles 2.1a, d, f) are also restricted to specifically sensitive zones, often associated with water. In many states, these localised and zonal programmes constitute the central thrust of AEP. This would certainly be the case for the British ESAs and the French *opérations locales*, which, apart from the *grassland premium scheme*, dominate French AEP both in the areas covered and in the numbers of contractants.

The organisation of Regulation 2078 programmes within the Member States is complex. No single application model emerges from the above review. A common distinction in organisational forms exists between 'broad and shallow schemes', which apply to large areas but seek no major changes to existing farm practices (and hence offer relatively low premiums to farmers) and 'deep and narrow' schemes which, focusing upon limited sensitive areas require more significant changes in farm management and, as a result, offer generally higher premiums. In their assessment of the environmental impact of certain EU agricultural measures, Baldock *et al.* (1998) offer a matrix of broad scheme types (Table 12.4). Many of the wide focus horizontal schemes are, in fact, frameworks within which a number of individual measures operate.

Each State has approached scheme organisation in a different way. UK and Danish ESAs share a commitment to pre-2078 modalities, with wide-focus schemes concerning identified sensitive areas wherein a variety of different, but cumulative, environmental objectives operate[54] – an approach that has been followed by the more recent programmes of Spain, Sweden and, in part, France. Germany and Austria (like Ireland and Finland which do not figure in this volume) have adopted broad frameworks (either at the national or at the regional level, or indeed both as in the case of Germany) which contain a number of (in many cases cumulative) sub-measures, some of which are spatially targeted, others of which apply to entire territories. Few countries, apart from Sweden, have followed France's lead in establishing a broad national scheme aimed at maintaining grassland systems, though all countries have some form of, often more targeted, grassland schemes.

---

[54] In Denmark, premiums for otherwise horizontal schemes are generally higher within ESAs.

Table 12.4 Types of scheme organisation following Member States' adoption of Regulation 2078

	Horizontal schemes	Targeted schemes
Wide focus	• ÖPUL (Austria) • KULAP (Germany) • MEKA (Germany) • GAK (Germany)	• ESA (UK) • ESA (Denmark) • ESA (Sweden)
More specific focus	• Organic schemes • Grassland Premium (Fr) • Landscape and biodiversity scheme (Sweden) • Spanish extensification scheme	• NSA scheme (UK) • Opérations locales (Fr) • Spanish pollution reduction measures

Source: adapted from Baldock *et al.*, 1998

The content of Regulation 2078 aid schemes

As we saw in the Introduction to this book, Regulation 2078 (Article 2) identifies a number of broad categories of activity for which participating farmers might be eligible to apply for aid schemes. From these, we might identify 12 specific goals or actions which we shall, for the sake of clarity, refer to as 'aid schemes':

1. the introduction or continuation of organic farming methods
2. reduction of fertilisers and/or plant protection products
3. extensification of arable land
4. conversion of arable land to extensive grassland
5. extensification of livestock production through the reduction of sheep and cattle numbers per forage area
6. maintenance of grassland schemes
7. preservation of rare breeds
8. protection of the environment and natural resources
9. upkeep of abandoned farmlands or woodlands
10. long-term (20-year) set-aside
11. management of land for public access and leisure
12. training of farmers

The range of measures

Under the terms of Article 3, Member States were encouraged to devise zonal programmes that encompassed the full range of possible activities listed above. The possibility also existed, however, for more specific measures to be set up in response to individual contexts. Drawing upon the Member States considered in this book, two observations on the types of scheme implemented can be made.

First, the scheme types identified in Regulation 2078 are not equally adopted among the Member States considered here. Of all the aid schemes currently available within the EU, only those seeking to assist farmers converting to organic production methods are directly comparable across states. Here, the commitment of Member States to such methods is highly variable. While some states restrict their aid schemes to conversion, others offer further premiums for the maintenance of organic production methods. The maintenance of extensive systems and reducing fertiliser and plant protection products are also widely applied, though not universally. Other schemes however, have only been adopted in some states (for example, the management of abandoned farm and woodland). Finally, a third set of schemes have had, to date, a relatively limited adoption, notably farmer training schemes, the encouragement of access to farm land and the preservation of rare animal species.

Second, few states have adopted all the schemes identified in Regulation 2078 in their five-year programmes. The most consistent adoption is found in Spain, France and Austria. Part of the explanation for this 'full' adoption, lies in the fact that these nations have notably used the framework of Regulation 2078 as the basis for constructing (Spain) or re-defining (France and Austria) their domestic AEP, rather than seeking to maintain a largely pre-existing set of instruments.

A different perspective on the measures adopted by Member States is provided by the Commission in their 1997 review of the application of Regulation 2078. Classifying the range of aid schemes into five broad groups, the Commission report identifies budget spending per group for the Member States (Table 12.5, which includes only the Member States forming part of the current study).

Table 12.5 confirms the highly variable application of Regulation 2078 across Member States and reveals strong national preferences in the types of schemes adopted. On the one hand, Sweden and France, for example, are characterised by the importance they place on schemes that seek to maintain existing environmentally friendly farming systems.

Table 12.5 Type of agri-environment measure as proportion of total budget for the Member States included in this survey (based upon expenditure for programmes approved by March 1996)

	A	Dk	F	G	Gr	P	Sp	Sw	UK
	%	%	%	%	%	%	%	%	%
Organic farming	17	24	3	1	14	4	4	15	2
Farming with environmental improvements	59	46	15	56	35	18	35	6	53
Maintenance of low intensity systems	21	16	79	21	0	68	15	71	30
Non-productive land management	3	14	3	21	50	6	42	1	14
Training and demonstration projects	0	0	1	1	0	4	4	7	0
Total	100	100	100	100	100	100	100	100	100

Source: EC, 1997a

The French figures illustrate above all the priority, in budgetary terms, given to the scheme for the maintenance of extensive husbandry practices (the *Prime à l'Herbe*). This single scheme, which extends to the entire territory, consumes around 60% of the total five-year budget eligible for co-funding (1,905 MECU). On the other hand, Austria, Germany and the UK have committed large portions of their agri-environmental spending to schemes that purportedly seek actual gains in environmental quality. Spain and Greece stand apart in the importance accorded to non-productive land management. In all states considered here, training and demonstration projects, whose adoption is optional on Member States under Regulation 2078, concern only a relatively small proportion of total budgetary commitment where they have been implemented at all. The variable weight given to the promotion of organic farming is also a characteristic feature of 2078 implementation, with Denmark allocating the highest proportion of its relatively small agri-environmental budget to organic production, followed by Austria and Sweden which, though they spend more on organic farming than Denmark, offer slightly lower proportions of their total agri-environmental budget to this sector. By way of contrast, the UK, France and Germany record low levels of spending. While these figures need to be treated with a large degree of caution (as the categories selected by the Commission are based upon the stated objectives of schemes and not necessarily upon the ways they are actually implemented on the ground), they nonetheless reinforce the notion of distinct national implementation strategies.

Specific measures designed to combat farm pollution, by reducing chemical entrants or by placing arable land in long-term set-aside, concern only a very small proportion of both national UAA and those proportions of the agricultural area concerned by agri-environmental schemes. This suggests a definite orientation for AEP as it is applied within the Member States; one that takes it away from those environmental concerns more commonly associated with regulatory control and towards a more flexible approach to broader rural management (including landscape and nature protection) on the one hand, and the maintenance of specific forms of extensive, low intensity agricultural enterprise (themselves critical elements in landscape dynamics), on the other.

While certain aid schemes specified in Regulation 2078 refer to specific actions, such as the reduction of livestock numbers for given forage areas, others are far more open, notably the use of 'other farming practices compatible with the requirements of protection of the environment and natural resources' (Article 2.1d) and the management of land for public access (2.1g). Here, we might argue, Member States have been able to adapt AEP more closely to their broader domestic agendas identified above. Hence, while the UK has maintained its independence by keeping its pre-2078 ESA structure in place as the flagship of its AEP (Whitby and Lowe, 1994), certain other post-1992 aid schemes have proved far less successful (see Ch. 6). In Spain, Portugal and France, meanwhile, paragraph 2.1d of the Regulation has been widely interpreted to include a variety of measures that seek to maintain traditional farm systems whose survival is considered important not only for landscape and environmental reasons, but also within the context of broader rural development considerations.

The aid scheme to protect landscape and natural resources covers, in reality, a vast panoply of different measures that target local landscapes (bocage systems, alpine pastures, wetlands, etc.), individual landscape features (stone walls, hedgerows, olive groves), specific sub-regional environmental management issues (forest fire management, desertification and land abandonment), the protection of individual species and ecosystems (bustards in Portugal, flamingos in south west France, plovers on the Yorkshire Moors), environmental pollution (water pollution, soil pollution) and public access. In many cases, particularly in the UK and in France, individual schemes combine these different objectives and are frequently associated with other programmes more closely linked to rural development initiatives such as the LEADER programme.

Similarly, the notion of *extensification* has been widely interpreted by the different Member States. To some degree, a catch-all concept, the principle of 'extensification' is based upon two assumptions; first, that by actively diffusing or dispersing the causes of environmental degradation, their impact will be lessened and, second, that the maintenance of existing extensive systems against intensification will maintain the relative integrity of landscape and rural conditions. States have thereby interpreted extensification in differing ways. For some, notably France but also Spain, Germany and Portugal, extensification has largely been interpreted in terms of the maintenance of traditional extensive husbandry systems. In other States, for example Denmark and also parts of Germany, extensification is more closely associated with de-intensification and active farm pollution reduction. For the former group of countries, extensification measures can be closely linked to less productive farm regions. In France, 45% of the land contracted under the aid scheme to maintain extensive husbandry systems lies in mountain zones and a further 36% in other LFAs.

Clearly, there are a great many different agri-environmental measures and aid schemes currently in operation within the EU as well as in other non-EU states such as Switzerland. We might ask ourselves whether these varied implementation strategies reveal any coherent pattern. Can one identify criteria that allow us to differentiate national responses in scheme adoption?

Here, we confront again the different national and sub-national traditions that were discussed earlier in this chapter. The presence of an established AEP prior to the adoption of the agri-environmental accompanying measures plays a key role in determining the national strategies of adoption, both through the definition of a distinct agri-environmental agenda and through the procedures and institutions linked to its implementation. In those states where agricultural modernisation and intensification have dominated (or still dominate) the recent agricultural policy agenda (Portugal, Greece parts of Spain and parts of France), progress in AEP development has frequently been slow in the face of entrenched sectoral opposition and domestic economic priorities. Alternatively, those states where an established domestic agri-environmental agenda already existed (Germany, Denmark and the United Kingdom) have often been pioneers in AEP, establishing a range of schemes prior to the EC/EU's involvement in this domain, though in the case of the UK, that pioneer role has been challenged with the emergence of the post CAP reform agri-environmental agenda. These latter nations display a more individualised strategy of adoption (ESAs in the UK and Denmark, or a set of highly individualised sub-national programmes such as the Bavarian KULAP) than the former group for whom EU policy has provided a framework for the initiation and development of national policy. The voluntary tradition of countryside management in the UK, one that lends itself to the approach enshrined in both Regulations 797/85 and 2078, contrasts not only with the regulatory tradition in France but also with the relative inexperience of the French farming sector in establishing contractual engagements for non-production related farm activities. The strong role played by certain agricultural organisations, notably the DBV in Germany which initially opposed AEP measures, contrasts with the initially weak involvement of farmers' unions in the agri-environmental debate in Spain. Different national patterns of AEP implementation thereby reflect different political choices. While Sweden has sought to use agri-environmental schemes largely to promote landscape values (see Ch. 4), Germany has focused its attention on reducing farm-based pollution and maintaining, in certain regions, a distinctive agricultural structure. The French *grassland premium scheme* can be seen in part as a compensation offered to extensive grass-based husbandry farmers for the fact that they gain little from other compensatory payment mechanisms offered in the reformed CAP of 1992. Many Spanish schemes similarly seek to 'protect' a particular model of south European extensive farming.

It is also evident that certain aid schemes have a limited pertinence in some countries. At a general level, aid schemes that seek the active de-intensification of agriculture are unlikely to attract many farmers in regions (and countries) where agricultural activities are not only already highly extensive, but are more likely to disappear altogether without some form of intervention. The preservation of rare breeds, it might be argued, becomes relevant only in those areas where particular agricultural systems have developed involving particular breeds (e.g. Portugal; see Ch. 11). The rules governing this particular aid scheme imply the existence of established networks or breeders and holdings. Access to farmland has likewise been adopted only where this is seen as a local issue. As the example of Sweden (and to some extent Switzerland) shows, some states have preferred to orientate their voluntary agri-environmental schemes towards specific aspects of landscape management, rather than to use it as a means of addressing the reduction of farm-based pollution, preferring to use a more regulatory approach for this latter concern.

Finally, though Member States have been required by Regulation 2078 to submit national agri-environmental programmes, the implementation and operation of AEP is essentially a sub-national and local concern. The extent to which major sub-national variations exist in agricultural, environmental and rural socio-economic conditions will have an effect upon the nature and the impact of agri-environmental schemes. If in the smaller European states (e.g. Greece, Denmark, Austria and to a lesser extent Portugal), national programmes display a greater coherence with a smaller range of dominant issues being pertinent across large, though frequently focused, areas of the national territory (such as the maintenance of traditional, low-density husbandry practices), large countries offering a varied geography, such as Spain, France and Germany, display significant internal variations in agricultural, environmental and rural conditions. The pertinence of a 'national' response to Regulation 2078 and the efficacy of national scheme types is thereby raised. The German experience, like the Spanish, has been highly regionalised, reflecting the federal structure of both states, but also reflecting the existence of multiple agri-environmental agendas within the single state. In its initial response to Regulation 2078, the French government proposed a series of 'regional measures' which would follow a nationally-defined set of contractual obligations. These have largely failed to attract large numbers of participants. By way of contrast, the locally negotiated schemes have, generally, been far more attractive to farmers and environmental interests alike.

The considerable variety in patterns of adoption in scheme models (and indeed in scheme objectives) is one of the most persistent features of EU AEP. While Regulation 2078 sets out broad intentions (Article 1) and identifies relevant undertakings (Article 2), what is clear from the above review and from the chapters contained in this book is that, though they might be defined at the European level and implemented at the national or regional level, agri-environmental schemes are essentially locally constructed mechanisms that respond to a wide variety of essentially local, and hence territorial, agricultural and environmental concerns.

Premium rates

The levels of payment made to farmers engaging voluntarily in agri-environmental aid schemes are, following Regulations 2078 and 746/92, established according to three criteria: costs incurred, income foregone and an incentive element (which must not normally exceed 20% of the former). As the Commission itself comments, "premia should be regarded as compensation for the costs of delivering environmental public goods and cannot be regarded as subsidies in an economic sense" (EC, 1997a, 5). Upper levels for payments were established by Regulation 2078 and subsequently amended by Regulation 746/96 (EC, 1996).

Within individual national or regional agri-environmental programmes, premia levels are either nationally or regionally fixed by relevant agricultural ministries or are locally negotiated (particularly in the case of highly targeted local schemes). The result is a highly complex pattern of payment levels with considerable variations and indeed inconsistencies in the levels of payments existing both between and within Member States (Table 12.6).

Table 12.6 Variation in maximum and minimum premium levels (in ECU) for certain aid schemes by country (data for 1996)

	Organic Farming	Landscape protection	Grassland management
Austria	350-750	38-575	25-300
Denmark	100-150	No data	100-250
France	106-712	up to 500	60-250
Germany	135-867	up to 750	135
Greece	100-200	420	No data
Spain	85-450	55-350	No data
Sweden	100-250	50-450	No data
UK	8-60	10-300	No data

Source: DGVI, 1999

To a certain degree, such variations are to be expected. Costs incurred, levels of income foregone, as indeed the notion of incentive, will vary from region to region according to a variety of factors including the type of agricultural activity, the degrees of constraint imposed as conditions, the different levels of charges faced by farmers and so on. Variations are thereby expected both between aid schemes (e.g. premium levels for the maintenance of extensive grassland husbandry will be lower than those for the conversion of olive production to organic techniques) and within aid schemes (e.g. within a multi-tier scheme, lower premiums will be offered for the basic tiers).

However, the regionalisation of agri-environmental programmes in certain states (for example, Germany, France, Spain) has led to inconsistencies, particularly among those schemes benefiting from locally negotiated premium rates. German *Länder* commonly have the possibility to raise nationally negotiated aid levels by 20% or to lower them by 40% – the highest premium rates often being recorded in the rich *Länder* of Bavaria, Hessen and Baden-Württemberg (see Ch. 7). In France, as in Spain, regional disparities might also occur, with farmers engaged in similar schemes being offered widely differing premiums in neighbouring regions, though this is often as much the result of budgetary constraints (over-spending on one scheme and under-spending on another) as any differing payment scheme.

In those countries and regions where priority has been given, often in the form of 'broad and shallow' schemes, to the maintenance of extensive traditional farming practices either in upland and/or LFAs (such as the UK and much of France, Spain and Germany), premium rates (and therefore budgets per ha) are likely to be lower than in those countries and regions where priority has been given to reducing pollution and landscape degradation linked to intensive production methods in smaller, more concentrated areas (areas of Denmark, Greece). Extensification schemes are highly varied in their premium rates reflecting their varied objectives. The maintenance of, and conversion to, organic farming methods require in general high premiums, and where such schemes are strongly supported (Austria and parts of Germany) ECU/ha rates are also likely to be high. Thus, at a comparative level, premiums offered in France, Spain, Portugal and, in particular, Denmark are, on average, lower than those offered in Austria and Germany. Although one would hesitate before drawing hard and fast conclusions from this (given the various caveats identified above), these high premium levels do suggest that, in the latter two states (Germany, Austria) different criteria are being employed in assessing costs and income forgone and/or that aid schemes are being cumulated in a fashion that permits substantial per ha payments to farmers.

The uptake of 2078 schemes

By mid 1997, just under one-fifth of all European farms had entered one or more agri-environmental schemes. A similar proportion of the agricultural area of the 15 Member States is currently under one or more agri-environmental contracts which pay, on average, around 117 ECU/ha/year (EC, 1997a). Such averages, though they imply a rapid and wide-scale uptake of agri-environmental schemes among European farmers, nonetheless mask considerable variations both within and between individual Member States. Using three basic indicators (the number of contracts established, the surface area under contract, expenditure per unit area and per scheme, and the various composites that these permit), we seek, in this section, to examine the geography of uptake across the EU and to explore reasons for the differential adoption of Regulation 2078.

It is worth pausing, however, to re-emphasise that the countries investigated here are located at different stages in the implementation of Regulation 2078. To date, only three Greek programmes have been approved (two horizontal and one vertical programme) despite the fact that at least three others have been under negotiation for over two years (see Ch. 5). Certain states have undergone profound agricultural transformation since their entry into the EU. Agri-environmental reform, following on the heals of rapid modernisation has had to be located within a broad trajectory of agricultural development and, following CAP reform, farm income support. Whereas this might potentially give rise towards an ecological modernisation of contemporary agriculture within these states (in that environmentally friendly practices become an integral part of agricultural development), the implementation of Regulation 2078 to date has been delayed by the administrative and financial complexities associated with, not only, a seemingly fundamental agricultural policy shift from farm structure to farm environment and landscape, but also with the institutional reforms and changes that have frequently accompanied it.

The last available figures at the time of writing (1999) maintain that around 1.8 million agri-environmental agreements have been established within the 15 Member States of the EU (Table 12.7). It is extremely hazardous, however, to suggest that this figure also represents the number of farms or farmers contracted. In certain states, particularly those that offer composite and multi-layered agri-environmental schemes (for example, the Irish REPS, the Austrian ÖPUL or the Finish GAEPS), individual farms may in fact have as many as six distinct agri-environmental contracts. This is clearly the case in Austria where some 430,825 contracts have been established despite there only being 222,000 agricultural holdings overall. The actual number of contractants to the ÖPUL programme is estimated at around 169,000 (see Ch. 9). The total number of Regulation 2078 aid scheme participants throughout Europe is therefore closer to 1.35 million, though even this figure might be an over-estimate.

Table 12.7 clearly reveals the uneven distribution of 2078 contracts across the EU. Germany is distinguished by a high number of contracts, though this is almost certainly a considerable over-estimation that can be explained by the cumulative nature of the two largest German schemes (KULAP and MEKA). Nonetheless, taken together, the states of Germany, France and Austria collectively represent 67% of all contracts to date within the EU (as well as 62% of the total budget, see below). By way of contrast, the four southern European states of Greece, Italy, Spain and Portugal account for only 16% of all contracts. This disparity is all the more striking when one considers that the latter four states account for almost 68% of all farms in the EU, while the former group represent only 23%. Such figures suggest that, in its current form, Regulation 2078 responds more to a northern European agenda than to a southern European one.

If we consider this distribution in greater detail (Figure 12.1), we

Table 12.7 Contracts to aid schemes under Regulation 2078 (situation at mid 1997)

State	Total number of 2078 contracts (April 1997)	Total number of farms (1995)	N° of contracts as % of total farms	N° of contracts as % of all EU15 contracts
	n	n	%	%
Austria	168,804	221,800	75.9	12.5
Belgium	1,242	71,000	1.7	0.09
Denmark	8,193	69,000	11.8	0.6
Finland	91,509 *	101,000	**	6.8
France	177,695	734,800	24.1	13.2
Germany	554,836 *	567,000	**	41.2
Greece	1,839	773,800	0.2	0.1
Italy	63,841	2,482,100	2,5	4.7
Ireland	23,855	153,400	15.5	1.7
Luxembourg	1,922	3,200	60.0	0.1
Netherlands	5,854	113,200	5.1	0.4
Portugal	125,479 *	450,600	27.8	9.3
Spain	29,599	1,277,600	2.3	2.1
Sweden	68,969	88,800	77.6	5.1
UK	21,482	234,500	9.16	1.6
Total	**1,345,119**	**7,341,500**	**18.3**	**100**

(*) While, in the majority of EU Member States, farmers generally enter single schemes, in these countries (or in certain regions within these countries) cumulative framework instruments operate with farmers potentially holding a number of contracts on their farms. The number of contracts exceeds the number of farms (as in the German *Länder* of Baden-Württemberg where some 234,279 contracts exist, the total number of farms being estimated at 101,600).

(**) Impossible to determine with any accuracy for the reasons given above.

Source: calculated from EC, 1997a; Eurostat, 1998; and data from individual chapters in this volume

observe an even stronger regional concentration of contractants in the southern and eastern German *Länder*, particularly Bayern and Baden-Württemberg (each of these *Länder* recording over 200,000 contracts), Austria, Luxembourg, northern Italy and central and southern France. Regions showing weaker proportions of farmers engaged in 2078 aid

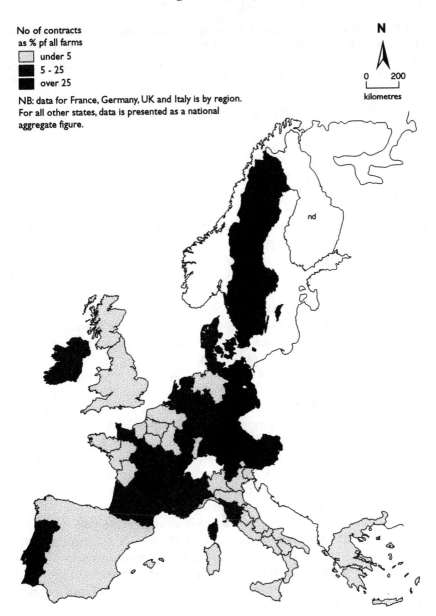

No of contracts
as % pf all farms
  under 5
  5 - 25
  over 25

NB: data for France, Germany, UK and Italy is by region.
For all other states, data is presented as a national
aggregate figure.

N

0   200
kilometres

nd

**Figure 12.1   Number of contracts as a percentage of total farm
numbers per region (data for mid 1997)**

Source: Unpublished statistics from EU and individual
Member States and Eurostat, 1998

schemes can be divided into two groups; those made up of the southern states (with the exception of Portugal and the Tuscany region of Italy) and those that comprise the principal arable regions of northern Europe (north eastern France, eastern England [though his does not appear in Figure 12.1], and northern Germany).

Those EU Member States having much of their UAA in upland and mountainous regions also show high proportions of their agricultural land placed within Regulation 2078 aid schemes (Table 12.8). Austria, Sweden and Finland all record over 50% of their UAA under agri-environmental contracts. The spatial impact of Regulation 2078 aid schemes is far more limited in the intensive lowland states of Denmark, the Netherlands and Belgium, where they fail to exceed 3.5% of the total agricultural area. The predominance of schemes aimed at maintaining extensive grassland-based farming activities in the former Member States, and the importance given to schemes aimed at reducing farm pollution in the latter, is a central element in this geographical variation. Indeed, with the exception of Luxembourg, the highest average areas per contract are found, unsurprisingly, in countries that have concentrated the bulk of their Regulation 2078 actions in maintaining extensive environmentally friendly forms of farming (Sweden, Ireland, France). In the French region of the Auvergne, in the heart of the Massif Central, the surface placed under the *Prime à l'Herbe* scheme amounts to around 60% of the total UAA. By contrast, within the predominantly arable Champagne-Ardennes region, the area contracted amounts to just 4.5% of the regional UAA. The UK operates a focused agri-environmental programme centred essentially upon ESAs. Although other aid schemes do exist beyond designated ESAs, these account for a far smaller proportion of the number of participating farmers and only 17% of the total UK agricultural area under contract (Buller, 1999b). The amount of land actually contracted as a proportion of the total UAA (8.1%) remains very low when held in comparison with France and Germany.

Given the wide variety of levels of farmer engagement across Europe and the substantial differences in Member State implementation strategies of Regulation 2078, it should hardly surprise us to also find considerable variations in the levels of payments to farmers (Table 12.9). Taking expenditure for the one year of 1997, average area based payments (as opposed to per head payments for livestock) range from 42 ECU/ha in France to 260 ECU/ha in the Netherlands, a difference that reflects once again the contrasts between the highly targeted schemes in the latter state, often designed to protect natural resources by active changes to farm practice on small farm holdings, and the horizontal schemes aimed at maintaining extensive practices on large holdings in the former. If these

Table 12.8   Area contracted under Regulation 2078 aid schemes (situation at mid 1997)

State	Total area under contract (April 1997) ha	Total national UAA (1995) ha	Proportion of total UAA under contract %	Average UAA per contract ha
Austria	2,500,000	3,425,100	72.9	14.8
Belgium	17,000	1,354,400	1.2	13.6
Denmark	94,000	2,726,600	3.4	11.4
Finland	2,000,000	2,191,700	91.2	21.8
France	5,725,000	28,267,200	20.2	32.2
Germany	6,353,000	17,156,900	37.0	11.4
Greece[1]	12,000	3,464,800	0.3	6.5
Italy[1]	977,000	14,685,500	6.6	15.3
Ireland	801,000	4,324,500	18.5	33.5
Luxembourg	97,000	126,900	76.9	50.4
Netherlands	31,000	1,998,900	1.5	5.3
Portugal	606,000	3,924,600	15.4	4.8
Spain	532,000	25,230,300	2.1	17.9
Sweden	1,561,000	3,059,700	51.0	22.6
UK	1,322,000	16,446,600	8.1	61.5
Total	**22,628,000**	**137,348,000**	**16.5**	**16.8**

(1) Contracted area data for Italy is for 1996, and for Greece for 1995.

Source: compiled by the author from EC, 1997a; Eurostat, 1998; and data from individual chapters in this volume

figures are subsequently related to the average amount of land engaged per contract, then a broad and albeit approximate assessment of the financial benefits of Regulation 2078 per farm can be estimated (Table 12.9, column 4). Here the differences between states and scheme priorities are less apparent. Ireland, Luxembourg, the Netherlands and the UK emerge as the states where contractants receive the highest payments per contract, while farmers in France, Portugal and Germany receive the lowest payments. In part,this is due to differences in average farm size, in part also to the types of schemes and premiums offered. The average contracted area per farm in the UK, for example, is notably higher than that in either Germany or France.

Table 12.9 Expenditure under Regulation 2078 (situation at mid 1997)

State	Total budget for 1997[*] MECU	Average payment per ha under contract (area schemes only) ECU	Estimated average annual payment per contract ECU
Austria	509	140	3,030
Belgium	3	84	2,415
Denmark	17	186	2,075
Finland	285	124	3,114
France	287	42	1,615
Germany	428	89	771
Greece	13	n/a	n/a
Italy	560	n/a	n/a
Ireland	134	147	5,617
Luxembourg	9	90	4,683
Netherlands	23	260	3,929
Portugal	77	137	614
Spain	72	81	2,433
Sweden	166	156	2,407
UK	70	55	3,258
Total	**2,652**	**117**	**1,972**

(*) This includes the EAGGF contribution and the national contribution estimated at 25% in Objective 1 areas and 50% in other areas.

Source: compiled from EC, 1997a; Eurostat, 1998; and data from individual chapters in this volume

A more detailed examination of the spatial distribution of 2078 expenditure, based on the total regional UAA rather than upon the contracted area (Figure 12.2), reveals a similar pattern to that shown in Figure 12.1 above. The mountainous LFAs of the eastern margins of the current EU, which include some of the richest German *Länder*, dominate the geography of Regulation 2078 expenditure. In regions where the take-up of agri-environmental schemes extends over most of the agricultural surface, the average payments per ha of total regional UAA attain up to 148 ECU in Austria, and 60 ECU in the German region of Baden-Württemberg. Only three southern regions (Portugal, Tuscany and Sicily) emerge as relative poles for agri-environmental spending (albeit with significantly lower

ECU/ha average payment rates at around 30 ECU), though central southern France also accounts for a fair share. Spain, Greece, most of southern Italy and much of lowland France are categorised both by low take-up rates and, as a consequence, by very low average levels of expenditure.

From the above assessment, it is apparent that the spatial impact of Regulation 2078 is far from evenly spread across the EU. In both relative and real terms, the primary beneficiaries in terms of uptake are Germany and Austria, with Sweden, France and Finland close behind (leaving Luxembourg aside). Within these 'beneficiary' states, the principal areas concerned are those lying in upland regions where extensive agricultural systems predominate. It is notable too, that the principal beneficiary states and regions are, for the most part, among the richer agricultural areas of Europe. With the possible exception of the French *Prime à l'Herbe* and parts of the Austrian ÖPUL scheme, which do show high take-up rates in some of the poorer mountain areas of Europe (though as premiums for grassland maintenance measures are frequently low, it is debatable if such measures have a major income effect), AEP implementation can, on the face of the above analysis, only be said to constitute a partial force for the redistribution of agricultural aid within European rural space. Finally, we need to note that many agri- environmental schemes also exist to reduce agricultural pollution in areas of arable production. These, however, are frequently highly targeted, considerably more expensive and involve relatively fewer contractors. As a result, they are perhaps less immediately visible in aggregate national or even regional figures.

Evaluation

One common theme that emerges from the bulk of the chapters in this book is the difficulty of assessing and evaluating the performance of Regulation 2078 over and above the kind of uptake statistics we have already considered in this chapter. Such statistics undoubtedly give an encouraging image of EU AEP. With around 17% of the EU UAA under contract and around 19% of EU farmers involved, AEP has clearly become a significant element both in European agricultural and environmental policy. However, within the context of agricultural policy, on the one hand, and environmental policy on the other, a number of questions remain to be asked. Has Regulation 2078 had an impact on improving environmental quality and reducing environmental pollution? Is the maintenance of environmentally friendly production systems a justifiable objective? Has Regulation 2078 contributed to providing an 'appropriate income for

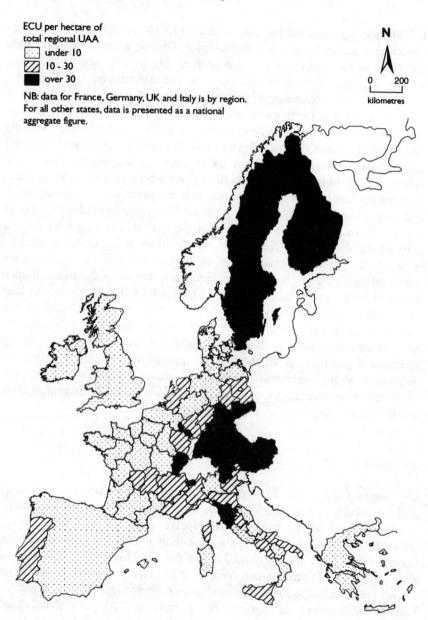

ECU per hectare of
total regional UAA

- ☐ under 10
- ▨ 10 - 30
- ■ over 30

NB: data for France, Germany, UK and Italy is by region.
For all other states, data is presented as a national
aggregate figure.

N

0   200
kilometres

**Figure 12.2 Estimated expenditure of Regulation 2078 aid as a
percentage of the total regional UAA (data for mid 1997,
except Italy, mid 1996)**

Source: Unpublished statistics from EU and individual
Member States and Eurostat, 1998

farmers' (Article 1)? Is it likely to yield durable and tangible gains in the move towards establishing and maintaining types of farming compatible with the requirements of environmental protection and upkeep of the countryside?

As the national reviews show, the answers for too many (if not all) of these questions are, for the moment, far from clear. It is noticeable that since their adoption in Member States, the bulk of agri-environmental aid schemes have not yet been subject to consistent and scientific monitoring procedures. Only in those Member States where pre-existing measures were carried over into new Regulation 2078 schemes, has any long-term monitoring been possible (e.g. MAFF, 1997b). It was, in part, to redress this that the subsequent Regulation 746/96 was drawn up. Yet by this time, many schemes had already been established without baseline studies of environmental state, or indeed of farmer practices, or without sufficient reflection as to the appropriateness of different assessment methodologies. We might suggest that this neglect derives principally from the fact that, in most states, AEP following Regulation 2078 has been adopted and implemented primarily as a component of agricultural policy and not as a component of environmental policy. Thus, it has been largely agricultural extension services or administrations that have been charged with promoting schemes and securing participants. As such, scheme performance has tended to be judged more in terms of participation and effects than upon impacts and effectiveness (EC, 1998). Regulation 2078 is itself very vague with reference to its own monitorability. Its exact goals are frequently imprecise and, while not being contradictory, make the adoption of a single common evaluation methodology very difficult (DGVI, 1999). It offers no targets, and neither do the bulk of national or regional programmes other than expenditure targets.

Many of the concerns expressed regarding the effectiveness of agri-environmental aid schemes focus upon their ability to deliver improvements in environmental quality. Yet, as the chapters of this book have amply demonstrated, the bulk of agri-environmental schemes (in terms of participant numbers and areas covered) seek to maintain existing practices, and consequently environmental conditions, rather than to incite actual changes to farm practices and farm land management. In a number of cases, even those aid schemes that seek the latter objective are often limited, in practice, to the former goal[55]. In the southern and mountainous countries of

---

[55] The UK ESAs are a case in point. Although they are considered as schemes designed to bring about actual environmental improvements, the largest numbers of participants nevertheless subscribe only to the lower tiers, limited essentially to the maintenance of existing practices (House of Commons, 1997; Hart and Wilson, 1998).

the Union, the agri-environmental agenda is often fundamentally different from that in northern Europe. Maintaining low intensity practices and thereby rural communities, or maintaining open pasture-land in an increasingly omnipresent forest landscape, are the dominant goals in those regions where agricultural modernisation has brought about rural abandonment and regional specialisation. In such areas, any evaluation methodology based upon assumptions of induced changes and improvements to the environmental state is likely to be of little practical value.

That having been said, the current pattern of AEP implementation today, at the end of its first five-year cycle, does raise a number of points of concern (Buller, 1999a). First, agri-environmental aid schemes do not, in their vast majority, address the issue of agricultural pollution, and this at a time when increasing public attention and political action is focused upon this very issue. It might be argued that aid schemes of this kind are not the best means to address such issues; the premiums would need to be much higher than is customarily the case (partly to overcome the financial advantages of following intensive practices), regulatory measures would be more suited to pollution control and making payments to farmers to reduce pollution would run contrary to the PPP. However, such arguments inevitably lead one to question the role and pertinence of AEP as a specific domain and its position within the broad spectrum of measures designed to integrate agricultural and environmental policy within the EU. Does it genuinely achieve this union, or is it not more likely merely to perpetuate a growing polarisation of European farm systems?

Second, there remains the critical question of the relationship of AEP, as enshrined in Regulation 2078, and the other, more central, regimes of the CAP. It is fair to say that much of the EU's AEP can be seen either as seeking to undo what the more traditional aspects of CAP have done and are still doing, or as compensating certain farmers for their ineligibility for other forms of, often more lucrative, CAP aid. Certainly, Regulation 2078 is an 'accompanying measure' to the CAP in that it too seeks to reduce agricultural surpluses by favouring more extensive forms of production. However, it is also, to some extent, an alternative and indeed, in some instances, "contradictory measure" (House of Commons, 1997, xvii) in that many schemes offer payments to farmers who, for whatever reason, decide not to intensify their production methods or to convert to organic farming. Extensive grassland maintenance schemes, for example, are widely seen, by farmers, as compensation for not receiving forage maize payments.

Third, as this chapter has demonstrated, EU AEP has been both conceived and implemented following an essentially north European agenda. Although some Mediterranean states (notably Portugal and Italy) have recorded high rates of uptake or expenditure, the emphasis increasingly being placed upon achieving verifiable improvements in environmental quality (e.g. OECD, 1997) ignores the perhaps more preoccupying scenario of the gradual disappearance of extensive farming systems and the rural social and economic fabric that they support. The twin functions of Regulation 2078 as an environmental instrument and as an income instrument (Priebe, 1997) are differentially emphasised at the national and regional levels. Whilst it might be tempting to seek aid schemes that deliver significant environmental and income improvements at one and the same time, the reality is more often one of choosing between, on the one hand, greater environmental benefits at specific locations (for example, reducing pollution) with less income benefits for the broader territory concerned or, on the other hand, lower environmental benefits (for example, maintaining existing grasslands) with more significant benefits for the local rural economy as a whole.

Finally, and leading on from the above points, AEP needs to be placed within the context of broader rural development policy. As yet, the links between the two are unclear, partly for the reasons evoked in the preceding paragraph, partly because in many states, rural development remains distinct as a policy domain from agricultural policy. We have shown in this chapter that Regulation 2078 does not, for the moment at least, appear to be a major force for the redistribution of agricultural aids across Europe. Of course, those areas and farms most concerned by arable area and set-aside payments do not generally emerge as major recipients of agri-environmental payments. However, not only are the latter, for the most part, vastly inferior to the former (the proportion of the EAGGF budget going to agri-environmental schemes being well under 5% of that proportion going to other forms of direct aid), but the regions benefiting the most from agri-environmental aid are, in many states, far from being either the poorest or the most threatened by environmental or farm income decline.

13 Conclusions: agri-environmental policy beyond Regulation 2078

Geoff A. Wilson, Henry Buller and Andreas Höll

In concluding this book, we return to the first EU agri-environmental regulation, that of 1985, now fifteen years old. Proposed by the UK, largely as a response to developments in its own internal agricultural policy agenda, that original legislation marked the start of a new component to EU agricultural policy in that it permitted Member States (and later co-financed such actions) to pay subsidies to farmers for the 'production' and maintenance of environmental goods. This was, at the time, wholly new territory both for many national governments and for the CAP and its political and administrative masters. Yet, as Potter (1998, 108), amongst others, has pointed out, this new component was wholly consistent with the "Green Europe model of agricultural development" of the time, one that sought to protect and maintain the European farming community and the 'countryside' that it shaped in a time of farm population contraction and growing budgetary constraints.

Fifteen years on, this central idea – that farmers have a key role to play in maintaining and in protecting a European rural environment that is largely the result of past agricultural endeavours and that they should receive payments for playing that role – occupies a central place in the *Agenda 2000* proposals, finally agreed upon by the heads of state and government of the EU Member States in late March 1999. That agreement maintained that 'agriculture must play its role in preserving the countryside and natural open spaces, and that it must make a key contribution to the vitality of rural life' (EC, 1997e, 1999a, 1999b). As the various chapters in this book have amply demonstrated, despite the considerable diversity of policy contexts, implementation models and scheme styles and foci, there is now across Europe a communality of concerns and responses to the challenge of reconciling and bringing together contemporary farming practices, environmental quality and rural development. Increasingly, agri-environmental policy is becoming the vehicle for that reconciliation.

The detailed analysis of the implementation of agri-environmental programmes in nine EU countries and Switzerland that this book has provided, reveal both the strengths and the weaknesses of current national experiences. Regulation 2078 has undoubtedly had some beneficial effects with regard to both raising farmers' incomes and contributing towards improved environmental management of the European countryside, but equally importantly it has served as a means of reasserting the positive role (both within and beyond the agricultural community) that farming has to play in maintaining both rural environmental quality and the rural economy. Ironically perhaps, farmers have, in an increasingly multifuntional European rural space, rediscovered their critical position as rural actors.

However, in this concluding chapter it behoves us to speculate how what has been in many Member States a five-year experiment in agri-environmental actions is to be taken forward. This is particularly important in light of the growing challenge to the much heralded, but rarely defined, 'European model of farming' from globalisation (in the form of reduced farm subsidy levels and declining product prices) and enlargement (in the form of the opening of the EU to new states of Eastern and Central Europe) – both of which form the key justification of the EU's *Agenda 2000*.

Agri-environmental policy and *Agenda 2000*

In March 1999, EU Agriculture Ministers reached agreement on further reform of the CAP as part of the *Agenda 2000* discussions. Although, the later meeting of the European Council watered down some of the measures agreed by the Agriculture Ministers, the ultimately accepted package of reforms aim at ensuring that European agriculture will become more competitive in both EU and global markets, at making farming more environmentally sensitive, and at providing better protection for farmers' livelihoods – issues, it is felt, that were not sufficiently addressed by the 1992 reforms. *Agenda 2000*, therefore, is a further step in the 'decoupling' of price support from production, accompanied by a step towards the use of environmental 'cross-compliance' which gives EU member states more power than the 1992 reforms to make most direct payments contingent on farmers meeting certain environmental requirements (Baldock, 1998).

The regimes subject to reform under *Agenda 2000* include the cereal, beef, dairy and wine sectors and will, therefore, affect many of the farming regimes discussed in this book. Specific decisions include, for example, reductions in intervention prices for butter and skimmed milk powder of 15% and 20% for cereals, thereby further aligning EU prices to world market prices. Similarly, for the beef sector the intervention price will be reduced by 20% to about ECU 2200/tonne. Bignal (1999) argues that there are two ways in which the environment may benefit from suggested changes in *Agenda 2000*. First, the introduction of direct measures targeted at environmentally friendly farming practices or at preventing environmentally damaging practices (the latter especially in intensive farming areas) could be a substantial step towards improved environmental management of the countryside compared to Regulation 2078. Second, indirect measures are likely to give greater support to farming systems with high ecological value (especially in extensive grassland systems in LFAs). Commentators currently argue that it is particularly the second type of measures which may be most favoured by member states and would further shift the balance of countryside protection mechanisms towards extensive low-intensity farming systems – thereby continuing the trend already outlined in many chapters of this book (see, for example, Chs. 2, 6, 7 and 9). As many authors in this book have already hinted at, this strategy may however penalise farmers on economically marginal holdings that are neither extensive nor intensive, which means that a substantial part of Europe's farming population may continue to slip through the protective 'agri-environmental net', both in terms of environmental protection and farm incomes.

Preliminary assessments of the implications of *Agenda 2000* suggest that the proposed changes to the arable sector will not lead to obvious gains for the European countryside, although it appears that *Agenda 2000* will further encourage the maintenance of extensive arable systems (e.g. important for Spain; see Ch. 8) and will possibly lead to reduced use of inputs and a further increase in organic farming (see also Chs. 7, 9 and 10). However, intensive and environmentally damaging arable crops such as silage maize, for example, will still be supported, and in some countries lower grain prices may result in farmers switching production to intensive dairying (e.g. Finland; Bignal, 1999). Similarly, the new dairy regime is unlikely to have major environmental implications. On the contrary, in some regions of the EU, the effects of lower milk prices may lead to more intensive dairying (Baldock, 1998). However, through new budgetary structures under *Agenda 2000* (so-called 'national envelopes'), member states may have more flexibility to introduce area payments with attached environmental conditions in the dairying sector (e.g. maximum stocking rates). Finally, changes to the beef sector are also unlikely to greatly influence intensive beef farms, and for some farmers increased headage payments per stock may even lead to increases in livestock densities. However, through the national envelopes individual member states will be able to attach specific stock density conditions to area payments.

From an environmental perspective, and in light of the discussion in this book, the new *Rural Development Regulation* holds most promise. This new regulation will include measures on forestry (incorporating policy mechanisms under the current Regulation 2080/92), early retirement for farmers (similar to the current Regulation 2079/92), compulsory agri-environmental measures (a continuation of Regulation 2078) and support for LFAs (European Commission, 1999b). The latter indicates that, for the first time, structural policy (e.g. LFA measures) will be integrated with socio-economic (early retirement) and environmental measures (agri-environmental schemes). This, it could be argued, will be an important step towards a more holistic treatment of structural, socio-economic and environmental problems in the European countryside. The new LFA measure, in particular, will have a clearer focus on the environment than earlier LFA policies, and in particular the environmentally damaging headage payments in LFAs are to be replaced by hectarage payments (see, for example, Ch. 6 on the damaging effects of headage payments in LFAs under Regulation 2078). The *Rural Development Regulation*, therefore, provides a clear shift in how livestock payments will be made, and should considerably reduce pressure on upland farms to stock to maximum levels. Thus, one single regulation will provide the framework hitherto provided by a mixture of regulations, thereby making implementation of future agri-environmental programmes easier, and simplifying both payment structures and management agreements for individual farmers. Chapters in this book have outlined how many farmers have particularly complained about the latter two issues within the framework of schemes implemented under Regulation 2078. However, implementation of environmentally friendly practices under the *Rural Development Regulation* will be made difficult by the relatively low available budget (only ECU 2.8 billion allocated for the period from 2000 to 2006).

Further environmental measures will be available through horizontal measures under *Agenda 2000*. These include the introduction of the principle of cross-compliance, payment ceilings for CAP subsidies per farm, and more subsidiarity to member states with regard to shaping direct payments according to their specific environmental and socio-economic needs through national envelopes. As both Baldock (1998) and Bignal (1999) have rightly argued, cross-compliance potentially will yield the greatest environmental benefits, as it may force farmers to adopt environmentally friendly farming practices if they wish to be eligible for CAP support. Interestingly, most member states now appear to be willing to accept the principle of cross-compliance, although there was much resistance in the early stages of the drafting of *Agenda 2000*. Specific codes of 'good practice' are still being negotiated (EC, 1999a, 1999b), but the codes may require farmers to retain and sustainably manage remnant semi-natural habitats on farms, to preserve field boundaries and other landscape elements, and to protect historic sites on their farms. However, to what extent existing opportunities of cross-compliance will be made use of will only become clear after establishment of the 'national envelopes'.

Plus ça change . . . .

In their 1990 analysis of early ESA policy in the UK, Baldock *et al.* (1990) identify what they see to be the 'familiar stamp of British incrementalism'. Do agri-environmental schemes, following Regulation 2078 and *Agenda 2000*, represent any genuine and durable reform in European agricultural policy? As the chapters in this book have pointed out, agri-environmental schemes have not challenged dominant agricultural models, but have rather sustained certain often more marginal farming systems and the countryside they produce from changes that are to a large degree consequent upon such dominant agricultural development trajectories (such as intensification and regional specialisation).

    Agenda 2000, driven as it has been primarily by financial, rather than agricultural, environmental or rural imperatives, cannot be regarded as a radical departure from the established CAP philosophy that has, from the outset, constrained the effectiveness of Regulations 797/85 and 2078 discussed in this book. It too, therefore, embodies incrementalism rather than reform – in part an inevitable result of having to reach policy compromises between an ever-increasing number of EU member states. Thus, while Regulation 797/85 'only' had to take into account the interests of 10 EEC member states at the time, the structure of Regulation 2078 was already made more complicated by the accession of Spain (see Ch. 8) and Portugal (see Ch. 11), while *Agenda 2000* currently has to take into account the views of 15 EU member states, with the likely addition by the year 2005 of another five countries (Hungary, Poland, the Czech Republic, Estonia and Slovenia) with highly disparate agricultural and environmental interests (Petersen, 1999).

    Many environmental actors (in particular environmental NGOs) have thereby criticised *Agenda 2000* for not going far enough. Bignal (1999, 1), for example, referred to the agenda as a 'halfway house', with some positive and negative elements with regard to environmental management of the European countryside. Despite the emphasis placed upon the central role of farming in protecting the rural environment, the anticipated budget for agri-environmental schemes and rural development remains small, around 10% of the total anticipated budget for the time period between 2000 and

2006, the bulk of the remainder being given over to market support. Contradictions persist in CAP support, for example through the continuing support of forage maize, despite not only the clear negative environmental effects of converting grassland to arable, but also because of the major differences in levels of support between pasture and forage systems.

The key challenge both for *Agenda 2000* and for future AEP, however, is not necessarily budgetary. Nor is it about offering a radical alternative to the current model of European agricultural support. Less about making distinctions than about uniting what have become, under the CAP but also as a result of evolving social and consumer trends, increasingly distinct rural concerns, future AEP needs to move beyond the strictly agricultural policy domain, wherein it currently lies, to embrace a far broader rural agenda. We would argue that, where they have taken place, the first steps along this path have been perhaps the greatest achievements of agri-environmental policy to date.

Bibliography

Abler, D. and Shortle, J. (1992), 'Environmental and farm policy linkages in the US and the EC', *European Review of Agricultural Economics,* vol. 19, pp. 197-217.

Adams, W.M., Bourn, N.A.D. and Hodge, I. (1992), 'Conservation in the wider countryside: SSSIs and wildlife habitat in eastern England', *Land Use Policy,* vol. 9, pp. 235-48.

Adams, W.M., Hodge, I.D. and Bourn, N.A.D. (1994), 'Nature conservation and the management of the wider countryside in eastern England', *Journal of Rural Studies,* vol. 10, pp. 147-57.

Agger, P. and Brandt, J. (1988), 'Dynamics of small biotopes in Danish agricultural landscapes', *Landscape Ecology,* vol. 1, pp. 227-40.

Aldinger, F. (1997), 'Entwicklung der Umstellungsbetriebe des EU-Extensivierungsprogramms in Baden-Württemberg: 5 Jahre danach', in: Nieberg, H. (ed.), *Ökologischer Landbau: Entwicklung, Wirtschaftlichkeit, Marktchancen und Umweltrelevanz,* Bundesforschungsanstalt für Landwirtschaft, Braun-schweig-Völkenrode, pp. 75-90.

Alphandéry, P., Bitoun, Y. and Dupont, P. (1990), 'Les agriculteurs et la sensibilité écologique', *Courrier de la Cellule Environnement de l'INRA,* vol. 90, pp. 14-5.

Alphandéry, P. and Deverre, C. (1994), 'La politique agri-environnementale communautaire et son application en France', *Recherches en Économie et Sociologie Rurales,* 1994, pp. 2-3.

Andersen, E., Primdahl, J. and Solvang, V. (1998), *Miljøvenlige jordbrugsforanstaltninger og de Særligt Følsomme Landbrugsområder 1994-96: evaluering af MVJ-ordningens iværksættelse og betydning,* DSR, Frederiksberg.

Associação de Agricultores do Campo Branco (1995), *Programa zonal de Castro Verde,* AACB (Boletim informativo), Campo Branco.

Baldock, D. (1990), *Agriculture and habitat loss in Europe,* WWF, Gland.

Baldock, D. (1994), 'New environmental schemes being approved', *La Cañada* 1, p. 5.

Baldock, D. (1995), 'Agriculture, CAP and biodiversity', in: Reus, J.A., Mitchell, K., Klaver, C.J. and Baldock, D. (eds.), *Greening the CAP,* IEEP, London, pp. 16-20.

Baldock, D. (1998), *The detailed Agenda 2000 proposals on agriculture: a first review,* Countryside Commission, London.

Baldock, D., Beaufoy, G., Brouwer, F.M. and Godeschalk, F.E. (1996), *Farming at the margins,* Agricultural Economics Research Institute, The Hague.

Baldock D. and Bennett, G. (1991), *Agriculture and the polluter pays principle in six EC countries,* IEEP, London.

Baldock, D., Cox, C., Lowe, P.D. and Winter, M. (1990), 'Environmentally Sensitive Areas: incrementalism or reform?' *Journal of Rural Studies,* vol. 6, pp. 143-62.

Baldock, D. and Lowe, P.D. (1996), 'The development of European agri-environmental policy', in: Whitby, M. (ed.), *The European environment and CAP reform: policies and prospects for conservation*, CAB International, Wallingford, pp. 8-25.

Baldock, D., Mitchell, K., von Meyer, H. and Beaufoy, G. (1998), *Assessment of the environmental impact of certain agricultural measures*, IEEP, London.

Barbut, L. (1997), *Le programme agri-environnemental de la région Franche-Comté: premiers éléments d'évaluation et enseignements méthodologiques*, Proceedings of the Société Française d'Économie Rurale conference 'Les MAE: Premiers Bilans', 3-4 November 1997, SFER, Paris, unpaginated.

Barceló, L.V., Compés, R., García, J.M. and Tió, C. (1995), *La organización económica de la agricultura española: adaptación de la agricultura española a la normativa de la UE*, Fundación Alfonso Martín Escudero-Mundiprensa, Madrid.

Barnes, P.M. (1996), 'The Nordic countries and European environmental policy', in: Miles, L. (ed.), *The European Union and the Nordic countries*, Routledge, London, pp. 203-21.

Barral, P. (1968), *Les agrariens francais: de Méline ^ Pisani*, A. Colin, Paris.

Beaufoy, G., Baldock, D. and Clark, J. (1994), *The nature of farming: low intensity farming systems in nine European countries*, IEEP, London.

Beopoulos, N. (1996), 'The impact of agricultural activities', in: Papaspiliopoulos, S., Papayannis, M. and Kouvelis, S. (eds.), *The state of the environment in Greece* (in Greek), Bothsakis Foundation, Athens, pp. 18-31.

Beopoulos, N. and Louloudis, L. (1997), 'Farmers' acceptance of agri-environmental policy measures: a survey of Greece', *South European Society and Politics*, vol. 2, pp. 118-37.

Beopoulos, N. and Skouras, D. (1997), 'Agriculture and the Greek rural environment', *Sociologia Ruralis*, vol. 37, pp. 255-69.

Berlan-Darqué, M. and Kalaora, B. (1992), 'The ecologization of French agriculture', *Sociologia Ruralis*, vol. 32, pp. 104-14.

Bignal, E. (1999), 'Agreement on Agenda 2000 in sight', *La Cañada*, vol. 10, 1-3.

Bignal, E. and McCracken, D. (1992), *Prospects for nature conservation in European pastoral farming systems*, Joint Nature Conservation Committee, Peterborough.

Billaud, J.-P. (1994), 'De la solution negociada de los conflictos a la negociation institucional', *Agricultura y Sociedad*, vol. 71, pp. 209-42.

Billaud, J.-P., Bruckmeier, K., Patricio, T. and Pinton, F. (1997), 'Social construction of the rural environment: Europe and discourses in France, Germany and Portugal', in: de Haen, H., Kasimis, B. and Redclift, M. (eds.), *Sustainable rural development*, Ashgate, Aldershot, pp. 9-34.

Billaud, J.-P. and Pinton, F. (1996), *Sociological enquiry into the conditions required for the success of the supporting environmental measures within the reform of the CAP: report on French case study*, Report to the DGXII of the European Commission, Contract EV5V-CT94-0372, Centre National de la Recherche Scientifique, Paris.

Birdlife International (1996), *Nature conservation benefits of plans under the Agri-Environment Regulation (EEC 2078/92)*, Birdlife International, Sandy.

Black, R. (1992), *Crisis and change in rural Europe: agricultural development in the Portuguese mountains*, Avebury, Aldershot.

BMELF [Bundesministerium für Ernährung, Landwirtschaft und Forsten] (1995), *Umsetzung der Verordnung (EWG) Nr. 2078/92 in der Bundesrepublik Deutschland*, BMELF, Bonn.

BMELF [Bundesministerium für Ernährung, Landwirtschaft und Forsten] (1997), *Pressekonferenz 'Agrarumweltprogramme in Deutschland'*, BMELF-Pressestelle (Pressemitteilung 12.8.1997), Bonn.

BMLF [Bundesministerium für Land- und Forstwirtschaft] (1996a), *Österreichisches Programm zur Förderung einer umweltgerechten, extensiven und den natürlichen Lebensraum schützenden Landwirtschaft*, BMLF, Wien.

BMLF [Bundesministerium für Land- und Forstwirtschaft] (1996b), *Ökologische Evaluierung des Umweltprogrammes (ÖPUL I) Band 1 und 2*, BMLF, Wien.

BMLF [Bundesministerium für Land- und Forstwirtschaft] (1996c), *Ökonomische Evaluierung des Umweltprogrammes (ÖPUL I)*, BMLF, Wien.

BMLF [Bundesministerium für Land- und Forstwirtschaft] (1996d), *INVECOS/ÖPUL I: Förderungsstatistik 1995 und 1996*, BMLF, Wien.

BMLF [Bundesministerium für Land- und Forstwirtschaft] (1997), *Lebensmittelbericht*, BMLF, Wien.

Bodiguel, M. and Buller, H. (1989), 'Agricultural pollution and the environment in France', *Tijdschrift voor Sociaal Wetenschappelijke Onderzoek van de Landbouw*, vol. 3, pp. 217-39.

Body, A. (1982), *Agriculture: the triumph and the shame*, Temple-Smith, London.

Boisson, J.-M. and Buller, H. (1996), 'France', in: Whitby, M. (ed.), *The European environment and CAP reform: policies and prospects for conservation*, CAB International, Wallingford, pp. 105-30.

Bowers, J.K. and Cheshire, P.C. (1983), *Agriculture, the countryside and land use*, Methuen, London.

Brandt, J., Holmes, E. and Larsen, D. (1994), 'Monitoring small biotopes', in: Klijn, F. (ed.), *Ecosystem classification for environmental management*, Kluwer Academic Publishers, Dordrecht, pp. 251-74.

Braudel, F. (1986), *L'identité de la France*, Artaud, Paris.

Briand, B. (1990), *Les position des différents acteurs de l'agriculture et de l'environnement sur l'article 19*, Unpublished paper to the bi-annual conference of the Société Française d'Économie Rurale 'Agriculture et la gestion des ressources naturelles', November 1990, Paris.

Brives, H. (1998), 'L'environnement: nouveau pré carré des Chambres d'Agriculture', *Ruralia*, vol. 2, pp. 73-83.

Bronner, G., Oppermann, R. and Rösler, S. (1997), 'Umweltleistungen als Grundlage der landwirtschaftlichen Förderung: Vorschläge zur Fortentwicklung des MEKA-Programms in Baden-Württemberg', *Naturschutz und Landschaftsplanung*, vol. 29, pp. 357-65.

Brotherton, I. (1989), 'Farming conflicts in national parks', *Journal of Environmental Management*, vol. 28, pp. 361-80.

Brouwer, F.M., Godeschalk, F.E., Hellegers, P.J. and Kelhot, H.J. (1995), *Mineral balances at farm level in the European Union*, Agricultural Economics Research Institute, The Hague.

Brouwer, F.M. and Lowe, P.D. (1998), 'CAP reform and the environment', in: Brouwer, F.M. and Lowe, P.D. (eds.), *CAP and the rural environment in transition*, Wageningen University Press, Wageningen, pp. 3-19.

Buckwell, A., Blom, J., Commins, P., Hervieu, B., Hofreither, M., von Meyer, H., Rabinowicz, E., Sotte, F. and Sumpsi Viñas, J.M. (1998), *Towards a Common Agricultural and Rural Policy for Europe*, European Economy, Reports and Studies, N° 5 (1997), Office for Official Publications of the European Communities, Luxembourg.

Buller, H. (1992), 'Agricultural change and the environment in Western Europe', in: Hoggart, K. (ed.), *Agricultural change, environment and economy*, Mansell, London, pp. 68-88.

Buller, H. (1997a), 'Regards croisés: Angleterre, Irlande, France', *Etudes Rurales*, vol. 141/142, pp. 171-4.

Buller H. (1997b), 'La fin du residualisme: rural policy evolution in France', *Built Environment*, vol. 23, pp. 221-8.

Buller, H. (1998a), *Green boxing the CAP*, Unpublished paper to the Third Environmental Summer Workshop, Centre Robert Schuman, Florence, Italy.

Buller, H. (1998b), 'Reflections across the Channel: Britain, France and the Europeanisation of environmental policy', in: Lowe, P.D. and Ward, S. (eds.), *British environmental policy and Europe*, Routledge, London, pp. 67-84.

Buller, H. (1998c), *Agrarianism, environmentalism and agri-environmental policy: towards a new 'territorialisation' of European farm systems*, Unpublished paper to the Royal Geographic Society's and Institute of British Geographers' Annual Conference, Guildford, January 1998.

Buller, H. (1999a), 'The agri-environmental measures', in: Brouwer, F.M. and Lowe, P.D. (eds.), *CAP regimes and the European countryside*, CAB International, Wallingford, pp. 121-44.

Buller, H. (1999b), 'Les mesures agri-environnementales en Grande Bretagne: enjeu national, politique communautaire', *Économie Rurale*, vol. 248, 35-41.

Buller, H., Lowe, P.D. and Flynn, A. (1992), 'National responses to the Europeanisation of environmental policy', in: Liefferink, J., Lowe, P.D and Mol, A. (eds.), *European integration and environmental policy*, Belhaven, London, pp. 175-95.

Bundesamt für Landwirtschaft (1990), *Direktzahlungen in der schweizerischen Agrarpolitik*, Eidgenössische Drucksachen- und Materialzentrale, Bern.

Bundesamt für Landwirtschaft (1997), *Direktzahlungen 1996 an die Landwirtschaft*, Bundesamt für Landwirtschaft, Bern.

Caillot, P. (1992), *Agriculture et environnement: les syndicats agricoles face au défi écologique*, Unpublished DEA Thesis, University of Paris X, Nanterre.

Carson, R. (1962), *Silent spring*, Houghton Mifflin, Boston.

CEDOC [Centro de Estadística y Documentación de Canarias] (1987), *Estadísticas básicas de Canarias*, Consejería de Economía y Comercio del Gobierno de Canarias, Las Palmas de Gran Canaria.

Cernusca, A., Bahn, M., Bitterlich, W., Newesely, C., Prock, S., Tappeiner, U., Sobotik, M., Buchgraber, K., Holaus, K. and Höller, P. (1997), 'Ökologie und Bewirtschaftung alpiner Ökosysteme', *Der Förderungsdienst*, vol. 1/97, pp. 20-4.

Charvet, J.-P. (1994), *La France agricole en état de choc*, Liris, Paris.

Christensen, N., Paaby, H. and Holten-Andersen, J. (eds.) (1993), *Miljø og samfund*, Danmarks Miljøundersøgelser (Faglig rapport N° 93), Roskilde.

Clark, J.R., Jones, A., Potter, C.A. and Lobley, M. (1997), 'Conceptualising the evolution of the European Union's agri-environmental policy: a discourse approach', *Environment and Planning A*, vol. 29, pp. 1869-85.

Cloke, P. and Little, J. (1990), *The rural state? Limits to planning in rural society*, Clarendon Press, Oxford.

Clunies-Ross, T. and Cox, G. (1994), 'Challenging the productivist paradigm: organic farming and the politics of agricultural change', in: Lowe, P.D., Marsden, T.K. and Whatmore, S. (eds.), *Regulating agriculture*, Fulton, London, pp. 53-74.

CNASEA [Centre National pour l'Amenagement des Structures Agricoles] (1993), *Rapport d'activité*, CNASEA, Paris.

CNASEA [Centre National pour l'Amenagement des Structures Agricoles] (1997), *Rapport d'activité*, CNASEA, Paris.

Collins, N. and Louloudis, L. (1995), 'Protecting the protected: the Greek agricultural policy network', *European Journal of Public Policy*, vol. 1, pp. 95-114.

Conway, R. and Pretty, J. (1991), *Unwelcome harvest*, Earthscan, London.

Cooper, N. (1999), *Street-level bureaucrats and the ESA scheme: the FRCA project officer in the UK*, Unpublished PhD thesis, Department of Geography, King's College London, London.

Coulomb, P., Delorme, H., Hervieu, B., Jollivet, M. and Lacombe, P. (1990), *Les agriculteurs et la politique*, Presses de la FNSP, Paris.

Country Landowners Association [CLA] (1997), Personal communication, CLA, London, March 1997.

Countryside Commission (1974), *New agricultural landscapes*, Countryside Commission, Cheltenham.

Courtet, C., Berlan-Darqué, M. and Demarne, Y. (eds.) (1993), *Agriculture et société: pistes pour la recherche*, INRA Editions, Paris.

Cox, G., Lowe, P.D. and Winter, M. (1985), 'Changing directions in agricultural policy: corporatist arrangements in production and conservation policies', *Sociologia Ruralis*, vol.25, pp. 130-54.

CPRE [Council for the Protection of Rural England] (1996), *Evidence submitted by CPRE to the Agriculture Committee Inquiry into Environmentally Sensitive Areas and other schemes under the Agri-Environment Regulation*, House of Commons, London.

CREM [Centro Regional de Estadística de Murcia] (1995), *Anuario estadístico de la región de Murcia 1994*, Comunidad Autónoma de la Región de Murcia, Murcia.

Curry, N. and Stucki, E. (1997), 'Swiss agricultural policy and the environment: an example for the rest of Europe to follow?', *Journal of Environmental Planning and Management*, vol. 40, 465-82.

DANI [Department of Agriculture for Northern Ireland] (1998), Personal communication, DANI, Belfast, May 1998.

Danmarks Statistik (1993), *Landbrugsstatistik*, Danmarks Statistik, Copenhagen.

Daugbjerg, C. (1998), 'Linking policy networks and environmental policies: nitrate policy making in Denmark and Sweden 1970-1995', *Public Administration*, vol. 76, 275-94.

Dax, T. and Wiesinger, G. (1998), *Mountain farming and the environment: towards integration*, Bundesanstalt für Bergbauernfragen (Research report N° 44), Wien.

De danske landboforeninger (1996a), *Landøkonomisk oversigt 1996*, De danske landboforeninger, Copenhagen.

De danske landboforeninger (1996b), *Statistik nyt N° 9*, De danske landboforeninger, Copenhagen.

De Juana, E., Martín-Novella, C., Naveso, M.A., Pain, D. and Sears, J. (1993), 'Farming and birds in Spain: threats and opportunities for conservation', *RSPB Conservation Review*, vol. 7, pp. 67-73.

De Juana, E., Santos, T., Suárez, F. and Tellería, J.L. (1988), 'Status and conservation of steppe birds and their habitats in Spain', in: International Council for Bird Preservation (ed.), *Technical publications vol. 7*, ICBP, Cambridge, pp. 113-23.

De Putter, J. (1995), *The greening of Europe's agricultural policy: the 'Agri-Environmental Regulation' of the MacSharry reform*, Agricultural Economics Research Institute (LEI-DLO), The Hague.

Deutscher Bundestag (1995), *Rahmenplan der Gemeinschaftsaufgabe 'Verbesserung der Agrarstruktur und des Küstenschutzes' für den Zeitraum 1996 bis 1999*, Deutscher Bundestag (Drucksache 13/4349), Bonn.

Deverre, C. (1998), 'La mise au propre de la nature: la construction sociale de la protection des milieux naturels de la steppe de Crau et des massifs boisés du Var', *Etudes Rurales*, vol. 141-142, pp. 31-49.

Díaz, M., Campos, P. and Pulido, J. (1997), 'The Spanish dehesas: a diversity in land-use and wildlife', in: Pain, D. and Pienkowski, M. (eds.), *Farming and birds in Europe: the Common Agricultural Policy and its implications for bird conservation*, Academic Press, London, pp. 178-209.

DGVI [Directorat Général VI] (1999), *Final report of FAIR Project CT95-0274 on 'Implementation and effectiveness of EU agri-environmental schemes established under Regulation 2078'*, DGVI, Brussels.

DoE [Department of the Environment] (1992), *Action for the countryside*, DoE, London.

Domingo, R. (ed.) (1994), *Anuario autonómico 1993*, Planeta-De Agostini S.A., Barcelona.

Donázar, J.A., Naveso, M.A., Tella, J.L. and Campión, D. (1997), 'Historical trends in extensive livestock farming in Spain: economic viability and the impact of the Common Agricultural Policy', in: Pain, D. and Pienkowski, M. (eds.), *Farming and birds in Europe: the Common Agricultural Policy and its implications for bird conservation*, Academic Press, London, pp. 124-49.

Drake, L. (1984), *Skötsellagen och naturvårdslagen i jordbruket: en välfärdsekonomisk analys*, Swedish University of Agricultural Sciences (Department of Economics and Statistics), Uppsala.

Dwyer, J. and Hodge, I. (1996), *Countryside in trust: land management by conservation, recreation and amenity organisations*, Wiley, Chichester.

EC [European Commission] (1985a), *Perspectives for the Common Agricultural Policy*, European Commission (COM[85] 333), Brussels.

EC [European Commission] (1985b), 'Council Regulation (EEC) N° 797/85 of 12 March 1985 on improving the efficiency of agricultural structures', *Official Journal of the European Communities*, vol. L 93 of 30.03.1985.

EC [European Commission] (1991a), *The development and future of the Common Agricultural Policy: reflections paper of the Commission*, European Commission (COM[91] 100), Brussels.

EC [European Commission] (1991b), *The agricultural situation in the Community: Report 1990*, Office for Official Publications of the European Communities, Luxembourg.

EC [European Commission] (1992a), 'Council Regulation (EEC) N° 2078/92 of 30 June 1992 on Agricultural Production Methods Compatible with the Requirements of the Protection of the Environment and the Maintenance of the Countryside', *Official Journal of the European Communities*, vol. L 215 of 30.07.1992, pp. 85-90.

EC [European Commission] (1992b), *Agriculture in Europe*, Office for Official Publication of the European Commuities, Luxembourg.

EC [European Commission] (1996), 'Council Regulation (EEC) N° 746/96 of 24 April 1996 laying down detailed rules for the application of Council Regulation (EEC) N° 2078/92 on Agricultural Production Methods Compatible with the Requirements of the Protection of the Environment and the Maintenance of the Countryside', *Official Journal of the European Communities*, vol. L 102 of 25.04.96, pp. 19-27.

EC [European Commission] (1997a), *Report from the Commission to the Council and the European Parliament on the application of Council Regulation (EEC) N° 2078/92 on Agricultural Production Methods Compatible with the Requirements of the Protection of the Environment and the Maintenance of the Countryside*, European Commission (COM[97] 620), Brussels.

EC [European Commission] (1997b), *Agriculture and environment*, Office for Official Publications of the European Commission, Luxembourg.

EC [European Commission] (1997c), *EAGGF Guarantee: 26th financial report*, Office for Official Publications of the European Communities, Luxembourg.

EC [European Commission] (1997d), *Agenda 2000: Agricultural Chapter*, DGVI, Brussels.

EC [European Commission] (1997e), *CAP 2000 working document: rural developments*, DGVI, Brussels.

EC [European Commission] (1997f), *The agricultural situation in the European Union: Report 1996*, Office for Official Publications of the European Commission, Luxembourg.

EC [European Commission] (1998), *Evaluation of agri-environment programmes*, DGVI (Working Document VI/7655/98), Brussels.

EC [European Commission] (1999a), *Berlin European Council Agenda 2000: conclusions of the Presidency*, DGVI (Agenda 2000 Newsletter N° 10), Brussels.

EC [European Commission] (1999b), *Agriculture Council: political agreement on CAP reform*, DGVI (Agenda 2000 Newsletter N° 11), Brussels.

Ellenberg, H., Rüger, A. and Vauk, G. (1989), 'Eutrophierung: das gravierendste Problem im Naturschutz?', *Berichte der Norddeutschen Naturschutzakademie*, vol. 2, pp. 5-9.

Eurostat (1996), *Farm structure survey*, Office for Official Publications of the European Communities, Luxembourg.

Eurostat (1998), *Agriculture statistical yearbook*, Office for Official Publications of the European Communities, Luxembourg.

Fasola, M. and Ruíz, X. (1997), 'Rice farming and waterbirds: integrated management in an artificial landscape', in: Pain, D. and Pienkowski, M. (eds.), *Farming and birds in Europe: the Common Agricultural Policy and its implications for bird conservation*, Academic Press, London, pp. 210-35.

Fernández, P. (1996), *Espacios naturales protegidos del estado español*, Federación de Parques Naturales y Nacionales-Agencia del Medio Ambiente de la Comunidad de Madrid, Madrid.

FoE [Friends of the Earth] (1992), *Environmentally Sensitive Areas*, FoE, London.

Fottorino, E. (1989), *La France en friche*, Lieu Commun, Paris.

Froud, J. (1994), 'The impact of ESAs on lowland farming', *Land Use Policy*, vol. 11, pp. 107-18.

Führer, J. (1997), *Interessenvermittlung und Steuerungsproblematik im agrarpolitischen Netz*, Peter Lang, Frankfurt am Main.

García Dory, M.A., Martínez, J.S. and Vela, S. (1985), *Sistemas ganaderos extensivos I*, Instituto de Economía Agraria y Desarrollo Rural del CSIC (Monografías IEA 11), Madrid.

GCT [Game Conservancy Trust] (1997), *Evidence submitted to the Agriculture Committee Inquiry into Environmentally Sensitive Areas and other schemes under the Agri-Environment Regulation*, House of Commons, London.

Geier, U., Urfei, G. and Weis, J. (1996), *Stand der Umsetzung einer umweltfreundlichen Bodennutzung in der Landwirtschaft*, Dr. Köster Verlag, Berlin.

Gerakis, P. (ed.) (1990), *Protection and management of the Greek wetlands* (in Greek), Aristotelian University of Thessaloniki, Thessaloniki.

Gibbons, D., Avery, M., Baillie, S., Gregory, R., Kirby, J., Porter, R., Tucker, G., and Williams, G. (1996), 'Bird species of conservation concern in the United Kingdom, Channel Islands and the Isle of Man: revising the Red Data List', *RSPB Conservation Review*, vol. 10, pp. 3-6.

Green, B. (1985), *Countryside conservation*, Allen and Unwin, London.

Groier, M. (1993), *Bergraum in Bewegung*, Bundesanstalt für Bergbauernfragen (Research report N° 31), Wien.

Groier, M. (1995), 'Agrarische Umweltprogramme in der EU nach VO 2078/92', in: Bundesministerium für Land- und Forstwirtschaft (ed.), *Grüner Bericht 1995*, Bundesministerium für Land- und Forstwirtschaft, Wien, pp. 47-8.

Groier, M. (1998a), *Entwicklung und Bedeutung des biologischen Landbaus in Österreich im internationalen Kontext*, Bundesanstalt für Bergbauernfragen, Wien.

Groier, M. (1998b), 'Der biologische Landbau in Österreich im Kontext der agrarischen Umweltpolitik', in: Agrarbündnis (ed.), *Der kritische Agrarbericht 1998*, Agrarbündnis, Bonn, pp. 321-31.

Grubb, M., Koch, M., Munson, A., Sullivan, F. and Thomson, K. (eds.) (1993), *The Earth Summit agreements: a guide and assessment*, Earthscan, London.

Gruber, W. (1992), *Die schweizerische Agrarpolitik vor einer ökologischen Neuorientierung?* Universitätsverlag, Freiburg.

Haber, W. (1971), 'Landschaftspflege durch differenzierte Bodennutzung', *Bayerisches Landwirtschaftliches Jahrbuch*, vol. 48 (Sonderheft 1), pp. 19-24.

Häfliger, M., Keusch, A., Lehmann, B. and Wolf, H.P. (1995), *Anpassungsschritte landwirtschaftlicher Betriebe zwecks Abbau der N-Emissionen: technischer Bericht*, Institut für Agrarwirtschaft der ETH Zürich, Zürich.

Hampicke, U. (1988), 'Extensivierung der Landwirtschaft für den Naturschutz: Ziele, Rahmenbedingungen und Maßnahmen', *Schriftenreihe Bayerisches Landesamt für Umweltschutz*, vol. 84, pp. 9-35.

Hansen, B. and Primdahl, J. (1991), *Miljøfølsomme områder: evaluering af MFO-ordningens iværksættelse og betydning*, DSR (Landskabsserie Nº 1), Frederiksberg.

Hanser, C. (1991), 'Berggebietsförderung und Ökologie: ein Widerspruch?', *Geographica Helvetica*, vol. 46, pp. 118-23.

Hart, K. (1997), 'The implementation and effectiveness of Regulation 2078/92 in the UK', in: Project FAIR1 CT95-0274: *Implementation and effectiveness of agri-environmental schemes established under Regulation 2078/92: first progress report to the European Commission*, Institut für ländliche Strukturforschung, Frankfurt.

Hart, K. and Wilson, G.A. (1998), 'UK implementation of Agri-environment Regulation 2078/92/EEC: enthusiastic supporter or reluctant participant?', *Landscape Research*, vol. 23, pp. 255-72.

Hasund, K.P. (1991), *Landskapspolitiken i Sverige 1960-90: en empirisk utvärdering*, Swedish University of Agricultural Sciences (Department of Economics), Uppsala.

Heißenhuber, A., Katzek, J., Meusel, F. and Ring, H. (1994), *Landwirtschaft und Umwelt*, Economica, Bonn.

Heißenhuber, A. and Ring, H. (1991), *Grundwasserschutz und Landbewirtschaftung: Wasserwirtschaftliche, pflanzenbauliche und ökonomische Aspekte*, Ulmer, Stuttgart.

Hellenic Zoological Society (1992), *Red Data Book of threatened vertebrates of Greece*, Hellenic Zoological Society and Hellenic Ornithological Society, Athens.

Hendriks, G. (1991), *Germany and European integration the Common Agricultural Policy: an area of conflict*, Berg, Oxford.

Hernández, Z. (1996), *Guía de Tenerife*, Editorial El País S.A. y Santillana S.A., Madrid.

Hervieu, B. and Lagarve, R.-M. (eds.) (1992), *Les syndicats agricoles en Europe*, L'Harmattan, Paris.

Hess, J. and Vogl, C. R. (1997), 'Biolandbau austriae: quo vadis?', in: Agrarbündnis (ed.), *Der kritische Agrarbericht 1997*, Agrarbündnis, Bonn, pp. 40-9.

HMILFN [Hessisches Ministerium des Innern und für Landwirtschaft, Forsten und Naturschutz] (1998), *Veränderungen in der Kulturlandschaft: Lebensraum Grünland*, HMILFN, Wiesbaden.

HMLFN [Hessisches Ministerium für Landwirtschaft, Forsten und Naturschutz] (1990), *Ökologie-Forum in Hessen Flächenstillegungen in der Landwirtschaft: Auswirkungen auf den Naturhaushalt*, HMLFN, Wiesbaden.

HMSO [Her Majesty's Stationery Office] (1986), *Statutory instrument 2253*, HMSO, London.

HMSO [Her Majesty's Stationery Office] (1996), *Environmental statistics 1996*, HMSO, London.

Hofer, E. (1998), 'Direktzahlungen und die aktuellen Spannungsfelder heute', *Agrarwirtschaft und Agrarsoziologie*, vol. 2, pp. 23-41.

Hofreither, M. and Rauchenberger, F. (1995), *Administrative versus ökonomische Einflüsse auf die Nitratbelastung von Grundwasser*, Bundesministerium für Land- und Forstwirtschaft (Project report for Research project 775/93), Wien.

Hoggart, K., Buller, H. and Black, R. (1995), *Rural Europe: identity and change*, Edward Arnold, London.

Höll, A. and von Meyer, H. (1996), 'Germany', in: Whitby, M. (ed.), *The European environment and CAP reform: policies and prospects for conservation*, CAB International, Wallingford, pp. 70-85.

Hondraki-Birbili, C. and Lucas, N. (1997), 'The integration of environment into agricultural policies for rural Greece', *Journal of Environmental Management*, vol. 49, 337-53.

Hoskins, W.G. (1955), *The making of the English landscape*, Hodder and Stoughton, London.

House of Commons (1997), *Environmentally Sensitive Areas and other schemes under the Agri-Environment Regulation*, HMSO, London.

House of Lords (1984), *Agriculture and the environment*, HMSO, London.

Hovorka, G. (1996), *Das Direktzahlungssystem in Österreich nach dem EU-Beitritt*, Bundesanstalt für Bergbauernfragen (Research report N° 37), Wien.

Hovorka, G. (1998), *Die Kulturlandschaft im Berggebiet: Politiken zur Sicherung von Umwelt- und Kulturleistungen und ländliche Entwicklung (OECD Fallstudie)*, Bundesanstalt für Bergbauernfragen (Research report N° 43), Wien.

IEADR [Instituto das Estruturas Agrárias e Desenvolvimento Rural] (1993), *Portugal agrícola*, IEADR, Lisbon.

IEADR [Instituto das Estruturas Agrárias e Desenvolvimento Rural] (1994), *Medidas agro-ambientais: proposta de aplicação a Portugal para o período 1994 - 1998*, IEADR, Lisbon.

IEADR [Instituto das Estruturas Agrárias e Desenvolvimento Rural] (1995), *Relatório de execução material e financeira*, IEADR, Lisbon.

IGN [Instituto Geográfico Nacional] (1992), *Atlas nacional de España: climatología*, IGN, Madrid.

Ilbery, B. and Bowler, I. (1998), 'From agricultural productivism to post-productivism', in: Ilbery, B. (ed.): *The geography of rural change*, Longman, Harlow, pp. 57-84.

INE [Instituto Nacional de Estadística] (1996a), *Anuario estadístico 1995*, INE, Madrid.

INE [Instituto Nacional de Estadística] (1996b), *Encuesta de población activa: segundo trimestre 1996*, INE, Madrid.

Ingelög, T., Thor, G., Hallingbäck, T., Andersson, R. and Aronsson, M. (1993), *Floravård i jordbrukslandskapet: skyddsvärda växter*, SBT-Förlag, Lund.

Institut Français pour l'Environnement [IFEN] (1997), *Comptes d'évolution de l'occupation des Terres*, IFEN, Orleans.

ITGME [Instituto Tecnológico Geominero de España] (1993), *La calidad de las aguas subterráneas en España*, ITGME, Madrid.

Jauneau, J.C. and Rémy, J. (1997), *L'application de l'article 19 dans le Parc Naturel Régional du Vercours: un goût d'inacevé*, Proceedings of the Société Française d'Économie Rurale conference (SFER) 'Les MAE: Premiers Bilans', 3-4 November 1997, SFER, Paris, unpaginated.

Jenkins, T. (1990), *Future harvests: the economics of farming and the environment*, Council for the Protection of Rural England, London.

Jones, A. (1991), 'The impact of EC set-aside policy: the response of farm businesses in Rendsburg-Eckernförde (Germany)', *Land Use Policy*, vol. 8, pp. 108-25.

Jones, A. (1994), *The new Germany*, Wiley, Chichester.

Jones, A., Fasterding, F. and Plankl, R. (1993), 'Farm household adjustments to the European Community's set-aside policy: evidence from Rheinland-Pfalz (Germany)', *Journal of Rural Studies*, vol. 9, pp. 65-80.

Jordan, G., Maloney, W. and McLaughlin, A. (1994), 'Characterizing agricultural policy-making', *Public Administration*, vol. 72, pp. 502-26.

Jordbrugsdirektoratet (1993), *Opgørelser over videreførte og nye MFO-aftaler for 1990 og 1991*, Jordbrugsdirektoratet (unpublished), Copenhagen.

Jungehülsing, J. and Lotz, J. (1997), 'Agrarumweltprogramme 1997', *AID-Informationen für die Agrarberatung*, vol. 5, pp. 4-10.

Karl, H. and Urfei, G. (1997), 'Ökonomische Effizienz von Umwelt und Naturschutzprogrammen im ländlichen Raum', in: Bauer, S. (ed.), *Märkte der Agrar- und Ernährungswirtschaft: Analyse, einzelwirtschaftliche Strategien, staatliche Einflußnahme*, Landwirtschaftsverlag, Münster-Hiltrup, pp. 111-31.

Klinkmann, D. and Tremel, S. (1995), 'Ökologischer Landbau im Rahmen des Extensivierungsprogramms in den neuen Ländern', *AID-Informationen für die Agrarberatung*, vol. 3, pp. 7-10.

Kluge, U. (1989), *Vierzig Jahre Agrarpolitik in der Bundesrepublik Deutschland (2 volumes)*, Paul Parey, Hamburg.

Knauer, N. (1989), 'Katalog zur Bewertung und Honorierung ökologischer Leistungen der Landwirtschaft', in: Streit, M. E., Wildenmann, R. and Jesinghaus, J. (eds.), *Landwirtschaft und Umwelt: Wege aus der Krise,* Nomos, Baden-Baden, pp. 179-202.

Knöbl, I. (1989), 'Das Bayerische Kulturlandschaftsprogramm', *Der Förderungsdienst*, vol. 11/89, pp. 336-40.

König, M. (1991), 'Flächenstillegung und Extensivierung in der Landwirtschaft', *Agra-Europe Bonn,* vol. 31/91, Dokumentation.

Köpke, U. and Haas, G. (1997), 'Umweltrelevanz des ökologischen Landbaus', in: Nieberg, H. (ed.), *Ökologischer Landbau: Entwicklung, Wirtschaftlichkeit, Marktchancen und Umweltrelevanz*, Bundesforschungsanstalt für Landwirtschaft, Braunschweig-Völkenrode, pp. 119-46.

Krammer, J. and Scheer, G. (1978), *Das österreichische Agrarsystem I*, Bundesministerium für Land- und Forstwirtschaft, Wien.

Lampkin, N. (1996), *European organic farming statistics*, University of Aberystwyth, Aberystwyth.

Land Use Consultants (1995), *Countryside Stewardship monitoring and evaluation: third interim report,* Countryside Commission, Cheltenham.

Landbrugs- og Fiskeriministeriet (1996), *Betænkning fra udvalget om natur, miljø og EUs landbrugspolitik,* Landbrugs- og Fiskeriministeriet, Copenhagen.

Landesamt für Naturschutz und Landschaftspflege Schleswig Holstein (1991), Extensivierungsförderung: Bilanz und Folgerungen, *Natur und Landschaft,* vol. 66, pp. 37-49.

Larrue, C. (1992), 'Le comportement des agriculteurs face aux mesures de protection de l'eau', *Économie Rurale,* vol. 208-209, pp. 42-9.

Lasanta, T. (1988), 'The process of desertion of cultivated areas in the central Spanish Pyrenees', *Pirineos,* vol. 132, pp. 15-36.

Louloudis, L. and Maraveyas, N. (1997), 'Farmers and agricultural policy in Greece since the accession to the European Union', *Sociologia Ruralis,* vol. 37, pp. 270-86.

Lowe, P.D. (1992), 'Industrial agriculture and environmental regulation', *Sociologia Ruralis,* vol. 32, pp. 1-18.

Lowe, P.D., Clark, J., Seymour, S. and Ward, N. (1997), *Moralizing the environment,* UCL Press, London.

Lowe, P.D. and Goyder, J. (1983), *Environmental groups in politics,* Allen and Unwin, London.

Lowe, P.D. and Ward, S. (eds.) (1998), *British environmental policy and Europe,* Routledge, London.

Lucas, P.H. (1992), *Protected landscapes: a guide for policy makers and planners,* Chapman and Hall, London.

Lundgren, L.J. (1990), *Miljöpolitik på längden och tvären,* Swedish National Environmental Protection Agency (Rapport 3635), Solna.

MacEwan, M. and Sinclair, G. (1983), *New life for the hills,* Council for National Parks, London.

MAFF [Ministry of Agriculture, Fisheries and Food] (1989), *Environmentally Sensitive Areas,* HMSO, London.

MAFF [Ministry of Agriculture, Fisheries and Food] (1995), *Environmental land management schemes in England,* MAFF, London.

MAFF [Ministry of Agriculture, Fisheries and Food] (1996a), *Evidence submitted to the Agriculture Committee Inquiry into Environmentally Sensitive Areas and other schemes under the Agri-Environment Regulation,* MAFF, London.

MAFF [Ministry of Agriculture, Fisheries and Food] (1996b), Personal communication, MAFF, London, June-December 1996.

MAFF [Ministry of Agriculture, Fisheries and Food] (1997a), *Going organic: Government announces details of review,* MAFF (Press release 221/97), London.

MAFF [Ministry of Agriculture, Fisheries and Food] (1997b), *South Downs ESA: report of environmental monitoring 1987-1995,* HMSO, London.

MAFF [Ministry of Agriculture, Fisheries and Food] (1998), Personal communication, MAFF, London, May 1998.

Mannion, A.M. (1995), *Agriculture and environmental change: temporal and spatial dimensions,* Wiley, Chichester.

MAPA [Ministerio de Agricultura, Pesca y Alimentación] (1990-94), *Anuario de estadística agraria 1988-92,* MAPA, Madrid.

MAPA [Ministerio de Agricultura, Pesca y Alimentación] (1994), *Programa de ayudas para fomentar métodos de producción agraria compatibles con las exigencias de protección del medio ambiente y la conservación del espacio natural,* MAPA, Madrid.

MAPA [Ministerio de Agricultura, Pesca y Alimentación] (1995), *Anuario de estadística agraria 1993,* MAPA, Madrid.

Marsden, T., Murdoch, J., Lowe, P.D., Munton, R. and Flynn, A. (1993), *Constructing the countryside,* UCL Press, London.

Meeus, J. H. (1993), 'The transformation of agricultural landscapes in Western Europe', *The Science of the Total Environment,* vol. 129, pp. 171-90.

Mehl, P. and Plankl, R. (1996), "Doppelte Politikverflechtung' als Bestimmungsfaktor der Agrarstrukurpolitik: untersucht am Beispiel der Förderung umweltgerechter landwirtschaftlicher Produktionsverfahren in der Bundesrepublik Deutschland', in: Kirschke, D. (ed.), *Agrarstrukturentwicklung und Agrarpolitik,* Landwirtschaftsverlag, Münster-Hiltrup, pp. 57-68.

Mengin, J. (1991), 'L'image du paysan dans la société française', *Économie Rurale,* vol. 201, pp. 37-40.

Metais, M. (1997), Unpublished address of the President of the 'Lègue pour la Protection des Oiseaux' to the Société Française d'Économie Rurale conference 'Les MAE: Premiers Bilans', 3-4 November 1997, Paris, SFER.

Miljø- og Energiministeriet (1995a), *Denmarks nature and environment policy 1995: summary report,* Miljø- og Energiministeriet, Copenhagen.

Miljø- og Energiministeriet (1995b), *Miljøindikatorer 1995,* Miljø- og Energiministeriet, Copenhagen.

Miljøministeriet (1994), *The Danish environmental strategy,* Miljøministeriet, Copenhagen.

Ministère de l'Agriculture (1980), *Activités agricoles et qualité des eaux (Rapport Hénin),* Ministères de l'Agriculture et de l'Environnement, Paris.

Ministère de l'Agriculture (1996), Unpublished statistics, Ministère de l'Agriculture, Paris.

Ministère de l'Environnement (1989), *L'Etat de l'environnement,* La Documentation Française, Paris.

Ministério da Agricultura (1991), *PEDAP 5 anos: direcção geral de planeamento e agricultura,* Ministério da Agricultura, Lisbon.

Ministério da Agricultura (1994), *Medidas agro-ambientais,* Ministério da Agricultura (Direcção de Serviços de Política Sócio-Estrutral), Lisbon.

Ministério da Agricultura (1995), *Plano zonal de aplicação para a área do Biótopo Corine de Castro Verde,* Ministério da Agricultura (Secretaria de Estado da Agricultura), Lisbon.

Ministry of Agriculture (1993), *General implementation framework for Regulation 2078/92* (in Greek), Ministry of Agriculture, Athens.

MOA [Ministry of Agriculture] (1989), *En ny livsmedelspolitik,* Allmänna Förlaget (Ds 1989:63), Göteborg.

MOA [Ministry of Agriculture] (1994), *Förstärkta miljöinsatser i jordbruket,* Fritzes (SOU 1994:82), Stockholm.

MOA [Ministry of Agriculture] (1995), *Jordbruk och konkurrens: jordbrukets ställning i svensk och europeisk konkurrensrätt,* Fritzes (SOU 1995:117), Stockholm.

MOA [Ministry of Agriculture] (1998), *Ett nytt svenskt miljöprogram för jordbruket för perioden 2001-2005,* Ministry of Agriculture (Dir 1998:11), Stockholm.

Montes, C. and Bernués, M. (1994), 'The Spanish national wetland inventory', in: International Wetland Research Bureau (ed.), *The status of wetland inventories in the Mediterranean region,* IWRB, Slimbridge, pp. 29-40.

MOPTMA [Ministerio de Obras Pœblicas, Transportes y Medio Ambiente] (1992), *Medio ambiente en España 1992,* MOPTMA, Madrid.

Moreux, I. (1994), 'Agriculture et environnement', *Structures,* vol. 5, pp. 45-50.

Morey, M. (1992), *Estudio integrado de la isla de Formentera: bases para un ecodesarrollo,* Ministerio de Obras Pœblicas y Transportes, Madrid.

Mormont, M. (1996), 'Agriculture et environnement: pour une sociologie des dispositifs', *Économie Rurale,* vol. 236. pp. 28-36.

Morris, C. and Potter, C. (1995), 'Recruiting the new conservationists: farmers' adoption of agri-environmental schemes in the UK', *Journal of Rural Studies,* vol. 11, pp. 51-63.

Morris, C. and Young, C. (1997), 'Towards environmentally beneficial farming? An evaluation of the Countryside Stewardship Scheme', *Geography,* vol. 82, pp. 305-16.

Mousset, S. (1992), 'Protection de la nature et agriculture dans le Parc National des Cévennes: bilan d'une expérience insolite', *Annales du Parc National des Cévennes,* vol. 5, pp. 223-43.

Müller, K. (1998), 'Hintergründe zur Ablehnung der Direktzahlungen 1973', *Agrarwirtschaft und Agrarsoziologie,* vol. 2/98, pp. 9-21.

Muñoz, A. (ed.) (1991), *Recursos naturales y crecimiento económico en el 'Campo de Dalías',* Agencia de Medio Ambiente, Sevilla.

Munton, R. (1983), 'Agriculture and conservation: what room for compromise?', in: Warren, A. and Goldsmith, F. (eds.), *Conservation in practice,* John Wiley, London, pp. 84-109.

Murdoch, J. (1995), 'Governmentality and the politics of resistance in UK agriculture: the case of the Farmers' Union of Wales', *Sociologia Ruralis,* vol. 35, pp. 187-205.

National Environmental Protection Agency (1990), *Fördjupad anslagsframställning,* National Environmental Protection Agency (Skrivelse 31.3.1990), Solna.

Naveso, M.A. (1992), *Proposal to declare the steppeland of Madrigal-Peñaranda as an Environmentally Sensitive Area,* Sociedad Española de Ornitología-Junta de Castilla y León, Madrid.

Naveso, M.A. (1993), *Zonal programe proposal for the La Serena steppe area in accordance with Regulation 2078/92/EEC,* Sociedad Española de Ornitología/BirdLife, Madrid.

NCC [Nature Conservancy Council] (1984), *Nature conservation in Great Britain,* NCC, Peterborough.

Neveu, A. (1993), *Les nouveaux territoires de l'agriculture française,* Uni-Editions, Paris.

Newby, H. (1980), *Green and pleasant land? Social change in rural England*, Hutchinson, London.

Nieberg, H. (ed.) (1997), *Ökologischer Landbau: Entwicklung, Wirtschaftlichkeit, Marktchancen und Umweltrelevanz*, Bundesforschungsanstalt für Landwirtschaft, Braunschweig-Völkenrode.

OECD [Organisation for Economic Co-operation and Development] (1997), *Environmental indicators for agriculture*, OECD, Paris.

Ollagnon, H. (1985), 'Agriculture et environnement: vers une gestion de la qualité', *POUR*, vol. 99, pp. 34-9.

Oñate, J.J., Malo, J.E., Suárez, F. and Peco, B. (1998), 'Regional and environmental aspects in the implementation of Spanish agri-environmental schemes', *Journal of Environmental Management*, vol. 52, pp. 227-40.

O'Riordan, T. (1985), 'Halvergate: the politics of policy change', *Countryside Planning Yearbook*, vol. 6, pp. 101-6.

Pain, D. and Pienowski, M. (eds.) (1997), *Farming and birds in Europe: the Common Agricultural Policy and its implications for bird conservation*, Academic Press, London.

Palacios, S.P. (1998), 'Farmers and the implementation of the EU Nitrate Directive in Spain', *Sociologia Ruralis*, vol. 38, 146-159.

Peco, B. and Suárez, F. (1993), *Recomendaciones para la gestión y conservación del medio natural frente a los cambios de uso relacionados con la política agraria comunitaria*, Instituto Nacional para la Conservación de la Naturaleza (unpublished), Madrid.

Pérez Trejo, F. (1992), *Desertification and land degradation in the European Mediterranean*, European Commission (Report EUR 14850), Luxembourg.

Persson, O.L. and Westholm, E. (1993), 'Turmoil in the welfare system reshapes rural Sweden', *Journal of Rural Studies*, vol. 9, 397-404.

Petersen, J.-E. (1999), *Overview of current and planned agri-environmental activities in the CEECs*, IEEP, London.

Pettursson, O. (1993), 'Scandinavian agriculture in a changing environment', in: Harper, S. (ed.), *The greening of rural policy: international perspectives*, Belhaven, London, pp. 82-98.

Pfadenhauer, J. (1988), 'Gedanken zu Flächenstillegungs- und Extensivierungsprogrammen aus ökologischer Sicht', *Zeitschrift für Kulturtechnik und Flurbereinigung*, vol. 29, pp. 165-75.

Plankl, R. (1996a), *Synopse zu den Argrarumweltprogrammen der Länder in der Bundesrepublik Deutschland, Maßnahmen zur Förderung umweltgerechter und den natürlichen Lebensraum schützender landwirtschaftlicher Produktionsverfahren gemäß VO (EWG) 2078/92*, Bundesforschungsanstalt für Landwirtschaft (Institut für Strukturforschung), Braunschweig-Völkenrode.

Plankl, R. (1996b), 'Die Entwicklung des Finanzmitteleinsatzes für die Förderung umweltgerechter landwirtschaftlicher Produktionsverfahren in der BR Deutschland', *Agrarwirtschaft*, vol. 45, pp. 233-8.

Popp, H, (1990), *Direktzahlungen in der schweizerischen Agrarpolitik*, Eidgenössisches Volkswirtschaftsdepartement, Bern.

Potter, C. (1986), 'Processes of countryside change in lowland Britain', *Journal of Rural Studies*, vol. 2, pp. 187-95.

Potter, C. (1988), 'Environmentally Sensitive Areas in England and Wales: an experiment in countryside management', *Land Use Policy*, vol. 5, pp. 301-13.

Potter, C. (1998), *Against the grain: agri-environmental reform in the United States and the European Union*, CAB International, Wallingford.

Potter, C. and Lobley, M. (1993), 'Helping small farms and keeping Europe beautiful', *Land Use Policy*, vol. 10, pp. 267-79.

Pretty, J.N. (1995), *Regenerating agriculture: policies and practice for sustainability and self-reliance*, Earthscan, London.

Priebe, H. (1985), *Die subventionierte Unvernunft*, Siedler, Berlin.

Priebe, R. (1997), *Evidence to the Agriculture Committee of the House of Commons on Environmentally Sensitive Areas and other schemes under the Agri-Environment Regulation*, HMSO, London.

Primdahl, J. (1996), 'Denmark', in: Whitby, M. (ed.), *The European environment and CAP reform: policies and prospects for conservation*, CAB International, Wallingford, pp. 45-69.

Primdahl, J. and Hansen, B. (1993), 'Agriculture in Environmentally Sensitive Areas: implementing the ESA measure in Denmark', *Journal of Environmental Planning and Management*, vol. 36, pp. 231-38.

Primdham, G. (1994), 'National environmental policy-making in the European framework: Spain, Greece and Italy in comparison', in: Baker, S., Milton, K. and Yearly, S. (eds.), *Protecting the periphery: environmental policy in peripheral regions of the European Union*, Frank Cass, Harlow, pp. 80-101.

Rabinowicz, E. and Bolin, O. (1998), 'Negotiating the CAP: the Nordic experience', *Swedish Journal of Agricultural Research*, vol. 28, 5-15.

Rammler, C. and Würflein, T. (1991), 'Untersuchungen zum Artenspektrum auf Brachflächen aus dem Flächenstillegungsprogramm der EG im Sommer 1990', in: Regierung von Mittelfranken (ed.), *Informationen zu Naturschutz und Landschaftspflege*, Regierung von Mittelfranken, Ansbach, pp. 3-25.

Rat von Sachverständigen für Umweltfragen (1985), *Umweltprobleme der Landwirtschaft (Sondergutachten März 1985)*, Kohlhammer, Stuttgart.

Rémy, J. (1997), 'La parcelle et la lisière', *Etudes Rurales*, vol. 141-142, pp. 85-108.

Reus, J.A., Mitchell, K., Klaver, C.J. and Baldock, D. (eds.) (1995), *Greening the CAP*, IEEP, London.

Rieder, P. and Anwander Phan-Huy, S. (1994), *Grundlagen der Agrarmarktpolitik*, Hochschulverlag, Zürich.

Robinson, G.M. (1991), 'EC agricultural policy and the environment: land use implications in the UK', *Land Use Policy*, vol. 8, pp. 95-107.

Robinson, G.M. and Ilbery, B. (1993), 'Reforming the CAP: beyond MacSharry', *Progress in Rural Policy and Planning*, vol. 3, pp. 197-207.

RSPB [Royal Society for the Protection of Birds] (1991), *A future for environmentally sensitive farming: RSPB submission to the UK review of Environmentally Sensitive Areas*, RSPB, Sandy.

RSPB [Royal Society for the Protection of Birds] (1997), Personal communication, RSPB, Sandy, May 1997.

Ruedig, W. (ed.) (1992), *Green politics II*, Edinburgh University Press, Edinburgh.

Ruíz, M. (1988), 'Agriculture and environment in less-favoured areas', *Agra-Europe London*, vol. 43, pp. 29-37.

Rundqvist, B. (1996), 'Sweden', in: Whitby, M. (ed.), *The European environment and CAP reform: policies and prospects for conservation*, CAB International, Wallingford, pp. 173-85.

SBA [Swedish Board of Agriculture] (1984), *Jordbrukets hänsyn till naturvårdens intressen*, SBA (Rapport 1984:1), Jönköping.

SBA [Swedish Board of Agriculture] (1996a), *Utvecklingen inom jordbruket*, SBA (Rapport 1996:5), Jönköping.

SBA [Swedish Board of Agriculture] (1996b), *The Swedish agri-environmental programme*, SBA, Jönköping.

SBA [Swedish Board of Agriculture] (1997), *Utvärdering och översyn av det svenska miljöstödsprogrammet*, SBA (Rapport 1997:10), Jönköping.

Scheele, M. (1996), 'The agri-environmental measures in the context of the CAP reform', in: Whitby, M. (ed.), *The European environment and CAP reform: policies and prospects for conservation*, CAB International, Wallingford, pp. 3-7.

Scheele, M. and Isermeyer, F. (1989), 'Umweltschutz und Landschaftspflege im Bereich der Landwirtschaft: kostenwirksame Verpflichtung oder neue Einkommensquelle', *Berichte über Landwirtschaft*, vol. 67, pp. 86-110.

Scheele, M., Isermeyer, F. and Schmitt, G. (1993), 'Umweltpolitische Strategien zur Lösung der Stickstoffproblematik in der Landwirtschaft', *Agrarwirtschaft*, vol. 42, pp. 294 -313.

Schulze-Pals, L. (1994), *Ökonomische Analyse der Umstellung auf ökologischen Landbau*, Landwirtschaftsverlag, Münster-Hiltrup.

Schweizerischer Bauernverband (ed.) (1996), *Statistische Erhebungen und Schätzungen über Landwirtschaft und Ernährung*, Schweizerischer Bauernverband, Brugg.

Schweizerischer Bundesrat (ed.) (1992), *Siebter Landwirtschaftsbericht*, Eidgenössische Drucksachen- und Materialzentrale, Bern.

Schweizerischer Bundesrat (ed.) (1996), *Botschaft zur Reform der Agrarpolitik; Zweite Etappe (Agrarpolitik 2002)*, Eidgenössische Drucksachen- und Materialzentrale, Bern.

Schweizerisches Bauernsekretariat (1990), *Die Rolle neuer Direktzahlungen in der künftigen Agrarpolitik*, Schweizerischer Bauernverband, Brugg.

Seibert, O. and von Meyer, H. (1987), *Zur Neuorientierung der EG-Agrarpolitik unter umweltpolitischen Gesichtspunkten*, Institut für ländliche Struktur-forschung, Frankfurt.

Shoard, M. (1980), *The theft of the countryside*, Temple-Smith, London.

Sinclair, G. (1983), *New life for the hills: policies for farming and conservation in the uplands*, Council for National Parks, London.

Sinclair, G. (1992), *The lost land: land use change in England 1945-1990*, Council for the Protection of Rural England, London.

Sironi, H. and Peter, D. (1993), 'Die Berglandwirtschaft in einem nicht-touristischen Bergtal an ihren ökologischen, sozialen und ökonomischen Grenzen: von einer sektoralen zu einer integral CH vernetzten Agrar- und Regionalpolitik am Beispiel des Safientals (GR)', *Geographica Helvetica*, vol. 48, pp. 135-41.

SOAEFD [Scottish Office Agriculture, Environment and Forestry Department] (1998), Personal communication, SOAEFD, Edinburgh, May 1998.

Société Française d'Économie Rurale [SFER] (1997), *Proceedings of the Société Française d'Économie Rurale conference 'Les MAE: Premiers Bilans', 3-4 November 1997*, SFER, Paris.

SS [Statistics Sweden] (1955), *Statistisk årsbok 1955*, Statistics Sweden, Stockholm.

SS [Statistics Sweden] (1990a), *The Natural Environment in Figures*, Statistics Sweden, Stockholm.

SS [Statistics Sweden] (1990b), *Statistiska Meddelanden*, Statistics Sweden (J 13 SM 9003), Stockholm.

SS [Statistics Sweden] (1990c), *Statistiska Meddelanden*, Statistics Sweden (Na 36 SM 9001), Stockholm.

SS [Statistics Sweden] (1995), *Jordbruksstatistisk årsbok 1995*, Statistics Sweden, Stockholm.

SS [Statistics Sweden] (1996), *Jordbruksstatistisk årsbok 1996*, Statistics Sweden, Stockholm.

Stedman, N. (1993), 'Conservation in National Parks', in: Goldsmith, F. B. and Warren, A. (eds.), *Conservation in progress*, Wiley, Chichester, pp. 209-40.

Streit, M. E., Wildenmann, R. and Jesinghaus, J. (eds.) (1989), *Landwirtschaft und Umwelt: Wege aus der Krise*, Nomos, Baden-Baden.

Strukturdirektoratet (1997), *Statistics on uptake of agri-environmental measures*, Ministry of Food, Agriculture and Fisheries, Copenhagen.

Strukturdirektoratet (1998), *Landbrugets strukturudvikling*, Ministry of Food, Agriculture and Fisheries, Copenhagen.

Suárez, F., Naveso, M.A. and De Juana, E. (1997a), 'Farming in the drylands of Spain: birds of the pseudosteppes', in: Pain, D. and Pienkowski, M. (eds.), *Farming and birds in Europe: the Common Agricultural Policy and its implications for bird conservation*, Academic Press, London, pp. 297-330.

Suárez, F., Oñate, J.J., Malo, J.E. and Peco, B. (1997b), 'La aplicación del reglamento agroambiental 2078/92 CEE y la conservación de la naturaleza en España', *Revista Española de Economía Agraria*, vol. 179, pp. 267-96.

Swedish Government (1994), *Vissa livsmedelspolitiska åtgärder vid ett medlemskap i Europeiska unionen (Government Bill)*, Swedish Government, Stockholm.

Syrett, S.J. (1995), *Local development: restructuring, locality and economic initiative in Portugal*, Avebury, Aldershot.

Thompson, P. (1995), *The spirit of the soil*, Routledge, London.

Tió, C. (1991), 'Reforma de la PAC y su impacto a nivel sectorial en España', *Información Comercial Española*, vol. 700, pp. 79-90.

Tucker, G.M. and Evans, M.I. (1997), *Habitat for birds in Europe: a conservation strategy for the wider environment*, BirdLife International, Cambridge.

Tucker, G.M. and Heath, M.F. (1994), *Birds in Europe: their conservation status*, BirdLife International, Cambridge.

Urdameneta, A. and Naveso, M.A. (1993), *Propuesta de programa de zona del área de las Bardenas Reales y del Vedado de Eguaras en aplicación del Reglamento CEE 2078/92*, Sociedad Española de Ornitología/BirdLife, Madrid.

Vail, D., Hasund, K.P. and Drake, L. (1994), *The greening of agricultural policy in industrial societies: Swedish reforms in comparative perspective,* Cornell University Press, New York.

Valladares, M.A. (1993), 'Effects of EC policy implementation on natural Spanish habitats', *The Science of the Total Environment,* vol. 129, pp. 71-82.

Vera, F. and Romero, J. (1994), 'Impacto ambiental de la actividad agraria', *Agricultura y Sociedad,* vol. 71, pp. 153-81.

Wagner, K. (1996), 'Regional differenzierte Wirkung des ÖPUL I', *Der Förderungsdienst,* vol. 7/96, pp. 207-9.

Wagner, K. (1997), *Ökonomische Auswirkungen der Grundwassersanierung auf die Landwirtschaft,* Bundesanstalt für Agrarwirtschaft (Publication N° 80), Wien.

Ward, N. and Lowe, P.D. (1994), 'Shifting values in agriculture: the farm family and pollution regulation', *Journal of Rural Studies,* vol. 10, pp. 173-84.

Waters, G. (1994), 'Government policies for the countryside', *Land Use Policy,* vol. 11, pp. 88-93.

Weinschenck, G. and Gebhard, H.-J. (1985), *Möglichkeiten und Grenzen einer ökologisch begründeten Begrenzung der Intensität der Agrarproduktion,* Kohlhammer, Stuttgart and Mainz.

Whitby, M. (ed.) (1994a), *Incentives for countryside management: the case of Environmentally Sensitive Areas,* CAB International, Wallingford.

Whitby, M. (1994b), 'What future for ESAs?', in: Whitby, M. (ed.), *Incentives for countryside management: the case of Environmentally Sensitive Areas,* CAB International, Wallingford, pp. 253-72.

Whitby, M. (ed.) (1996a), *The European environment and CAP reform: policies and prospects for conservation,* CAB International, Wallingford.

Whitby, M. (1996b), 'The prospect for agri-environmental policies within a reformed CAP', in: Whitby, M. (ed.), *The European environment and CAP reform: policies and prospects for conservation,* CAB International, Wallingford, pp. 227-40.

Whitby, M. and Lowe, P.D. (1994), 'The political and economic roots of environmental policy in agriculture', in: Whitby, M. (ed.), *Incentives for countryside management: the case of Environmentally Sensitive Areas,* CAB International, Wallingford, pp. 1-24.

Wilhelm, J. (1995), 'Zu große Mitnahmeeffekte', *DLG-Mitteilungen,* vol. 12/95, p. 62.

Williams, A.M. (1992), 'The Portuguese economy in transition', *Journal of the Association of Contemporary Iberian Studies,* vol. 5, 30-9.

Wilson, G.A. (1994), 'German agri-environmental schemes I: a preliminary review', *Journal of Rural Studies,* vol. 10, pp. 27-45.

Wilson, G.A. (1995), 'German agri-environmental schemes II: the MEKA programme in Baden-Württemberg', *Journal of Rural Studies,* vol. 11, pp. 149-59.

Wilson, G.A. (1996), 'Farmer environmental attitudes and ESA participation', *Geoforum,* vol. 27, pp. 115-31.

Wilson, G.A. (1997a), 'Factors influencing farmer participation in the Environmentally Sensitive Areas scheme', *Journal of Environmental Management,* vol. 50, pp. 67-93.

Wilson, G.A. (1997b), 'Selective targeting in Environmentally Sensitive Areas: implications for farmers and the environment', *Journal of Environmental Planning and Management*, vol. 40, pp. 199-215.

Wilson, G.A. (1997c), 'Assessing the environmental impact of the Environmentally Sensitive Areas scheme: a case for using farmers' environmental knowledge?', *Landscape Research*, vol. 22, pp. 303-26.

Wilson, G.A. (1998a), 'Agri-environmental issues in Germany', in: Unwin, T. (ed.), *A European Geography*, Longman, Harlow, pp. 154-7.

Wilson, G.A. (1998b), 'The Environmentally Sensitive Areas Scheme in the UK: success or failure?', in: Bowler, I. R., Bryant, C. R. and Huigen, P.P. (eds.), *Dimensions of sustainable rural systems*, Rijksuniversiteit Groningen, Groningen, pp. 121-34.

Wilson, G.A. and Bryant, R.L. (1997), *Environmental management: new directions for the twenty-first century*, UCL Press, London.

Wilson, G.A., Lezzi, M. and Egli, C. (1996), 'Agri-environmental schemes in Switzerland: Euro-(in)compatible?', *European Urban and Regional Studies*, vol. 3, pp. 205-24.

Wilson, G.A., Petersen, J.-E. and Höll, A. (1999), 'EU Member State responses to Agri-environment Regulation 2078/92/EEC: towards a conceptual framework?', *Geoforum*, vol. 30, pp. 185-202.

WOAD [Welsh Office Agriculture Department] (1998), Personal communication, WOAD, Cardiff, May 1998.

WWF [Worldwide Fund for Nature] (1997), Personal communication, WWF, Godalming, May 1997.

Zeddies, J. and Doluschitz, R. (1996), *Marktentlastungs- und Kulturlandschafts-ausgleich (MEKA)*, Ulmer, Stuttgart.

Index